KU-602-065

LOVE WORDS

The Self and the Text in
Medieval and Renaissance Poetry

Mariann Sanders Regan

Cornell University Press
Ithaca and London

216289

Cornell University Press gratefully acknowledges a grant from the Andrew W. Mellon Foundation that aided in bringing this book to publication.

Copyright © 1982 by Cornell University Press

All rights reserved. Except for brief quotations in a review, this book, or parts thereof, must not be reproduced in any form without permission in writing from the publisher. For information address Cornell University Press, 124 Roberts Place, Ithaca, New York 14850.

First published 1982 by Cornell University Press.
Published in the United Kingdom by Cornell University Press Ltd., Ely House, 37 Dover Street, London WIX 4HQ.

Excerpts from "Escotatz, mas no say que s'es" by Raimbaut D'Orange from *Lyrics of the Troubadours and Trouvères,* translations by Frederick Goldin, copyright © 1973 by Frederick Goldin, are reprinted by permission of Doubleday & Company, Inc.

Quotations from *Troubadours and Eloquence* by Linda M. Paterson, © Oxford University Press 1975, and from *Dante's Lyric Poetry,* edited and translated by Kenelm Foster and Patrick Boyde, vol. I, © Oxford University Press 1967, are used by permission of Oxford University Press.

International Standard Book Number 0-8014-1415-6
Library of Congress Catalog Card Number 81-15186
Printed in the United States of America
Librarians: Library of Congress cataloging information appears on the last page of the book.

QUEEN MARY
COLLEGE
LIBRARY

To Thomas Greene

Contents

Preface

How do we go about interpreting literature? Not so long ago, we still had a manageable confusion of theories to offer in answer to that question. But today our theories have grown into a rich chaos that would seem to take us far beyond any dreams of synthesis or agreement we may once have had. There is no end to our researches, as Montaigne observed. Students of contemporary literature about literature need hope, good humor, and energy to find their way among the structuralists, deconstructionists, deformalists, neo-Marxists, neo-organicists, and all those others who would provide directions for literary interpretation. Although these reductive labels can unfairly disguise the individual efforts of many fine writers, the labels do fairly suggest the present situation—that these "schools" are poised in their separation from one another, with few theoretical bridges.

During my explorations of these contemporary theories, I was often confronted by two apparently contradictory tendencies among them: in some approaches, it seemed, scholars worked toward finding some version of a *central meaning* in a literary text; in others, they worked just as hard to demonstrate that such central meanings are illusory, that no such central meaning is possible. This difference impressed me, and it reminded me of some questions I had been formulating about the nature of the self, through readings in psychoanalytic literature. For object-relations theorists suggest a kind of *center* for the self, too—a center that is in one sense indispensable and yet in another sense illusory and impossible. The debates about the self and the literary text can appear to resemble each other: does the literary text move toward or away from a central meaning? does the self in its psychic topography move toward or away from a central meaning? These questions can suggest paradoxes essential to the human condition, paradoxes that can make selves and texts baffling to interpreters. But we might achieve a certain clarity by admitting these paradoxes and looking at them more closely. In this way, by elaborating these basic resemblances between the literary text and the self, I have worked toward a new theory of literary interpretation. I have tried to indicate some possible bridges among the current theories, and even to suggest how some of the current models of interpretation might be woven into one another. The results of my efforts are in the first two chapters here, which sketch a new poetics. The next four chapters illustrate and develop this poetics through the works of four poets.

This book is meant for all those readers interested in selves or in texts, and I have tried to keep such a general audience in mind. I have intended the progression of my argument to be clear and logical to the general reader, even though I often deal with irrational and affective matters. And I have tried to keep the main terms of my critical vocabulary sensible and direct, even though I must often allude to some intricate terms from current theories. No school of literary or psychoanalytic interpretation is here duplicated—so far as I know—but I hope that my interpretive model is compatible with a number of these schools, broadly speaking, and I hope that students of poems, literary theory, psychoanalytic theory, language, and philosophy will all find ideas here to interest them.

Love poems, so often concerned to put into words what cannot be put into words, seem especially well suited to demonstrate this new poetics, and Renaissance love poems are those I happen to know most closely. Therefore, this poetics is worked through the love poems of Arnaut Daniel, Dante, Petrarch, and Shakespeare, in Chapters 3 through 6. For the more general reader, I have included translations to make these particular readings accessible. And for the student of medieval and Renaissance literature, I have tried not to exclude historical or generic readings, but merely to take up the business of interpretation from a somewhat broader vantage point.

Thus in my title I would offer the book to all who study words of love, to all lovers who practice "wording," to all who love words, and to all who do not, "who pay no praise or wages, / Nor heed my craft or art." For although this book is a worded labor of love, it holds, with Melville's Ishmael, that "whatever is truly wondrous and fearful in man, never yet was put into words or books."

I am grateful to the American Council of Learned Societies for the 1977–78 fellowship that allowed me time to write this book, and to Fairfield University for research funds and a one-semester sabbatical in 1977. And I thank Lynn Bennett for her cooperation and patience in typing a difficult manuscript.

My debts to teachers and colleagues reach back a number of years. The late William Blackburn, who introduced me to Renaissance literature when I was an undergraduate at Duke University, first interested me in the poetry of idealized love. At Yale graduate school, Thomas Bergin graciously allowed me to audit his graduate course in the Provençal troubadours, and Bart Giamatti was generous with his time in discussing the Bernart de Ventadorn chapter of my dissertation. Harold Bloom has given kind support in many ways, including his helpful remarks on the first two chapters of this book. I am grateful to Geoffrey Hartman and the members of his 1977 NEH summer seminar in modern literary criticism for lively discussions that nourished my developing theories of interpretation. My most substantial debt, which I acknowledge with great pleasure, is to Thomas Greene. I was fortunate to be a student in his Renaissance literature seminar at Yale, to work on my dissertation under his supervision, and later to visit his graduate seminar in the Renaissance love lyric. He has generously read and commented upon a large part of this manuscript. He has been a continuing support, inspiration, and guiding influence, and his contributions to whatever virtues there may be in this book are beyond measure.

My friends and family have my heartfelt thanks for seeing me through the experience of writing this book. Celia Wells, as colleague and friend, has offered steady encouragement as well as useful comments on several of the chapters. My sister, L. B.

Sanders, has contributed her helpful perspectives and her proofreading skills. This book would not exist were it not for the daily support, tireless listening, and well-considered advice of my husband, Richard. And finally, I thank Timothy and Jennifer Regan for their tolerance and patience.

MARIANN SANDERS REGAN

Fairfield, Connecticut

LOVE WORDS

1 The Literary Text as Self: Toward a Psycho-ontological Hermeneutics

> You could not discover the limits of soul, even if you traveled
> every road to do so; such is the depth of its meaning.
> —Heraclitus, Fr. 42

Verbum Infans

Careful students of the psyche have always found that sooner
or later in their discourses upon the nature of the psyche or self,
they arrive at some enigmatic, unanalyzable core of being that
does not seem to yield to words. Freud would sometimes evoke
Eros and Thanatos in such a stalemate, but at other times he
could simply throw up his hands: what *did* women want? why
were some analyses interminable, like draining the Zuyder Zee?
do *all* interpretive paths lead to darkness? Certainly his analytic
guidelines took him quite a distance before he reached these
passes, but he reached them, nonetheless. Today we still await
the definitive geography of the psyche, the final mapping onto
words: in our expanding awareness of the gap between signifier
and signified, we wonder not so much whether we can explain
the self in Freudian terms, but whether we can explain the self in
terms at all. The self in its essence recedes and is opaque; like
Heidegger's Earth it wants to shine undisclosed, and it shatters
every attempt to penetrate it. We strain to match language to our
being and feel that we have failed in the task. Secularization
seems not to have solved our questions about our individual
identities, nor to have brought widespread agreement among

Epigraph   Philip Wheelwright, *Heraclitus* (New York: Atheneum, 1964), p. 58.
He translates the Greek *psyche* as "soul," *logos* as "meaning."

the vocabularies of the human sciences. Like many today who would not attempt to catch the self in rational discourse, James Hillman teaches us to abide within the "permanent ambiguity of metaphor," psychologizing in infinite regress to the gods within ourselves.[1] Ernest Becker concludes that we terrorize each other from our hunger for "immortality power," itself an "invisible mystery" transmitted among persons not in words but in fantasy[2]—which is to say again, with full anthropological documentation, that we hang in dreams on the back of a tiger. And in quest of self, an animal metaphor often seems to work at least as well as a mechanical one, while Self, the ultimate elusive Signified, seems to remain just out of reach.

Some would move to chronological origins for the explanations and causes of the self, but when they move closer to the enigma it is no clearer, only larger and more overbearing. When we try to make infancy speak to us, we are tasked with wording that preverbal pair, mother and child—and we cannot. Margaret Mahler judges that her extended studies of mothers and infants have "provided a glimpse into that bedrock of mental life that does not divulge its content and nature by verbal means—the 'unrememberable and the unforgettable.'"[3] When Freud works to unmask Mona Lisa's smile by revealing the kisses of Leonardo's mother hidden behind it, he merely gives us, as Paul Ricoeur shows, a redoubled enigma: "Lost like a memory, the mother's smile is an empty spot in reality. It is the point where all real traces get lost and the abolished memory borders on fantasy."[4] Like a sacred center amid our secular explanations, the image of mother and child seems to hold us still; we do not know quite how to say what this two-in-one being is, but we sense that we may find the self there. Even Freud, who after all had much more to say about fathers than about mothers, would like to preserve the relationship between mother and male child in pure affection, exempting it from the universal *homo homini lupus*.[5] Melanie Klein extends Freud's thoughts on narcissism and mourning, arguing that to love oneself is to love another "inside" oneself, and further that at the core of self is an irreducible primal dyad of child and mother. More recently, René Spitz, Margaret Mahler, Otto Kernberg, and numerous others have elaborated our knowledge, our inferences, and our questions about this dyadic core. When Martin Buber says that reality is something a man must search out in the eyes of his fellow man, he invokes again for us the infant, searching for himself in the eyes of his mother. What is more, our rise from void into infancy also suggests our enigmatic ontology, for "the silence which is death is also our mother."[6] We seem to embrace both lifegiving and deathgiving mothers, to weave them both into our sense of self, so that such concepts as Erik Erikson's "basic trust" are always implicated with their darker alternatives. The self mediates between void and infancy, still impenetrable. No wonder that structuralists would like to dissolve self and install Language as the ultimate Signified, for language can be almost readily drawn into manipulable sign systems. Yet fortunately or unfortunately we all still inhabit selves and resist full absorption into the Language System.

Still, our efforts to put ourselves into language are indefatigable. Our continuing infancy trails clouds of terms, as poets and philosophers, psychoanalysts and biologists, work to explain ourselves to ourselves. Perhaps our technologies do pursue our infant dreams of domination, as many would say; but surely our humanities elaborate even more the efforts to understand our whole range of infant dreams. The texts and artifacts that we accumulate take us back to primal questions; our art, in particular, shows us intuitively married to our beginnings, as though we would force Wordsworth's Child to speak. Ernst Kris extends the "flexibility of repression" theory and would see an artist as bringing his own infancy to his creation; Anton Ehrenzweig, among others, claims that all creative artists identify with the womb.[7] The formalist Viktor Shklovsky believes that through *ostranenie* (defamiliarization) the literary text delivers the reader again into an awesome childhood. And to Owen Barfield, an "almost universal consciousness" places the golden age of poetry, premetaphoric and alive with Figures, in the infancy of society.[8] To move forward in artistic creations seems inevitably to be drawn also backward to cultural and personal infancy, as though we were invoking our histories to weigh upon us before we reconceive our infant enigma within new matrices of words.

Insofar as we can reach understanding, it will be self-understanding within a dialectic of archaeology and teleology, according to Ricoeur; our interpretations must discover a semantics of desire in cultural figures and symbols that *simul-*

taneously repeat childhood and explore adult life. That is, we cannot symbolize ourselves as adults without reaching backward to childhood mysteries; on the other hand, we can understand the infant enigma of self only indirectly, by constructing texts as we move inevitably forward in time. "There is no direct apprehension of the self by the self, no internal apperception or appropriation of the self's desire to exist through the short cut of consciousness but only by the long road of the interpretation of signs."[9] Ricoeur, like Heidegger, will not reify meaning: the unconscious finds only its distortion in language, while words, the only way toward self, prove unending detours. Our simultaneous progressions and regressions of words or signs or spirit figures are to Ricoeur a *Bewusstwerden* or speaking without end; they will never discover the self in its completion. Walter Benjamin has figured the pathos of our attempted self-understanding, with its conflated progress and regress, in his "Angelus Novus": this angel of history gazes fixedly toward the past, as though wishing to become absorbed in its aura, while a storm from Paradise propels him "into the future to which his back is turned," and the debris of civilization accumulates at his feet.[10] Yearning backward, he is swept forward. Here we are, we selves, always pulled toward our unspoken origins and blown away again, always compelled to start afresh, to make new metaphors like Nietzsche's intuitive man, even to create new hypotheses and scientific theories, and then to watch them harden into mobile armies of truths at our feet, while we are drawn once more to that infant start we thought we had made. Like the angel, we want to be in touch with our past that is Paradise, our secret core of self, but words never seem to assure this touch for us, as we always hope they might.[11] And in our efforts to word the self we question today whether we can ever find the right relationship between language and being; many deal in violent deconstructions of language, rending the accepted woof of ideas. Jacques Derrida tells us that we falsely presume language is able to fit being: "Being presents itself in language precisely as that which opens it up to non-language."[12] His *archi-écriture* itself cannot hold presence. And Derrida may share with us all the nostalgia for a constant understanding of self, even if that understanding must be out of words. On the final page of *Glas,* after the exhilarating and disturbing sparagmos of intertextuality, appears an interlude among the debris in a passage from Nietzsche: "Wir reden nicht zueinander, weil wir zu vieles wissen —: wir schweigen uns an, wir lächeln uns unser Wissen zu" (We speak not to one another because we know too much: we gaze silently on one another, we smile our wisdom to one another). Here is intuitive wisdom and affirmation in that revealing "wir," an unwordable and silent dual unity like that of mother and preverbal infant, where at the sunrise of self wordless reciprocal smiles and gazes can signify our original boundless *yes*—"das ungeheure, unbegrenzte Ja-. . . ."[13] One finds "wir" among multiple echoes, deferred selves, texts in *différance*—a secure, constant, but silent pair.

If every literary theory is drawn from a canon of texts, mine results from a study of lyric poetry, especially Renaissance lyrics. I would suggest that the literary text can be an equivalent self. In this book, I mean to test this idea with some of the numerous poems that have suggested it to me; these relevant lyrics are, in this study, "text." Perhaps all texts must be equivalent selves— *Glas,* for example—or perhaps, on the other hand, other genres besides lyric poetry are exempt from this analogy. These are questions for other books. Here, I call the literary text an equivalent self in that both self and text are ongoing active constructions near a crucial enigmatic "core" that provokes words but does not finally yield to them. The literary text does not *capture* a given self, such as the author, any more than one enigma can capture another; rather, it makes up a self out of words, constitutes a being-in-words. It *acts* or *works* like a self in certain basic motions and limitations whose explanation will occupy the rest of this chapter, and it is the evocative failure of words to reach the infant enigma of self—not their explanatory power—that helps to promote the equivalence between text and self. It may seem at first that we can immediately apprehend a text through the meanings of its words, but text-interpretation, like self-interpretation, can prove a long detour of signs. For central to text, as to self, is an infinite and infant core that is resistant to words. Thus I would not claim that a particular text mirrors or models a particular self, although biographical details can be helpful; for I believe we cannot expect to find a fully explainable self "behind" the text, a self that we can solve forever with words. Because selves cannot be fixed in words, this expectation would be illusory; the otherwise flawed "autonomous object" theories of the text were suggesting its futility. Self and text are enigmatic at heart, and no interpretive words can dispense with either one. To speak of a "valid" interpretation of a literary text is as presumptuous as to claim a "valid" interpretation of another human being. Rather, the selves that are texts *work as presences upon* the selves that are readers: texts *presence* readers, in an act of being that is both given and received.

To call the literary text an equivalent self is neither to idealize nor to hypostasize the text. We cannot always call a text balanced or harmonious or even sane if we are to admit all the pathos of its discourse; the text will show the risked possibility of being— not the perfection of being—for like the self, the text has a conflicted ontology. Often in the poems relevant to this study, the text demonstrates a felt inadequacy to express its own enigmatic core; it shows a sense of its own obverse—death-of-text— in its questioning. We see the text in impending dissolution, not the text as reified beauty, and the self-awareness of its own fragile construction can paradoxically become the strength of a text. What is more, the text does not hold still for us like a thing before our eyes and emotions. In the fixed black lines of a text, an ongoing motion can be implied, just as a portrait, though fixed in its lines, can somehow evoke the mobility, the feeling tone and varied expressions of a human face, drawing our empathy from self to self.[14]

The chapter title refers to my use of psychoanalytic metaphors to interpret the being-in-words of the text as an equivalent self, as a partly explainable construction in words "around" an enigmatic core irreducible to words. For self and text can share some of the common motions and limitations that are explored by psychoanalytic theories. My interpretations of texts and selves, however, despite my use of theories considered "scientific," are not intended as full wordings or explanations; rather, I mean to evoke these texts as selves, and in response to their presences, to construct a new presence, another text and self. Perhaps literary study is at best an articulate initiation into the varied presences of texts. Derrida tells us that what we term "Hegel" is a construction of ours on a work called, by metonymy, "Hegel," and that self is the work of a text. Similarly, any full interpretation must be a construction of the reader, by the reader; the semantics of a text must be the semantics of reader as Self, the ultimate Signified and the only ground we have for meaning. To pursue finality in Aristotelian rationalism or validity, or an averaged Superreader, or a Language System is to assume that only definitive and wordable results make the activity of reading and interpretation worthwhile. We might as well presume our own immortality. Rather, the Self is the measure of all things, the maker of meanings within its own mortal freedom.

First I will sketch certain directions and limitations that all selves have in common, and that contribute to the ultimately enigmatic nature of the self. Then I will outline the possible resemblances between text and self.

Self as Source

We begin our identities by primal identification. With mother's milk we take in a caring maternal presence as psychic nourishment: no matter how much tangible food they are given, infants cannot survive unless they are given sufficient maternal presence as well. In order to be, we must first be presenced. Spitz puts it succinctly: "although the innate equipment is available to the baby from the first minute of life, it has to be quickened; the vital spark has to be conferred on the equipment through exchanges with another human being, with a partner, with the mother. Nothing less than a reciprocal relation will do."[15] For in that preverbal and prerational ocean we are the caring presence, and nothing else is: the enigma at the infant center of self is, first, Maternal Source.[16] This Maternal Source is not the literal mother we can recognize as adults, or even as young children; rather, it is the infant's self-as-Source, his own dawning being that is to him inextricable from a nourishing immanence felt to be infinite. Source is the original *Erlebnis* or lived experience; it is the infant's sustaining dream of life that must coincide with his emergent self. "From the beginning the child molds and unfolds in the matrix of the mother-infant dual unit."[17] The infant receives Maternal Source coenesthetically and extensively, as though within a common membrane of mother and child, with a quality colored by the mother's affects;[18] as Freud (1930) perhaps began to infer from Romain Rolland's convictions, being for the infant is boundless, oceanic.

This sense of a Present Source, given even before we can disentangle "self" from "other," remains crucial to self, a persistent infancy in our aliteral reality—here, at least, Freudians and Jungians seem in agreement. The primary narcissistic ego loves the ideal beloved object, maternal presence, that it has put into itself; when, as Freud tells us, men strive to be their own ideal once more, they strive in this way finally to be that "other," that loving Source.[19] Recent theorists stress the universal and inevitable psychic internalization of the maternal presence. Fromm recommends learning to mother oneself; Erikson regards "basic trust" as crucial to the self; Klein believes that all selves must take the sense of a "good breast" or "good mother" to their centers. In Mahler's terms, the self accumulates a "sufficient reservoir of that basic trust . . . which provides the solid base from which to reach out confidently into the 'other-than-mother' world."[20] Heinz Kohut's term for this internalized presence, self-and-Source, seems to be the "idealized self-object," archaic, omnipotent, and grandiose. Jacques Lacan's "moi" is a formulation of this dual unity that emphasizes its insidious nature: the self is mirrored in the maternal (Imaginary) other and thus caught in primary self-alienation. And the work of the Jungian Anima (Great Mother, Soul) is to infuse all selves with Maternal Source: "No longer is it a question of whether I believe in soul, but whether soul believes in me. . . . My so-called personality . . . depends altogether upon the gift of belief in myself, a faith given through anima in my worth as carrier of soul . . . her intense daydream is my 'me-ness.'"[21] That is to say, if she were not to dream of us, we would, like Alice, go out like a candle; we lodge this Maternal Source at our centers, we look for ourselves in her eyes. We require her to extend to us our sense of self. From the beginning, we intuit ourselves to be as-Source, a boundless warp and woof of self and Source, and we cannot put aside this original intuition of eternity. Our ontology belongs to our "everlasting longing for the actual or coenesthetically fantasized, wish-fulfilled, and absolutely protected state of primal identification (Ferenczi's absolute primal omnipotence . . .), for which deep down in the original primal unconscious, in the so-called primarily repressed realm, every human being strives."[22] Or, in somewhat less affecting terms, the "basic good self-object constellation" is "the nucleus of the self system of the ego," and there is a persistent intrapsychic tendency for defensive regressive refusion of good self and object images.[23] Simply, Maternal Source persists as though "within" each of us. Furthermore, we cannot reason this enigma of self-and-Source, for rational discourse can hardly re-present the direct Presence that engenders self. Neo-Freudian theorists try to interpret the infant's body-language, or read "regressive manifestations" backward to reach an understanding of preverbal phenomena, and most admit, like Helen Durkin, that our conception of infancy "is based on a mixture of observed fact, established inference, and assumption," and that our subsequent discourse is a matter of translating our "empathic observation of infants" into adult words. And even at best, we could not see the infant building the *core* of his self-representation.[24]

Yet this unwordable direct Presence, our ontological sense that we are as Source, sets us in an endemic motion toward others throughout our lives; in these others we are by nature always trying to rejoin Source, to become first and final Presence. We see sexuality, for example, as a mingling of self and Source: the two shall become one flesh; the lonely halves will make one hermaphrodite again. Freud compares coital satisfaction to the bliss of a nursing infant; Jean Laplanche, reading Freud and extending his implications, discusses the propping (*étayage*) of the sexual drive on the vital function: "Sexuality in its entirety is in the slight deviation, the *clinamen* from the [vital] function." He uses orality or breast-sucking as the archetypal example of this propping, and he posits the universal "seduction of maternal care."[25] Genital and anal stages replay the oral stage, a theme with variations; oedipal is grounded in preoedipal. We are drawn toward a succession of others, a lifetime of others, who we feel will keep giving us ourselves as Source; we continue to assimilate and to be assimilated.

Spitz teaches us that in the affective climate of infancy, the affective exchange between infant and mother, "begins the process which will transform the infant into a human, into a social being, into the zoon politikon in the human sense." The smiling response, in particular, is the "prototype and premise of all subsequent social relations."[26] We sense that we belong to Carlyle's "universal world-tissue," for we embrace group, nation, mankind as presences dear to us, in order to weave ourselves back into that seamless cloth of self and Source. Merleau-Ponty believes that the syncretic system "me-and-other," the *vie à plusieurs* that is synonymous with infancy, leads to a "segregation of individuals that is never completely finished," and that our syncretic sociability persists despite the "third-year crisis."[27] Philip Slater remarks that the group leader is typically sensed as a maternal presence, a breast absorbed over and over again and never destroyed, for interaction in training and therapy groups is most often "focussed at the oral level," and the members of a group will react aggressively when they feel this nurturance is being withheld. And to Norman Brown, "The authorities are the authors . . . the 'nursing fathers' of the Old Testament and of the New England Puritan political theorists. . . . The transition from matriarchy to patriarchy is always with us, and gets us nowhere."[28]

If our fundamental sense of self is like a spell cast by the unique maternal human face, Spitz suggests a paradigm situation for this original spell-casting when he describes the infant gazing unswervingly at his mother's face while nursing, so that he is brought to diacritic perception by the one sign Gestalt that reassures him of her vital presence.[29] Becker, adding the terms of other disciplines, observes that the life force continues to "personalize" for us as adults in a unique human face, so that a special individual like a shaman or demagogue can dominate as if by a psychological spell. Becker's lifelong studies in anthropology and psychology have convinced him that man's most crucial desire is to rejoin Source—that is, to tap the "life force" or "immortality power" through his social structures and rituals. Man is moved to fuse with leaders and national ideals because he "wants to merge with a larger whole . . . to serve the cosmic powers" even when the powers call for war. In this way he ensures organismic self-perpetuation and denies death: "man is an animal who has to live a lie in order to live at all."[30] He projects his lasting infant need for immortal Source onto his group, his *alma mater,* his country. Thus Kernberg can offer object-relations theory as a "major integrative framework" linking the psychosocial and subjective approaches to human life with the intrapsychic structures of the metapsychology—"a crossroad where instinct and the social system meet."[31] And we sense Maternal Source also in landscapes, omphaloi or navel stones, genius loci or world-soul, Eliade's sacred spot to which we return, Benjamin's "aura" inseparable from original place. Wordsworth's generous maternal Nature, inducing preconscious epiphanies more profound than will or imagination can contrive, is fitted to the mind like Maternal Source. Our thoughts seem naturally to lead us to infinities and eternities. In our central infancy, we are all Faustians, and all believers; we would all become as little children in order to say to the moment, with Goethe's Faust, "Verweile doch" (Stay awhile!—*Faust* I. 1700). Even Claude Lévi-Strauss finds a structuralist epiphany "behind" the phenomena: "suddenly time and space are mingled. . . . I feel myself bathed by a deeper intelligibility in which ages and places reply to each other and speak languages reconciled at last."[32] We feel ourselves pulled to the mingled space and time of infinite self-as-Source, whence we came: since Source sets our being in motion, we find it impossible fully to convince ourselves that Source is truly impossible.

Moreover, in our conflicted ontology we do not always sense this essential Source as peaceful and loving. This Source that enables self can also be felt as alien and threatening, the first intruder into self; the lifetime of others we meet can suggest to us this alien Source as well. Durkin believes that the mother is "the first compelling power in human experience" and that an aspect of experience with her is always "terrifying and infuriating"; indeed, the thesis of Durkin's book is that the "idea of a group activates in the adult individual traces of the preoedipal mother image and the fears connected with it, causing him to become relatively submissive to the group and unusually suggestible."[33] Laplanche discusses sexual excitation as an "alien internal entity" introduced into the child by the mother. Freud's superego is Source turned traitor: perhaps our severe desire to *be* one with the lifegiving Source, or our helpless sense that we *are* one with her, brings Source as monitoring enemy into the self. Spitz quotes Freud (1895), that the "original helplessness of human beings is thus the primal source of all moral motives." Klein believes that no matter what the style of mothering, inevitable ontological conflicts with the maternal presence will lead to the universal neuroses and psychoses of infancy. For not only are such disturbing aggressive impulses as greed and frustration inherent in feeding, but even the most lavish mothering seems to awaken the infant's primal envy: "The very ease with which the milk comes . . . gives rise to envy because this gift seems something so unattainable."[34] She implies that like Satan in heaven, we must always feel ourselves impaired by our Source, two where we would be one; the mystery of our iniquity is that we want to give life to ourselves, to succeed in the *causa sui* project. Our intimated failure is our hatred of Source, and our fear of hatred. For since self is as-Source, our psychic efforts to banish or destroy Source can only backfire, in the complex ways psychoanalysis has traced and interpreted: after all, we would not really like to banish or destroy ourselves, or at least we do not sustain such a wish for long. Thus the repressed Source returns to our sense of self, darkened to terror by our inevitable rage— the endopsychic rays that torment Schreber, wife of God, mocking and impregnating him, soul-murderers.[35] We placate our own Source, offering scapegoats, sacrifices, war, ourselves. If as infants we wish mother rent in pieces, we wish therefore our own dismemberment, and thus the vengeful fragments of Source return to haunt the self. *Verwerfung* (repression) and *Verneinung* (denial, negation) are rifts in self-being; they take away self with Source. As Freud concludes in his essay on negation, "So it *is* his mother."

Language and Self-as-Source

Our endemic motion to rejoin Source fills our attitudes toward language. The current scholarly controversies about whether we have made language or it has made us, whether we speak or are spoken—these debates themselves testify to our ongoing *causa sui* questions before language as maternal presence, mother tongue, great reservoir *langue,* original surplus of signifiers. It suits our infant ontology to claim that we can make words flesh: "The first active extroceptive stimulus would be the voice," according to Merleau-Ponty. The mother's manner of divining her infant's needs has been called "intuitive" and "near-clairvoyant," and thus the acoustic stimuli she offers the infant, the prelude to his speech, must belong to this sense of an entirely communicative presence.[36] "At bottom, it is not only the word 'mama' that is the child's first; it is the entire language which is, so to speak, maternal," Merleau-Ponty explains. Words spring from Maternal Source, and by this route words become personal presences to us. Barfield posits an adamic language of flesh and blood in which words were living Figures, "the echoing footsteps of the goddess Nature."[37] We feel that our words, like our societies or ideals or loved ones, might embody the lifegiving Source for us, and we sometimes affirm that they have done so. But which word is flesh? we may well ask, as we continue to move through new words to new claims of Presence. Perhaps for the newborn infant who moves his lips to his mother's voice, while the motherness of language becomes his sense of self—perhaps words for him are Presence. But newborn infants yield to the winds of time. Self must be as-Source, but self *is not* Source. It is the enigmatic *sense* of self that is not thoroughly separable from Source, and the *senses* of words, not words themselves, that can seem to belong to Presence. In schizophrenia, one may not perceive any separation of words from presences and may continue to be, like the newborn, spoken. Some might call this dedifferentiation Truth. But if this be Truth, most of us are fallen from it; we sense that words, although they may reach to touch infinite self-as-Source, must stop short of their intent and leave "beyond" them an untouched mystery. That is, we realize that our claims for a flesh-and-blood language are not literal; we speak in metaphors, of a direction toward presences and Presence.

Because words fail ultimately to hold Presence, the unexpressed presence or sense of the word—as though just "beyond" it—can seem to us all the stronger. Unheard melodies are sweeter: *because* they seem to us only traces of presence, words can evoke the goddess Nature herself. The memory trace of a parent, Freud tells us, can be crueler or kinder than the actual parent; just so, words in their incompleted motion toward Presence can carry extra charges. We can, like Barfield, hypothesize the infancy of language, but we cannot inhabit it. The transcendental referent of language may be, as Lacan says, the lost object at the center: exactly because words must lose the "object," Source, our necessarily transcendental sense of self-as-

Source continues to linger about the word. Words become haunted, and haunt us, insofar as they try but fail to reach Presence. Interpretive paths can never lead to full light: our sense of self-as-Source remains luminous just beyond our failing words. As Ricoeur says, the dynamics of our psyche is across a hermeneutics, but we can never reach it by a hermeneutics. Words and selves are as-Source, pulled toward a sensed infinite Source without ever arriving there.

Self away from Source

From the first day of life, we begin to lose the maternal presence, partially and temporarily at first, then more completely. Even as we feel eternally joined to lifegiving Source, then, we begin to sense ourselves also in inevitable motion away from Source. Klein and other theorists believe that the infant at the "depressive" stage, the main crisis of infancy, gradually becomes able to perceive Maternal Source as a whole, a losable entity; this is no accidental trauma, but a shock integral to the formation of all selves.[38] The infant undergoes primal bereavement for self-and-Source, a kind of primal meditation upon his own death. Here we learn our identities by difference and differentiation from the whole, by loss of being: we feel "self" as distinct from infinite life, abandoned to mortality. As we move away from that vital oceanic presence, in the same motion we fear to lose our own infinite centers. Even as we try to lodge that felt eternal Presence at our centers, we sense also what it would be to have no psychic nourishment—an empty "core." The infant enigma at the center of self is not only Source, but also this unspoken sense of thorough absence, self-as-Void. According to Hillman, "it is not upon life that our ultimate individuality centers, but upon death. . . . Pathologizing . . . leads the soul into the deepest ontological reflection," with fantasies that lead right out of life. Our experience in the world is an experience of not-ness, "a matter of multisided disillusionment based on expectation."[39] The profundity of the psyche is an abyss. In order to be selves, we must sense ourselves as incomplete, devouring a void, in Sartre's existential need, Lacan's *béance*.

Just as we continue in life to move toward others who mean to us self-as-Source, so we cannot help finding also symbols of our separation from Source, our Void. For we project our lasting infant sense of not-being that remains central to us. Poor Pip, abandoned by the whaleboats in mid-ocean: "the intense concentration of self in the middle of such a heartless immensity," exclaims Ishmael, "my God! who can tell it?" (chap. 93, *Moby-Dick*). Perhaps like Ahab we choose scapegoats and wage wars to exorcise this very sense of "creature inferiority," as Becker calls it, this sense of radical separation from immortality. Kohut, writing of narcissistic rage, emphasizes our fierce resistance to this intimation of Void: "Human aggression is most dangerous when it is attached to the two great absolutarian psychological constellations: the grandiose self and the archaic omnipotent object."[40] Freud tells us in "Mourning and Melancholy" that when we mourn a lost beloved, we also mourn ourselves; we must somehow deliver ourselves again into life by reattaching libido to others, and perhaps to the internalized image of the beloved as well. Klein would add that adult mourning recalls infant primal mourning. Thus the self, cast into extrauterine time, is caught in motion until death between self-as-Source and self-as-Void. The enigmatic self moves in both directions.

Language away from Source

We sense language to move in both these directions, too. We hope without believing that words will hold lifegiving Presence, and we simultaneously fear that they will be only black lines, swept toward Void, empty shells testifying that they can never rejoin Source. If language is maternal it is also, like the maternal presence, punctuated by ominous gaps that bespeak our primal bereavement, self from Source. Ferdinand de Saussure and his followers have proposed that words find their identity in difference, in separation from an undifferentiated whole: selves learn their identity in the same way. Some reserve of anxiety is necessary for language formation, and language, reciprocally, shadows primal absence. Unlike Nature, language seems to admit a vacuum: Kenneth Burke, in *Language as Symbolic Action*, defines language as the possibility of the negative, suggesting that negation is of the very essence of language. *Fort!* first, then

Da! The fall from Source into selves, the "I" distinct from "you," is intrinsic to language; between selves, there can be no zero-degree writing. Derrida continues to show us that words cannot outrun their shadow of unmitigated absence, their *différance:* since words, like selves, are caught in time, there is no way, ever, to make meaning or Presence reside in the spoken or written word, and there never has been such a way. Like selves, words cannot make Presence stay: "the This of sense, which is 'meant,' cannot be reached by language."[41] Nietzsche declaims in *Truth and Falsity* that the route from nerve stimulus! to percept! to sound! to idea! is absurd, no route at all but a series of illusory leaps.

Language leaps to Source but lapses, caught in two motions like the self. For even while they seem haunted by Presence, metaphor and metonymy can certify absence, their own inadequacy and duplicity. Condensation and displacement, the metaphor and metonymy of dreams, can distance, distort, confirm absence even while they seem to burden us with demonic presences. They label wish as wish: it is only a dream. Behind our rebus-dreams and our language, it is not hard to glimpse the abyss. But if words are only planks over an abyss and will not, as Paul Valéry says, bear our full weight, we are always putting up new planks, or treading lightly upon the old ones. Our words remain, deferred in meaning but still visible, still audible; they resist unrelieved absence. Words, like selves, negotiate the wide reality between Source and Void.

Self-texture

The unwordable enigma central to self includes two involuntary motions, then: self-as-Source and self-as-Void. Either motion by itself is self-contradictory, and combined they are all the more perplexing. Yet these two motions do prescribe to self its voluntary, deliberate task: a self *is* special real activity, individual work between the metaphors as-Source and as-Void. To be a self is to weave together in a continuing new texture these senses of primary presence and primary absence; a self must negotiate a chiasmus of *absent presence* and *present absence.* Mahler teaches us that the drive for and toward individuation in the infant is an innate, powerful given; we might say that in individuation, paradoxically, one is driven toward one's own voluntary, deliberate work, the texturing of one's own self. And Void and Source work as limits, not goals, for each would dissolve self. Mahler describes the "rapprochement crisis" of infancy as "an oscillation between the longing to merge blissfully with the good object representation, with the erstwhile (in one's fantasy, at least) 'all good' symbiotic mother, and the defense against reengulfment by her, which could cause loss of autonomous self-identity." Slater designates the poles of ambivalence equally feared by groups: loss of individuality and too great a degree of individuation.[42] Self must be created between the limits of Source and Void.

Thus if there is a teleology of self, it is in the very texture of the weaving peculiar to each self, the inner stresses of the ongoing construction. Object-relations theorists imply such a texture peculiar to each self, while their language shows the difficulties involved in naming an *agent* for the texturing. At this "bedrock of mental life" agents are especially hard to find. In fact, the early psyche seems in these theories to command only the passive voice: "physiological functions and somatic behavior . . . modified in preobjectal interchanges with the mother and endowed with psychic content, *are transformed into* psychic ego nuclei," and these nuclei "*are pulled together*," forming the rudimentary ego.[43] In other words, the autonomous functions of the ego, as Mahler says, can unfold only with maternal sustenance; only with the realization of Source can the self in any sense take hold of its own texturing. But when self does take hold, it becomes *sui generis,* by virtue of this very texturing. Spitz puts it this way: "while being itself the product of the integrative forces which operate in living matter, the ego in its turn becomes a gravitational center of organization, coordination, and integration." And Kernberg states that identification systems are precipitates of the ego "around which cognitive functions and adaptive aspects of defensive functions construct a secondary, stable interstitial web. . . . This web gives strength to the whole ego structure."[44] Ultimately, of course, maternal affects feed all this integration: one might say that Maternal Source organizes the self's ability to organize.

Resulting intrapsychic textures become individual, identifiable. In the final phase of rapprochement, Mahler states, each child finds his own particular style of being. The self in individuation, despite those inevitable motions toward and away from Source, chooses specific others to individualize those motions, and the ensuing world of "internalized object representations," as Kernberg says, becomes unique to each self. And there is no question of closure, short of death; selves can become ever more intensely individual. For by its nature, self is not a perfectible or justifiable activity; to call self a "dialectic" would imply some envisioned synthesis, some absolute and final form. But the self never reaches any unity; it weaves on through time. "Soul, to Heraclitus, is quality, substance, and activity in one . . . a dynamical something, always tending by a sort of inner urgency to become other than what it was and is."[45]

Thus the self becomes *absent presence,* never full Presence or Source. That is, in order to be, the self must be centered by an infinite presence acknowledged to be a metaphor, by an irreducible illusion of self-and-Source that cannot be reasoned. Freud tells us that to the ego, living means the same as being loved by the super-ego—an internalized mana figure, an absent Source, a phantom. The "all good" symbiotic mother can of course never be confirmed in reality, for she is not subject to time or space, much less to human failings: but in central fantasy she becomes indispensable, the crucial *absent presence.* Despite Roy Shafer's good sense in criticizing Freudian spatial metaphors, we can hardly eradicate this intrapsychically realized, nuclear internalization metaphor without destroying self, however firmly we may acknowledge it as metaphor. Neurosis, Otto Rank says, is the incapacity for illusion: the self must hold this acknowledged metaphoric presence by the main strength of its unconscious imagination. Thus Klein concludes that the infant can surpass the "depressive position" only and specifically by capturing this "image" of Maternal Source, by introjecting the "good mother imago." Later theorists essentially agree: they seem to concur that however intricate the vicissitudes of intrapsychic development, however highly integrated the internalized representations and the drives, there must always remain a stable, good, even ideal internal image of the mother. Mahler and others suggest that even though the development of object constancy and individuality involves the fusion of aggressive and libidinal drives—the integration of "good" and "bad" mothers into one whole—object constancy nevertheless "*depends upon* the gradual internalization of a constant, positively cathected, inner image of the mother." And Spitz says simply that when instinctual drives, good and bad objects, are fused into a single mother, "the good object predominates in the fusion."[46]

Continuing threats to this sustaining *absent presence,* both from unmodified "bad imago" and unfused aggressive drives, may always act to blur or shatter the image, and with it the self. As McDevitt states, "the mental representation of the mother may be so buffeted by violent and angry feelings that the stability of this image, at least from the libidinal as opposed to the cognitive side, is disrupted.[47] The image of self-as-Source appears to be the essence of our reality, an incarnate ocean that we must *seem* always to carry with us. Without this illusion—for one could not call it a literal memory, a matrix of facts—our lifegiving interactions with others and even with ourselves are put in jeopardy. We weave ourselves around memory-traces, preserving ourselves by preserving an aura of our lost Source.

At the same time, we cannot really fulfill our motion to refind the lost Source unless we suffer loss of self, psychic dissolution, the "one annihilation" of Shelley's *Epipsychidion.* Human beings are made human, according to Lacan, by the desire for nondifference that is really annihilation. Dante must leave that last *fulgore* in Paradise if he is to write the *Commedia.* Full Presence can be both ecstasy and the terror of engulfment: "The joyful fantasy in silence is that one will find mystical union with others without boundary dissolution . . . —in other words, a kind of intrauterine condition. The dark counterpart of this is boundary destruction in a state of utter isolation—the worst of both worlds. This is the terror of silence."[48] Our momentum toward Source can be equivalent to a motion toward the Void, and in our being we wander from both Source and Void that center us, traveling and working, never drawn finally into the vortex. Thus Laplanche can distinguish Eros as life-force from Freudian "sexuality," for the latter can be an unbinding, an entropy, a dissolution that threatens the margins of self.[49] As in Renaissance popular wisdom, perhaps, selves can move toward death through sexual intercourse, losing days of life and drops of blood.

Thus self becomes also *present absence,* a present being distinguishable from Source. The self must grieve for the absent Source in order to be self; that margin of separation from Source will preserve self even while it carries the threatening sense of Void. Time confounds in order to give; self needs the accumulating distance from Source in order to exist. For the lifegiving Source, after all, is also alien; in that primal pairing we are impaired, and Satan is the departing child who does not want to be told what is good for him: "Evil be thou my good." Hostility toward all others, as fundamentally alien, pervades even the most tender relationships, Freud says, and the Unconscious will murder even for trifles. The infant in primal envy feels overwhelmed by the real maternal presence. Thus the self moves to its own presence—its *present absence*—where that central Presence is, only and fortunately, a metaphor. Yet the self cannot sustain the complete absence of Source, in reality *or* metaphor, without its own obliteration. For disappearance of the imaged Source would invoke the Void within and without; that is, the self that will experience presences, others, Eros, Agape, or any psychic sustenance, must experience them finally through the infant self-as-Source, the aura and image of maternal Presence. Full absence—the shattered or lost image of lost Source—is the Everlasting No, the unmothered infant, Cocytus, divine mistrust, a psychic death-in-life. Kierkegaard writes that the child who is taught to walk by a mother who is not the "loving mother" has "no beckoning encouragement, no blessing at the end of the walk. . . . For now there is fear that envelops the child. It weighs him down so that he cannot move forward. There is the same wish to lead him to the goal, *but the goal becomes suddenly terrifying.*[50] If Derrida is suggesting that we should work to free ourselves completely from this inner metaphor of Presence, perhaps he is unwittingly suggesting that we work to destroy ourselves. If we are, as Merleau-Ponty suggests, to inhabit our world instead of simply manipulating it, we must ourselves be inhabited by Source, by imaginative memories of Presence. The self acts to hold *absent presence* within its own *present absence.*

Self emerges and keeps emerging through time as a new textured presence, inherited from a vital Source but distinct from Source and from all other selves. Self is a new reality woven from a metaphoric field, between self-as-Source and self-as-Void. To

Freud, the ego is first and foremost a bodily ego, the projection of a surface: the self is a woven construct with its own boundaries and its own particular texture, but the infinite recesses of an involuntary, enigmatic ontology lie as though "within" those boundaries. The new presence of self, however, is not a metaphor: "The 'I' is the one personification whose necessary perspective is to take itself as literally real."[51] Self is a real finitude, taking on shape in time and changing in time, grounded upon an unreal sensed infinity.

Text as Equivalent to Self

Text can be equivalent to self in several essential ways—for instance, in its birth, its involuntary motions toward Source and Void, its defining activity, its idiosyncratic texture, its interaction with other selves. We can gather many of these equivalences into five categories:

1. *A text can appear to be the child, or even the double, of its creator.* We have not yet found the precise mechanism to describe poetic creation, and we may never find it, but our metaphors for the creative act often seem to resemble one another. We imply that author is to text as mother or maternal father is to child; sometimes we even suggest that the text-child is the "true" author himself. Theories of poetic creation often speak of a crisis that seems a labor of delivery, a birth ritual: the enraptured states of Platonic fury and inspiration by the Muses, or Coleridge's "I AM" of the esemplastic imagination, representing the birth of the mind to the mind. We say that a "regression in service of the ego" provokes a reassembly or rebirth of the self. Ernst Kris adds, "In the typical case the work becomes part of and even more important than the self. Narcissistic cathexis has been shifted from the person of the artist to his work." Narcissism is reborn, Freud says, in the love of the parent for the child; Ben Jonson bids farewell to his seven-year-old son, his best piece of poetry. More radically, Ehrenzweig hypothesizes that the artist projects himself as though into his own womb, then allows his own psychic dissolution, and finally reintegrates the fragments in the art work.[52] After completing his early story "The Judg-

ment," Franz Kafka exulted "how for everything, for the strangest fancies, there waits a great fire in which they perish and are resurrected."

Some would claim that a text truly *is* its author, in all essential qualities. To Susan Sontag, the greatest art seems "secreted"; Suzanne Langer calls the poet's creation "a piece of virtual life"; William Wimsatt concludes, "The human psyche makes a poem out of itself."[53] The popular idiom shares the notion that self and text are all but identified: we are reading Shakespeare, we say, or writing a paper about Melville. When Lacan says that the search for self in psychoanalysis reveals a language, or that the unconscious is structured like a text, we are not sure whether he is overstating the case, provocatively. And Derrida offers, even more directly, "la parole est sujet"—that is, one has a self only by the work of a text. Yet others would keep some minimal distance between self and text, however unmeasurable. Ricoeur, following Saussure and Benveniste, believes that the symbolism of the unconscious is not a linguistic phenomenon *stricto sensu,* but infralinguistic and supralinguistic:[54] that is, text and self do not merge identities even if they are precisely alike. The authors of the "intentional fallacy" theory would probably agree here, severing text from author at the umbilical cord: each clears its own space.

If we say that a literary text can be an equivalent self, we might embrace many of these similar intuitions about the relationships possible between text and author. A given text may indeed be an exact mapping of the author's psyche at that moment of creation, but until the uncertain day when we can read the language of the unconscious directly, we need not say that a text "represents" or "models" a particular self. Rather, text and self, however closely their precise textures may or may not happen to agree, can be equivalent to each other. Each is a linguistic *and* translinguistic texture, actively negotiating enigmatic senses of self-as-Source and self-as-Void; each works a chiasmus of *absent presence* and *present absence;* each is a real finitude grounded upon an unreal sensed infinity. Each cannot be finally resolved in the rational discourse of interpretation. Psychohistory can evoke fascinating family likenesses between author and text, but it cannot thoroughly resolve either author or text.

2. *A text can be an active being-in-words of* absent presence *and* present absence, *with its own ultimately unworded sense of Source and Void.* Not only since Romanticism has the literary act been a raid on the absolute. In any age a lyric poem, through the constructed enunciative posture of the lyric "I," will often reach to hold absolute Source within its words. The text can seem alive with that intuition of sustaining, infinite experience that lies at the enigmatic heart of every self. Just as this intuition of Source is worked through specific others by the self, so the specific words of a text can be textured to suggest unwordable Source. There need be no formula predicting precisely how others for self, or words for text, carry this felt Source—in what selection or combination, what trope or symptom. For to understand one self only another self will suffice: we rely upon sensitive and competent readers to intuit the absolute self-as-Source evoked by a given text, and to read their intuition for us through the individual complexities of the text. Certainly these readers need to become as familiar as possible with appropriate historical periods, literary conventions, languages, or rhetorical devices, so as to educate their intuitions—but this is "connaissance," finally, and not "science"; definitive objective knowledge does not lie at the end of this path. For even the most competent reader before a text is, finally, one self confronting another self. To ask how a reader can intuit a text's intuition, how he can sense the attempt to reach absolute self-as-Source "through" the words of a text, is to ask just how one senses a certain psyche "through" a familiar human face and voice, or how in childhood we come to know those special presences around us. If we can sense the presence of a literary text as another self, our sense is no less real for being arational.

A text cannot exist without words; thus the absolute Source sensed through a text has been somehow brought there by the words, word combinations, word structures. For the author, as for all selves, words can seem to belong to Source, and values, truths, and presences can seem to reside in words and texts. Thus each author, a self in motion toward others to rejoin Source, finds around him a world of luminous words caught in the same motion: whether these words come from literary predecessors, poetic conventions, religions, governments, customs, legends, or eccentric personal history, they can seem immanent, nourishing, and eternal. The words and texts of a given author's signifying universe[55] can represent to the author the intuitions of Source shared by a certain culture or literary tradition at a given moment; thus the care of words, as for Petrarch, can mean the care of soul, and all the more so if it is community-soul or world-soul at issue. And since these words will never seem quite adequate to our unspoken sense of Source, they can become for the author enhanced with a halo of Presence, a dimension of Source they cannot quite capture. Thus the author's signifying universe may lie in words because it lies beyond them: Kenneth Burke suggests that things can be the signs of words, that "nature gleams secretly with a most fantastic shimmer of words."[56]

These charged words, radiant with their failed effort to reach Source, pass from the signifying universe through the crucible of the author's own sensibilities, his own individually worked sense of Source, his "interstitial web." Then, recombined and reworked, in old or new structures, with familiar or unfamiliar metaphors, rhymes, and figures, and sometimes among newly invented words, the words of the signifying universe reappear in the author's newborn text. If the author has made a text that is an equivalent self, he will have shaped these charged words with their new context to suggest *a sensed infinity that grounds the new text, that enables it to be present.* The lyric "I" will seem to intuit some eternity, some lifegiving value or presence, that lies just past the limit of his words. Nourished by this sense of Source, the new text comes to resemble lived experience; it seems to have an awareness of its own being, like an image in a mirror. The text, a being-in-words, can have by virtue of those words its own infant and enigmatic core, its own ultimately unworded sense of Source.

Thus the text can become *absent presence,* centered by an infinite Presence it can never embrace in words. Like a human self, then, the text is not isolated or autonomous, but is given its being: text draws its sense of self from Source. The unworded enigma crucial to a text can be, first, text-as-Source. Yet there is only a *sense* of Source, an *absent presence,* the re-presented infinite Source in the text as effigy, as metaphor. Text cannot *be* Source in full presence, although some selves may claim this full thaumaturgy for text—Word of God, made flesh. Like any self, like the literal mother, a text can be read or received as though it were Source, received as the infant receives maternal presence—but no text *is* Source. The structuralist effort to reabsorb texts into a Language System perhaps masks such a claim to refind the lost Source as Language, despite all texts and selves. Fredric Jameson says of structuralism, "this theory of models cannot recognize itself for a model."[57] To preserve text as equivalent self, we must stay among models and metaphors: if we claim that a text *is* Source, even if that Source be Language, we move closer to the effective annihilation of texts, and we lose our sense of responding to texts as selves.

For text becomes also *present absence,* its own Presence, distinguishable from that nourishing illusion of Source that seems to center it. A poem, through the lyric "I," can seem aware that its own being-in-words cannot really grasp full lifegiving Presence. The shadow of primal separation, always with language, follows the words and word structures of the author's signifying universe into his text, so that a felt motion toward total absence complements their motion toward Presence. Thus these charged words, reshaped and textured by the author with their new context, come to suggest their own final separation from infinite Source, threatening the new text and placing its being in question. When Valéry says that poetry never speaks but of absent things, he seems to describe poetry as Derrida has more recently described *écriture,* as a structure with a center that is deficiency, not being.[58] The unwordable sensed Void at the core of a poetic text is perhaps more evident to us today than ever, but it is no real news; we were told before now that the poet never affirmeth, and therefore never lieth. In the terms of modernity, "literature never pretended that sign and meaning did coincide," and poetic language names a void with ever-renewed understanding.[59] The words of a poem, like the self, negotiate between Source and Void: the lyric "I" seems to live in vigorous hope of embracing Source with words, while simultaneously fearing that words will fail entirely of Presence.

The separated self, grieving for Source, seems threatened—yet it is preserved, through that saving margin of separation, as itself a new presence distinct from lifegiving but alien Source. And so it is with equivalent self: the text that seems to disclose its own finitude, that includes its own deconstruction and demystification, somehow becomes all the stronger for this awareness. Hanna Segal, applying Klein's psychoanalytic theories to aesthetics, believes that when the artist allows the complete cycle of the "depressive position" to be revealed in his work—the destruction of Source, the terror and chaos of full mourning along with the reparation of "good imago" in the construction of the art work—he creates a profound aesthetic experience for audience or readers.[60] After all, the text that self-consciously divides itself from Source is no longer impaired; it has a presence, however vulnerable, of its own. Derrida himself, by his long and energetic questioning of language, deflects all words from presence or present: the more he questions, the more firmly he establishes himself, Derrida, as a new presence, a text that we call by metonymy "Derrida." Murray Krieger, in a fine chapter that takes issue with Derrida by supplementing him, puts it well: "Strangely, existential absence only reinforces aesthetic presence, though at the cost of compelling that presence to doubt itself."[61] The new text as equivalent self is fed, paradoxically, by a sense of absence, by division from Source and fear of Void.

The text that affirms its own presence by acknowledging the absent Source may move toward proclaiming its own immortality, if we follow its texture closely enough. Yet a text cannot claim full absence, the lost image of the lost Source: without its words a text cannot be, and words cannot outrun their glow of Presence, just as they cannot escape their shadow of Void. Text is caught between absence and presence, like the self, and becomes an active chiasmus-in-words of *absent presence* and *present absence*.

3. *The text as immanent new presence is real, self-selective, idiosyncratic, and vulnerable in time.* Like the self, the literary text can be a literal reality built of metaphors, a finitude structured about a sense of infinity. We seem often to think of the text as physically present, like a person: to us as to Milton, a good book is the life-blood of a master-spirit. Word as flesh, text as body: the text becomes an unyielding tangible fact, both as black lines on the page and as the sensual, tactile range of the words, fantasy incarnate in an equivalent self. As Gaston Bachelard puts it, "je suis fait de la matière de mon rêve." The words of the world are fulfilled in the flesh of the poem, the absolutely concrete text

that is the measure of all things. As Barfield says, "The world, like Dionysus, is torn to pieces by pure intellect; but the poet is Zeus; he has swallowed the heart of the world; and he can reproduce it as a living body." Sigurd Burckhardt discusses the corporeality of the text; cut these words and they bleed. The poem becomes what Freud might call a body-ego, its own surface and boundaries projected as the density of inner space. The sense of a physical body must be crafted by the psyche, like a poem; reciprocally, a poem must hold a living presence with the physicality of the text. A poem on the page, deliberately insulated and framed by its margins, seems to appropriate its own space as would a physical body, self-defined and aloof from surroundings. "I view verbal form as an author's projection of a self-protective and self-generative space that transcends or escapes historical time.... Perceived as an external structure, verbal space becomes an emblem for the physical structure we inevitably carry with us."[62] In our own continuing motion toward Source or Presence, we seem almost naturally to respond to a text as though it were a soul incarnate—immediately before us, as we suppose, even though we know we must work to recover a suitable cultural context. Petrarch begins his letter to posterity, "Greeting.—It is possible that some word of me may have come to you...."

The text cannot generate its own psychic and corporeal substance, but draws, chooses its life from the others that words are, and, "beyond" them, from Source; in a glass-bell divided from the world of texts and signifiers, the literary text could not be born. The text does not create itself, then. However, it does select itself, fundamentally: the voice of the text, author and lyric "I," determines absolutely *which* others from the signifying universe will belong to the text. Just as a human self appropriates a variety of others in its motion toward Source, choosing among them which others it will "be" or find itself in, so a text can freely choose the materials for its own texturing—using, for instance, a rigidly exclusive or voraciously inclusive vocabulary—and thus can determine its own composition. Thus text and self are free without complete autonomy; although they must be as-Source, made of others, no one can predict *which* others. Poetic form and convention can in this way belong to the text's identification with other texts; form need not be a "defense" against disturbing content, but can be part of the motion toward others that is necessary for self-formation.

Moreover, the text controls entirely the manner in which it carries these others (and, thereby, Source) into itself. The author not only chooses which set of poetic rules to follow, but he may also invoke rules only to break them. Morse Peckham even concludes, "the role of the artist requires him to break prescriptive rules about form. There are no exceptions."[63] The poem may fragment accepted truths and forms in order to restore and re-create them, like Klein's infant in reparation, or like a human body breaking apart and reconstituting food. "The poem is a structure of signifiers which absorbs and reconstitutes the signified."[64] That is, others undergo a sea change when they nourish the self; a poem is not determined by its sources, nor can its possible meanings be completely validated by its cultural contexts. Contexts do feed the poem, of course, and must therefore inform the competent reader, for there is no such thing as self-sufficient autonomy of text, a text uninfluenced by its age. But in its freedom to omit or admit specific others found in its cultural context, and in its particular work with those others, a poem can be a law unto itself, equivalent to a human self. Although heavily contextual interpretations may try to force-feed a poem, readers will not be long convinced by them; for the poem, a selective self, can resist and change details from its contexts.

In those words freely selected to compose its own being-in-words, the text weaves its own identifiable fabric—one of a kind, like the human psyche. Whatever the text is not, it *is* this activity of texturing, these unpredictable and arbitrary combinations of rhetorical forms, syntax, neologisms, new metaphors. By naming particular absences and presences, the text weaves itself, limited only by full absence and full Presence in its freedom to make meanings. To say that text and self must *conform* to the relational or structural Truth of the Symbolic Order, as Lacan says, is to preempt this basic freedom to texture, this freedom to construct a net of verbal and psychic relationships that is in some saving measure peculiar to oneself. Within this freedom, within the wide reality between Source and Void, self and text can be voluntary, joyous, playful. A text can find its own voice: even if all selves must negotiate a chiasmus of absence and Presence, each text as self may discover its own unchartered lines within this chiasmus, adventuring in the gaps between words and within words. A paragraph of Heidegger is recognizable as Heidegger and Heidegger only, no other self. The pleasure of the text is the pleasure of meeting another self whose texture differs from one's own—a self who perhaps "resists the intelligence / almost completely." The new presence of a text that can burden and fascinate a reader is, precisely, a new texture, a way of putting things that is a way of negotiating one's own being. These idiosyncratic textures resist being completely worded by interpretation; no matter how much one explains or describes them, these textures recede, belonging only to themselves because they are, essentially, selves. Perhaps it is this singular identifiability that elicits our judgment "classic," rather than any objectifiable criteria of excellence: Shakespeare, a voice aloof and strange beyond all interpretive words of other selves. Perhaps only texture immortalizes, as we discover there the possibility of birth, a presence newborn from the same old material of words.

Finally, the text as equivalent self is a risked and interminable construction, alive with the pathos of mortality and time. The formal closure of a text need not signify resolution, and symmetry in structure need not imply ideal harmony or balance. Although the self may be finite in space, closed upon itself like a human body, the activity of self is not perfectible or unchanging, except by the accident of death. If the space of the poem is a moment for the self, it can be nonetheless a moment in motion, conscious of its own passing, and spatial "unity" may only intensify this sense of temporal incompleteness, the poem's projection toward the future. Some theorists would say that a poem's rigid form can constitute a manic denial of change and bereavement, a frozen presence or verbal icon made to negate absence: to these theorists, poetic form would be defensive. But others, such as Suzanne Langer and Ella Sharpe, contend that the rhythms of a poem can be organic rhythms (feeding or sexual rhythms) and thus time-bound and Heraclitean, nothing so permanent as their change. No sense of an ending is implicit in such life rhythms, but ongoing self-elaboration, repeated processes. The objectivity of the text is an illusion of self-sufficiency and completeness, to Stanley Fish; the real literature occurs within the developing responses of the reader as they succeed one another in time.

43

These temporal contingencies of the text, the unique syntactical threading that each text weaves into its own voice, can accumulate a texture but not unity. Unity is arbitrary, like death—a break in the rhythm, a closing couplet that creates a synchronic pattern in retrospect.

Edward Said remarks in a discussion of Jean Piaget that the writer's own career, haunted by antecedence and the future, can gradually become his all-encompassing subject.[65] The literary text as self can indeed be haunted by the future, by its persistent sense of its own unfolding, its full being always deferred and deflected from its words. The poem is the work of a self continuing to take place: its finitude in space is its only and arbitrary completion, no matter what matching images one finds within it. As Hegel has said, "Wesen ist, was ist gewesen" (Being is what has been). If rhymes are a manic illusion of closure, perhaps the rhythms of organic process are the continuing reality. Insofar as a text becomes aware of its own suspense within time, it mourns its failure to reach permanent rest, infinite Source. Poems about poetry become poems about the self in its birth, unfolding, and mortality, "what is past, and passing, and to come." Since discursive language, in its rationality and sanity, can hardly address this existential mourning for Source that is self and text, a poem's language can carry an extra affective charge: a poem can be a little mad in its pathos.

4. *Along lines of literary tradition and influence, subtexts can be lifegiving presences, sources like Source, in the birth of new texts.* The texts of an author's signifying universe can be to him immanent presences, some more powerful upon him than the rest. The texts with which he identifies most closely, which reinforce most acutely his own sense of Source, become the most influential subtexts for his new text. In this way a text can hold the *absent presence* of its most vital subtexts: just as a human self is nourished continually by an unwordable sense of Source, so a text can seem to be sustained by the "aura" of its subtexts, not quite analyzable, a luminous Presence of subtext just beyond accidents of particular wording and phrasing. Further, insofar as a subtext is not limited to certain definite words in the new text, the inherited Presence of the subtext will be the more affecting, the more aureatic. Nietzsche contends in *The Use and*

Abuse of History that the literally reproduced dead are "mummified" in antiquarian history, *there* without being vitally *present*. So it is with past and present texts: extensive literal quoting seems to weaken and deanimate both subtext and text, to cancel the sense of presence. Thomas Greene describes two types of humanist imitation that employ literal reproduction—the first in reverential rewriting and the second in syncretic allusions from heterogeneous models: when the fact of the subtext is thus taken in without its life, the vital Presence of the subtext can hardly survive within the newly textured presence, and there can be no real mediation between past and present texts.[66]

Yet if the subtext cannot be distinguished as literal passages or allusions, perhaps the assimilation of the old presence by the new is more complete; the subtext can persist as an "aura" or *absent presence* irreducible to words, and the new text thereby earns a more definite presence of its own. The subtext is both within the new text and distant from it: it shines through the new text like that absent original Source that enables the new text to be, and yet the body of the subtext is unrecoverable from the new text, removed in history. The new text knows the loss of the subtext, the irresolvable temporal gulf between text and subtext, as all texts and subtexts seem caught in common historical motion toward a feared and unspoken Void. "One giant calls to another across the waste space of time." And this is for the best, because the new text trying to *be* subtext or Source, in extensive imitation, is in danger of losing its own voice. Although the use of convention can seem to confer immediate identity upon a text, lending it a sense of Source through a whole family of other texts, overly prescriptive conventions can constrict the new text as self-selective and idiosyncratic, until it becomes difficult to sense a new voice beneath inherited artifice. The text, like Nietzsche's weak man, is in danger of being extinguished by its own history, its own monumental presences: "Let the dead bury the living." Literary classics are imposing selves, the life force personalized in the human text, great presences that we invest with mana power; the new text must resist its drive to rewrite them, in order to preserve its own limited freedom as equivalent self.

Thus the new text becomes *present absence*, its own presence, realizing its separation from subtext-Source in a crisis equivalent to bereavement, succumbing to the distance of time and history in an effort to find its own voice. Nietzsche tells us that the right use of history is the critical use of history. And in dialectic imitation, the fourth type of humanist imitation proposed by Greene, the new text seems to leave itself open to potential criticism embodied in the subtext, as though trying to elicit some response from the subtext. The new text, aware that it does not hold the subtext-Source, now faces the subtext as separate self, finding equivalence and respect through differences. It is in this context of primal separation that we might understand the struggles described by Harold Bloom between "strong" poet and predecessor poet. For the strong poet can endure the necessary absence of subtext in the presence of the new text, the *clinamen* or departure from the subtext; the vessel self-and-Source must be broken to enable the poet. The new text must experience the subtext, in some measure, as alien. This experience may be only a nostalgic awareness of distance, like Dante's sense of Virgil—or it may be a radical misreading; or Heidegger's proposed violence to the subtext; or an insight into the subtext's central blindness, as Paul de Man describes; or Derrida's technique of deconstruction. The new text cannot leave the subtext unchanged; just as the maternal image is destined to be dismembered by the psyche, so it is often some iconoclasm that helps deliver the new text into its own being. Still, the new text cannot endure the full absence of all subtexts without its own death. Some cultural image or memory of lost subtext-Source must be preserved, for we need some greatness prior to our own in order to have a dialogue, a culture, or a tradition for our response, as Geoffrey Hartman suggests: otherwise, "das leblose Einsame" would remain, a Golgotha of imagination, a death-in-life for the new text.[67]

The literary text as equivalent self actively weaves the *absent presence* of subtext-Source into its own *present absence;* the unwordable "auras" of subtexts can participate in the enigmatic sense of Source central to a new text. Thus the anxiety of influence and the love of imitation are always both threads in the fabric of the new text, for the one complements the other in the chiasmus that is the self. The new text acts in affection for its subtexts and in alienation from them, both incorporating them and relinquishing them to form its own idiosyncratic texture. As

the past grows in weight and complexity, new textures may become impossibly hermetic presences. But if we ask to what end is
literary tradition, the poem, or the self, we are surely trying to
solve our vulnerability to time by a contrived teleology, like a
couplet at the end of a sonnet. The mortal freedom to make
one's own texture is the only teleology self and poem have, or
are. Such final goals are evocations of a Source that cannot be
realized without loss of self.

5. *In reading, the text can be swept into the reader's motion toward
Source, so that the text as equivalent self can act as a presence upon the
reader.* Despite our arguments about critical method and our
meticulous rereadings to support our arguments, we still read
first as infants, drinking in the presence of the text as we do the
original maternal presence, looking for ourselves in evocations
of Maternal Source. The texts we choose to devour most fully
are those that can best replenish our own central nourishing
metaphor of self-as-Source: some books are to be tasted, others
chewed and digested. "Till then, I cleave to you, o double-
breasted book."[68] Our identifications with personae and characters belong to our central enigma, that we are as-Source, reaching to others and Source to find ourselves. "Everyone remains
filial on the deep level where literature is registered."[69] To read
deeply, we reinvoke this most basic filial receptivity, entering a
preconscious or prelogical state as though spellbound before a
vital Presence. The surplus of signifiers that is the poem seems
to absorb us and rearticulate us in shamanistic magic, Lévi-
Strauss's "symbolic efficacity."[70] We seem to be entranced by the
text, and we in turn cannot word what it is that entrances us, that
casts this spell to which we so naturally succumb. In reading a
book, says Georges Poulet, "I am on loan to another . . . the I
who thinks when I read the book is the I of the one who writes
the book . . . a work of literature becomes at the expense of the
reader a sort of human being, suspending the reader's life for a
while."[71] As we loan ourselves to a text and become as-Source
again, we seem to slide into an ocean of Presence, an infinity.
Stanley Fish believes that in a dialectical experience of reading
one moves, or is moved, to an antidiscursive and antirational
view of the world, with an all-embracing unity.[72] Similarly, Murray Krieger speaks of the mythic and sacramental moment of the

aesthetic experience, where space and time seem to dissolve. And if words cannot fully express us, if they can only gesture toward enigmatic selves but not hold them, words can become all the more sacramental, luminous with uncontained Presence: self and text can *seem* to merge with each other at their centers, through an infinite well of Presence. In this magic interchange, immanent being seems passed from self to self: he who touches my book touches me. The reader, in metaphor, takes the text into himself; he becomes the *absent presence* of the text he reads.

Unlike Don Quixote, though, most readers do not try to become the text itself. It is a contrived and self-induced spell, after all; since we know that we only *seem* to lose ourselves, we can save ourselves from the overbearing full presence of the text. We are not in full belief, but in a willing suspension of disbelief, an acknowledged wish; in Kris's terms, we are in a safe range of aesthetic illusion, between "underdistance" and "overdistance."[73] Norman Holland and Marion Milner have also investigated this mixed nature of our aesthetic responses: we *let* the boundaries between self and text seem to melt away, in a seeming trespass of both selves, planning all the while to return to ourselves. We are drawn to Source ultimately in order to nourish our own centers.

The reader becomes then the *present absence* of the text, his own presence, distinguishable from the text and not determined by it. As Roland Barthes reminds us while he discusses shifters, "The *I* of the one who writes *I* is not the same as the *I* which is read by *thou*."[74] From the felt moment of sacramental unity with a literary text, the separate readers fall away, refinding themselves in the gap between reader and text, and reconfirming themselves in the disagreements among their text interpretations. Reader and text, each chiasmic realities around a metaphoric infinity, can only *seem* to reach an eternal truth of interpretation together. For we are selves only insofar as we are away from Source, separate from text; in this world of selves there can be only misreading and blindness, whatever else we may call them. If we all shared valid, absolute, fully worded and definitive interpretations of all literary texts, we would belong to an oceanic Language-numen, one annihilation of distinct selves. But readers, as selves, are continually weaving the shadow of primal separation into their own textures, continually putting their own mode of being into question. The text that questions its own being brings us thereby to question ours, in our own finite solitude and vulnerability. Alone with the text, we are alone with ourselves in a "symbolic process of self-confrontation in which infantile solutions are resisted even as they are indulged."[75] In this self-awareness we must meet the crisis of infancy that prefigures all other crises, the division of self from Source, and thus we renew our irreducible and central fear of Void. The affective disturbances of the text must find their meaning in the reader, the separated self, alone with his necessary illusion of eternity. "The world, unfortunately, is real; I, unfortunately, am Borges."

The reader's worded interpretation of a text can then become a new text, a new presence and another equivalent self, an active chiasmus of *absent presence* and *present absence* that is real, self-selective with regard to the interpreted text, idiosyncratic, and vulnerable in time. Not all critical texts are thus equivalent selves, nor are all poems, but perhaps the more imposing ones are. A text interpretation can thus be a self-construction or self-weaving; the accumulated texts and text interpretations that form our culture and tradition are presences, selves directed towards other selves, separate even though they share intuitions of Source. According to Lacan, words are always for the imaginary "other"; similarly, to Merleau-Ponty language is an *opération à deux,* in which the subject carries himself toward the one who is hearing. Thus only selves, and not systems, are privileged to enter the hermeneutic circle, for only selves have the necessary intuition to sense what the text is, and to let the text be, weaving its presence into their own interpretations. As Culler explains, "linguistic analysis does not provide a method by which the meaning of a text can be deduced from the meaning of its components."[76] Meaning cannot be made objectively common to all selves; interpretation belongs in the woven chiasmus of the enigmatic self.

2   *Poet-Lover*

The hermeneutics of the previous chapter can belong to Renaissance love lyric texts as equivalent selves. For like the self, the Poet-Lover longs to be forever with that engendering Source. Central to lyric, as to self, is an enigmatic and unspoken core (*infans*), resistant to interpretive words, including two primal and involuntary motions "out of" words: the longing for Source, for that anticipated blissful union with the beloved that would dissolve the text's being-in-words, and the dread of Void, of the full absence that would destroy the text (see above, pp. 21–30). More simply, we might name this infant and enigmatic "core," with these defining and chronic involuntary motions, *Lover*. If we can thus name these crucial and irreducible directions common to self and lyric text, without isolating or reifying "the Lover" as an abstraction, we might, in the same spirit, note that the beloved is usually evoked by these lyrics as their sustaining and unwordable Source, in response to their ontological infant longing. If we could adequately translate to the surface the matrix sentence structured far beneath the words of these lyrics, it would resemble the statement, "I am the beloved, and without the beloved I am not."

Moreover, the love lyric text, like the self, is inclined to take up the challenge posed by its own involuntary longing and fear. That is, the text is moved to individuate, to negotiate its own being-in-words between the silent limits of Source and Void, creating voluntarily and deliberately its own particular chiasmic texture of *absent presence* and *present absence* (see above, pp. 30–35). We might name this independent focus of initiative, this impulse or motion toward self-texturing, *Poet,* and thus again without reification we would call *Poet* the obvious care and concern for the wordwork, the planing and the polishing. Of course, it would be foolish even to try to isolate, within the verbal texture, *Poet* from *Lover*: these are simply names for impulses each appropriate to all the words, not sharp-edged critical tools that can divide some signifiers from others. *Poet* and *Lover* are both everywhere and nowhere in a given love lyric—they are not things, or even personae, but desires, interests, motivations "behind" processes, *Triebe* (drives) of poetics.

Finally, the motions we name *Lover* and *Poet* result in the activity that is the lyric text, the new self as contingent and ongoing work, the texturing of *absent presence* and *present absence* (see above, pp. 37–40). Thus the lyric, like the self, is not hypostasis or idealization, but activity, work: we name the text activity Poet-Lover because the speaking "I" is disclosed even as he speaks, generating the tissue of words that we know him to be, that sum our knowledge of him. If we seem to name the poem by its speaker, as though in synecdoche, it is because we must take all the words of the poem, even the rhymes and rhetorical schemes, to carry the full intentionality of the "I." We have the voice of a poem, not the voice in a poem—even if we find historical or biographical correlatives, even if the speaker is a fiction or a deception, even if he is a hollow "I," as Paul Zumthor would have him, speaking the *registre.* Furthermore, we would do well to keep questioning the intended meaning structured beneath that hyphen, in that term "Poet-Lover" that students of these lyrics have been unwilling to conflate or relinquish. For example, the hyphen might "mean" that neither *Poet* nor *Lover* is finally dispensable in the creation of text as equivalent self, despite various critical suggestions that, in a given poem, statements about poetry are really metaphors for statements about love, or vice versa, statements about love are really metaphors for poetic composition. Or again, the hyphen might indicate some implicated conflict between *Poet* and *Lover,* as though for instance the care for words could usurp or invalidate the expressed longing for wordless union with the beloved. These are questions that will continue; they will still be with us in the following chapters, as we look more closely at the individual textures of particular lyrics. But for now, we will discuss in broader

51

terms the Poet-Lover as an equivalent self, by exploring further the *Lover* and *Poet* motions as they are typically revealed in the text-milieu (texts, subtexts, contexts) of Renaissance love lyrics.

First, we must fully acknowledge that our understanding of *Lover* in these lyrics, despite and because of the verbal texture, is ultimately empathetic and intuitive—not clinical, or rational, or verbal. We respond to his enigmatic and involuntary motions from our own persistent core *infans;* our sustaining sense of Maternal Source receives that sense of Source evoked by the lyric. That is, the longings appropriate to *Lover* are finally not imposed by some neurotic medieval custom, some "infantile mother fixation" that can be verbalized, solved, and dispatched, but by our ontology. *Lover* is disclosed as a condition we recognize to be our own—not uncanny, after all, but *heimlich.* Margaret Mahler states that condition succinctly when she writes that our "smooth and consistently progressive personality development" is all but impossible, for "separation and individuation derive from and are dependent upon the symbiotic origin of the human condition, upon that very symbiosis with another human being, the mother. This creates an everlasting longing for the actual or coenesthetically fantasized, wish-fulfilled, and absolutely protected state of primal identification . . . for which deep down in the original primal unconscious, in the so-called primarily repressed realm, every human being strives."[1] She is saying, in effect, that we each still have, as though "deep down," primally repressed, and "within" the spatial self, that "everlasting longing" for Maternal Source, that *Lover* in motion, vestigial but crucial *daimon.* There seems perhaps an inner limit to our rational and verbal despatialization of our selves, for the self strives inwardly toward the sensed eternal grace of its own origins. Here, perhaps, Eros and Agape meet. Indeed, Peter Dronke calls *amour courtois* a universal emotion, and H. I. Marrou concludes that courtly love is "un secteur du coeur, un de ses aspects éternal de l'homme."[2] The maternal presence is not simply one of several love objects we may be unfortunate enough to "overvalue," but a repressed memory of infinity that we each *are,* at some irreducible psychic center. We know by empathy that there is no final way to cure *Lover,* to resolve self or lyric.

Moreover, the unspoken longing of self and text, *Lover infans,* is also the longing for unspoken Source. The *Lover* of these lyrics, a "core identity" of longing,[3] is transverbal and preverbal motion, both far beyond and deep within the words; in the central momentum of this fantasy, *Lover* belongs with a permanently unknown and unwordable beloved Source. Of course, the lyrics in this motion are rightful heirs of Platonic texts, where "becoming like God" is an *arrheton*, unspoken, and of Augustinian texts, where God is known in silence, and in heaven all languages cease.[4] But more than this, the lyrics are equivalent selves, moving in words in order to move "out of" words or "past" words to the beloved, evoked as Source of being-in-words. Thus Peire d'Alvernhe's *amic* and Jaufré Rudel's *amor de lonh* are "intentionally inexplicit" beloveds and Raimbaut d'Aurenga's *saber ver* is the private, true, and unspoken state of his feelings about his lady, never revealed in the words of the poem.[5] Indeed, conventions of secrecy like these may belong not only to supposed social customs of "courtly love," but perhaps more vitally to *Lover infans,* to the unspoken maternal center of self, poem, Poet-Lover:

> But that fourth Mayd, which there amidst them traced,
> Who can aread, what creature mote she bee,
> Whether a creature, or a goddesse graced
> With heavenly gifts . . .
> [*Faerie Queene* VI. x. 25]

The *Lover* motion of these lyric texts has finally, in the last resort, no care for words. The failure of words promotes the equivalence between self and text, which both exist in diacritic, worded separation from that central, "coenesthetically fantasized" Source. We find "in" the lyric only hope, memory, intimations of immortality, *absent presence:* the very existence of the lyric, being-in-words, signifies that *Lover* moves there, in everlasting longing. The words of these lyrics are dispensable, Augustine's *signum proprium* pointing to truth but not encompassing Truth, words designed to vanish in the silence of the Present beloved. The worded text yearns towards its own dissolution.

Of course, we can and must still admire the *Poet* of these lyrics, the obvious care for an intricate verbal texture with overdetermined particular meanings, multiple allusions to real referents. James Wilhelm has demonstrated how adroitly a single word in one of these lyrics can refer at once to two realities—for example, to a secular text by Ovid and to a religious text by Augustine.[6] *Poet* cherishes the subtle, even duplicitous wordwork that often evokes realities—such real sociological events as the decline of feudalism and the rise of the petty nobility, perhaps such real customs as "courts of love," and even real encodings of doctrine (Neoplatonic, Bernardine, Catharist, Averrhoistic) in real texts. For example, the division between concupiscence and charity, as present in theological texts, is a worded reality that may be pertinent to the verbal texture of these lyrics. But we must not confuse admiration of *Poet* with verbalization of *Lover*. However exhaustively we discuss the intricacies of the wordwork, we cannot think to catch *Lover* in our interpretations, for *Lover* longs to be and belongs with Source, unspoken. *Lover* will not yield to our painstaking explanations of the "nature of love," our ideologies. Perhaps this very effort to conquer *Lover* with words has led to the infamous and interminable controversy about the precise definition of "courtly love": we ask whether *fin' amors* is in truth sensual or spiritual, while *Lover* persists as somatopsyche, a primally repressed infancy common to self and text.[7] One cannot find a worded, doctrinal response when Raimbaut d'Aurenga's Poet-Lover implores God never to let love decline and kisses vanish, or when Bernart de Ventadorn's Poet-Lover tells us that his lady's body is as white as the snow at Christmas:[8] one may speak perhaps of appropriating religious terms, or perhaps of parody or irony (and this speaking may be difficult enough), but it is futile to try to fix the resulting "nature of love" here described. When we say that Marcabru's *Jois, Sofrirs,* and *Mesura* are designed to resemble Pauline fruits of the Spirit—*caritas, gaudium, pax, patientia*—we are dealing in comparative nuances of texts, but we are not fully verbalizing the "nature of love" in either Marcabru or Paul: we intuit *Lover* there, both despite and because of our interpretive words. The nuances we discuss do not explain *Lover* but merely evoke some of those unexplainable motions "in" us; the nuances of verbal texture belong to Poet-Lover, the activity of the text. Linguistic density will seem to lead us closer to the heart of the matter, but in words we must always stop short of the full journey. Even while the significant and real verbal difference of lyric texts continue to occupy us, we can recognize there *Lover*, vital and irreducible, in genuine and present motion "beyond" those differences of words.

Poet with Lover

We may intuit *Lover* most easily when *Poet* moves in conjunction with *Lover*, in certain features of the metaphoric language shared by the poems of this lyric genre. For in this tradition, ranging from troubadour cansos and stilnovist canzoni to Petrarchan and English sonnets, the poems do coalesce into a broadly unified text-milieu with its own set of conventions, literary sources, and metaphoric language—a text-milieu understood as the wide background of the lyrics discussed in the following chapters. There is no abstractable "definition of love" here, yet there is a large common ground of metaphors, hyperboles, paradoxes, and other tropes that work to disclose the undisclosable *Lover*. We can find analogues to the conventional metaphoric language of these lyrics in some metaphoric terms used by object-relations theorists to describe psychic processes—for example, fusion, symbiosis, incorporation, or identification. There is no question here of clinical "explanation"; one merely notes the broad similarity of vocabularies and concepts, between on the one hand neo-Freudian theory, and on the other the wide pool of conventional figures of speech where *Poet* and *Lover* move in conjunction.

The presiding metaphor of this group is fusion, the imagined ultimate merging of self with beloved Source. In object-relations theory the fusion metaphor can be used almost synonymously with the "primal identification" or "primal omnipotence" in the Mahler passage quoted above: these theorists seem to mean by "fusion" what we have been calling full Presence, the original and impossible state of oneness with Maternal Source that all selves must continue to desire. Kernberg uses this metaphor, for instance,when he describes a stage of intrapsychic development like Klein's "depressive position," in which higher level integrations are accompanied by fantasied representations of the now lost "ideal object" and the "ideal state of self" that would make the individual "acceptable to, close to, and in the last resort, symbolically re-fused with the ideal object (the unharmed, all-loving, all-forgiving early mother image)."[9] Certainly in the text-milieu of these love lyrics, fusion metaphors are pervasive and insistent—indeed, perhaps so thoroughly indispensable that they all but vanish in the background. Few would question that in these poems supreme bliss is typically understood as the ever-to-be-accomplished final assimilation of loving self to beloved. This fantasied ideal state is secure in the most varied representatives of these lyrics: the troubadours' *joi* requires this faith, but so does Shakespeare's "marriage of true minds," and in Donne's "The Extasie" love "interinanimates two soules" while hands are "cimented" and eyes are "upon one double string," to fuse two selves together. *Lover* moves in these lyrics, the hope that love will cure the separated self. Moshé Lazar, who stresses the sensual aspects of *fin' amors*, nevertheless also speaks in terms of a complete union: "The *fin' amors* of the troubadours was precisely that total love, of heart and body, which was realized in the state of *joie*, in *totius personae concessione finitur* [it is completed in the yielding-up of the whole person]."[10]

Moreover, the language of fusion is prominent in the varied texts usually acknowledged as possible subtexts for troubadour lyrics and their successors—in the doctrines of the Marianists, the Cathars, the Bernardine mystics, and in numerous medieval writings influenced by Neoplatonism, such as those by Avicenna, Ibn Hazm, Boethius, Augustine, Aquinas, Dante, and later Ficino and his followers. In Plato's *Theaetetus*, the philosopher's life according to *arete* is "assimilation to God,"[11] and for Ficino the single soul describes a *circuitus spiritualis* from One to Many and back again, from first to final assimilation. In Castiglione's *Book of the Courtier*, another descendant of these texts, the Platonic kiss is the union of two souls; Emilia Pia tells Aretino that the lover's soul should never think of anything but to be transformed into the soul of his beloved.[12] Again, for Ibn Hazm love is "a conjunction between scattered parts of souls that have become divided in this physical universe," and union with the beloved is "a miracle of wonder," before which "the intellect stands abashed."[13] Bernard, speaking of the *Song of Songs*, says that the love between Christ and the soul is "a truly spiritual contract, more than a contract, an embrace, which makes one spirit of two."[14] Indeed, in these texts the interpreted distinctions between "lower" and "higher" types of love often seem to be signified by grades of intensity in this metaphoric language of fusion. Since *Lover infans* moves in everlasting longing, it may be that the more assured the promise of fusion, the more exalted the "nature of love" available for discursive commentary. Topsfield, in a recent reading of several major troubadour poets, proposes that they are searching through sensual, imaginary, and visionary "planes" of *Amors* for ultimate happiness, *lo mielhs* in some version of union with the lady. And *fin' amors* grows closer to the love of God as the union sought grows less elusive and more secure, until finally in the thirteenth-century stilnovist poems, love of God itself becomes the ideal.[15] Similarly, the palinode speaker will often seem to exchange beloveds in quest of the one most "pure" in both Freudian and Christian senses—most likely to be everlasting, primally omnipotent. Kohut remarks that Christianity leaves open to the self "narcissistic fulfillment in the realm of the merger with the omnipotent self-object, the divine figure of Christ," and that the idealized self-object belongs to Freud's concept of "purified pleasure."[16]

Bodies and physical matter, time and change, are inconvenient to the vital imagination of eternal fusion. Thus to avoid sexual love may be also to avoid time, and to encourage the promise of eternity. As Jonathan Saville remarks, Time, the separator, once invoked is not able to be stopped; the grief in the *chanson* for what one does not have becomes in the *alba* the grief for what one must lose.[17] Andreas' version of sexual or "mixed" love "quickly fails, and it lasts but a short time."[18] Through privation one can protect the imagination of infinite Source, of eternal life. For as the Sophia Maria of the Gnostics symbolizes, eternal sexual desire is, at least, eternal. To Uc Brunec, "the greatest gift of love, men would rather hope for than attain," for when love has no further to go, it "turns into despair, and the lover blames what once he loved." Guiraut Riquier states that if one went no further than the kiss, love would never end and never die.[19] Paolo and Francesca went further than the kiss, and were rewarded in their *contrapasso* with permanent impermanence, swept forever by black winds and severed forever from Eternal Love. And the Cathars reach perhaps the human limit of simultaneously despising the physical and yielding the individual self to Source. In their Manichean revulsion against corporeality, they would evade sexual fulfillment even unto genocide: "Dualism necessarily disapproves of the propagation of the species." Eros meets Thanatos in this faith, and only death can fulfill the soul's desire to redissolve itself in Unity—indeed, death redeems the sin of birth and returns souls to "the One of luminous indistinction."[20] The pleasure of actual physical love seems to pale beside the ecstatic imagination of fusion with this luminous Source.

Perhaps the metaphors of symbiosis are born from the threat implicit in this hope-filled language of fusion. Mahler admits that in object-relations theory, symbiosis is a metaphor, or a term adopted from biological reality: that is, the self can cling to the maternal presence as though to life itself, as though existence were impossible outside the common membrane, or symbiotic orbit, of self-and-Source. Indeed, for the infant the metaphor makes itself eventually real: anaclitic depression, caused by removing the mothering person in the infant's first year of life, is manifest in "weepiness, apprehension, withdrawal, refusal to eat, sleep disturbances, and eventually stupor."[21] *Pace* Shakespeare's Rosalind, then, infants do die of love, and the symbiotic terms of the lyric present the languishing lover as a living metaphor, like the infant, of psychic starvation: he weeps, he is timid and fearful, his vital spirits withdraw to his heart; he eats little, watches all night, calls upon death. Thus in the rehearsed symptoms of *amor hereos* or love-melancholy, as old as Graeco-Arabic medical theory, *Lover* and *Poet* can move together in the lyrics. Avicenna analyzes this disease in *The Canon of Medicine,* warning that a lover who receives no recognition from his lady may well succumb to love-melancholy or *ishq,* a disease of the imagination leading finally to death.[22] Thus Chaucer's Troilus raves; thus Raimbaut d'Aurenga refers to "my lady from whom I cannot part"; thus Peire d'Alvernhe laments a love too pleasing, "that a man fears that he will perish at the moment when he must depart from it."[23] These passages may carry sexual innuendoes, and indeed, in *amor hereos* sexual hunger and hunger for Presence are not far apart: the lovers die for lack of succour, and only *joi* can nourish them back to life, renewing their flesh and spirit.

As a survival measure, then, the self moves to internalize Source, in both neo-Freudian terminology and love lyric convention. *Lover* and *Poet* meet now in metaphors of incorporation:

the self fantasizes that it takes in the sustaining Presence, as if by mouth, and that it lodges this Presence at its center, as if in the belly. These mental representations, inseparable from instinctual drives, seem to be born with the infant's first feedings, and thus to operate by analogy with feeding. And so with *Lover*: a love potion is something one drinks, after all, and in a common allusion to Tristan, Raimbaut d'Aurenga concludes, "since I have drunk that love, I must love with secrecy." Even more typically, the lover is sustained by the lady's glances, smile, or kind words in this way: such language of nourishment is common in Petrarch's *Canzoniere*, and his predecessor Peire d'Alvernhe writes, "I feel and seek that love in which there is nothing awry, a love in which my fair hopes may nourish me."[24] To feed on love, one *drinks in* the beloved, as the infant *drinks in* the maternal presence, in a metaphor that sustains all human reality. And if one displaces the incorporation metaphor slightly upward from the scene of the infant nursing at the breast, one arrives at that most familiar of all love lyric conceits, the original scene of spell-casting: the lady's image travels through the lover's eyes and becomes fixed in his heart. Some versions of the enamorment scene emphasize the heart's receptivity, as it welcomes the image or even preconceives it: in quest of life, one needs and wills to take this presence in. Yet often, too, enamorments seem fated, catching the lover by surprise in a vulnerable moment, and then determining him: love seems to *happen* to one, like Source to infant, beyond one's ability to choose. It may arrive in a variety of ways—Cupid's arrows in the lady's darting glance; a face in a mirror, a picture, or a vision; destiny implanting the image at birth—but the invariant in this metaphor is the full image itself, secured virtually forever in one's heart.[25] Just so, the infant unconsciously devours an image, and the maternal "ego-ideal" becomes part of the id. At best, this seems a means of possessing *joi* permanently: the lady, internalized, becomes one's sole hope and inspiration.

The self can also appropriate Source by trying to become identical to Source: the metaphor here is mimesis to the point of metamorphosis, transfiguration, the growth of a new identity. Thus the child unconsciously aspires to imitate the good mother or parent, trying thus to assume the maternal identity as his own, and in Lacan's "stade du miroir" (mirror-state) one conceives one's best self, as a whole, to be the ideal Imaginary Other. Likewise, to Guillem de Peitau, in a stanza sometimes taken as the credo for *fin' amors,* the lady's *joi* can create a whole new self, making the wise foolish, the courtly churlish, the churlish courtly.[26] *Joi* can work for good or ill in this stanza, but conventionally the transfiguration is for good, and the lover is ennobled by the lady's best qualities. Since she possesses all the virtues, love bestows all the virtues, in authors so various as Ibn Hazm, Aimeric de Peguilhan, Andreas Capellanus. And one recalls Boccaccio's Cimone, whom love of Iphigenia converted almost magically from a brute to a wise gentleman (*Decameron* V. 1). Perhaps those familiar ethical qualities of *fin' amors—pretz, mesura, cortezia, jovens, valors—*are often judged hardly translatable or wordable because they belong to that "primal identification" with Source, beyond words. Often these virtues seem to carry with them a sense of completion and peace: Topsfield, enumerating some attributes of the *fis amaire* specified by Marcabru, explains that they allow the lover security, wholeness, harmony within himself and esteem in society.[27] Part is made whole. And the metaphor of identification is reinforced by conceiving these transforming virtues as public. Helen Durkin, Philip Slater, and others believe that all selves in groups perform finally for the maternal presence they sense there, created by the projection of their own desire; the child imitates the good mother *for* the mother, seeing himself in the mirror-state as though with her eyes. The model is audience; one's identification is affirmed, approved by the original. Thus Peire d'Alvernhe takes the lady's virtues as tantamount to poetic inspiration and, as it were, plays them back to lady and audience: "she has given me the gift which, from here to Tyre, makes me supreme over the poets, great and small." For to please lady and audience is to guarantee serenity, wisdom, and happiness, poetic and courtly success. It is in mockery of such conventional affirmations that Raimbaut d'Aurenga tells his lady, "you make me compose. . . . And I am such a foolish courtly singer that they call me *joglar.*"[28] But such games of performance belong essentially to an earnest effort: *sub specie ludi* the game of self is being played, and to win is to close the distance between self and Source, in full and acclaimed identification.

Mimesis and incorporation are often combined in the meta-

phoric language of these lyrics. Surely Plato and Augustine
are relevant subtexts here, in the broad equivalences of these
metaphors: for Plato, the hungry soul in a state of *aporein* (helplessness) takes in a nourishing Idea of the Good that becomes a
divine center, firmly lodged within the soul as a model for the
soul's development; for Augustine, again, the soul receives
God's identity as its own center, intuited *verbum mentis* toward
which the soul then strives in love and knowledge.[29] Frederick
Goldin in *The Mirror of Narcissus* uses Augustine's texts to help
interpret certain love lyrics of this tradition, and the paradoxes
Goldin explores so well in the lyrics are the ones suggested by
the interplay of incorporation and mimesis. He says of the
troubadour in love, "his heart and mind contain the image that
grants him its qualities";[30] that is, he loves the image of the
beloved Source within himself (incorporation) and, in the next
step, loves the image of his own ideal self, cultivated in the image
of Source (identification, mimesis) and always to-be-affirmed by
the approval of the lady herself. The man mirrors the lady, and
the lady is in turn an image of his future perfection. Yet this
mirror seems to me not, as Goldin calls it, a "secular ideal." For
whether this image is credited, or whether it is doubted and then
acknowledged as a valuable lie, in either case it is the continuing
sense of the image's timeless perfection—its immunity to the
temporal and secular—that gives it value. Doubt may be confirmed even while fantasy persists, as Philip Slater suggests in
observing that groups never truly "outgrow" the fantasy of the
group leader as God, however often they symbolically divest him
of his powers: "The greater the discovered reality, the more
deeply and securely entrenched the religious fantasy becomes.
By detaching reality from it, the fantasy is purified and intensified."[31] In psychic reality free from time and place, we all move
with *Lover infans* toward Source as boundless and magical, not
limited and secular: surely it is that sense of enraptured completeness, infinity, that made "courtly love" seem to Averroës
and C. S. Lewis a dangerous competitor with Christianity. Goldin says of the lady's image: "It is really unreal, but really perfect."[32] Selves are a real finitude grounded upon an illusion of
infinity, but an illusion that feels real—really perfect.

　　There are often other linguistic devices in a given lyric, besides these metaphors of fusion, symbiosis, incorporation, and

mimesis, that can reveal *Lover* and *Poet* trying to hold beloved Source completely "in" the words, in perfect imitation, and yet failing. One recalls Geoffrey de Vinsauf's hope, in *Poetria Nova,* that words might be entirely transparent to meaning; that words might fit perfectly the imaginative conception, *prius archetypus;* that the theme of the beloved as *fons* (fountain) might be channeled completely into the brook of words, *rivus fontis*—distilled, not distorted; and that the performer's voice might become an image of that reality the song expresses.[33] This hope of fusing words to Source as "meaning" or "matter" may be rare in contemporary rhetorical theory, but it is frequent in this lyric textmilieu. And precisely this hope charges with Presence those tropes that can seem to announce the failure or inadequacy of words: hyperbole, paradox, ellipsis, synesthesia, and other devices that serve to keep beloved Source just past the words, in the aura of the words. Of course, these devices culminate in the inexpressibility tropes worked intensively by Dante and Petrarch. Certainly, stylistic devices are "not anything formulable in the abstract, but must always be felt and tested against the background of the particular psychic climate."[34] Yet often in the psychic climate of a given lyric can be the necessity that language prove insufficient, leaving Source as *absent presence.*

And this unwordable Source makes itself known throughout the wordwork, where *Lover* and *Poet* move together; Source can imbue a text with those indescribable qualities of coherence, affective energy, presence, intentionality. For the lyric text as an entity is preserved by curious and timeless formal patterns, those poetic orderings and integrations that elude full explanation, just as the self is preserved by an "interstitial web" or organizing principle enabled by maternal affects. Thus Marcabru and Peire d'Alvernhe, perhaps following Quintilian, believe that words and phrases should be well linked, and a poem elegantly bound up—and the connotations of such terms as *entier, frag, integra,* or *dissolutus* may be moral as well as aesthetic, for they refer to more than simply verbal integration.[35] All the symmetries of a poem, all the equivalences displaced on contiguity, all the echoes and parallels in syntax, semantics, and phonics, can both arise from Source and move with *Lover* toward fusion with Source. Perhaps because Maternal Source is the original "expectation" for all selves, the repetitions of a poem therefore arouse expectations and then fulfill them, creating verbal equivalents of the infant's "'confident expectation,'" as Mahler says, of the mother's nourishing responses, necessary for the integration of the self.[36] One thinks of Dante's poem of threes, reaching toward the triune God of a triune cosmos. One thinks of Molinier's *Leys d'Amors,* rigorous guidelines for Old Provençal poetics and grammar that become, in the metonymy of the title, an equivalent to perfectionism in love itself.[37] Moreover, if vowel and consonant patterns in poetry can have (between certain limits of crudity and refinement) a magical or hypnotic effect,[38] perhaps it is because they evoke that first syncretic magic of the infant, who receives the world, feeding, in rhythmic oral gestures, the prototype in action of these vowel and consonant patterns. Spitz reminds us that the infant continually receives coenesthetic signals on the level of deep sensibility, including categories of "rhythm, tempo, duration, pitch, tone, resonance, clang," and others that Western man elects to deemphasize in his concentration upon diacritic perception; perhaps the self, beginning with the rhythmic and repetitive sounds of a child's babbling monologues, will continue to "coenesthetically fantasize" that primal identification with Source through word patterns.[39] Surely our response to poetic rhythms is largely unconscious, or at least unexplainable: we allow ourselves to be cradled in these rhythms, set to their tune.

Through these means, even an operative center can be "core" presence or Source for a text, not as "content" but as maternal integration, the motivation for the careful patterning, as though some fantasy of ongoing verbal responsiveness had been taken into the belly of the text, to become the model for the text's developing identity. Perhaps the sense we are bound to make, along with our significant differentiations, is maternal, and texts like selves must retain a rudimentary sense of Source, to integrate and unify. Thus Jakobson finds spatial centers and Jan Mukarovsky temporal, dynamic ones, but all find centers. Marshall Edelson says, of the sound patterns in a poem by Wallace Stevens, "speech like music may be a means to the symbolization or presentation of tumescence-discharge-detumescence or anticipation-climax-relaxation *through sound alone.*"[40] Or, one might add, hunger-feeding-satiety. Our verbal patterns continue to take us back to unstated Source, maternal "home base."

We move in words out of the differences that words make, to that coherent and rhythmic maternal presence where we feel we belong.

Thus the secondary processes of poetic control, order, regularity, symmetry, and even rationality can themselves feed the deepest primary process desires for the rhythmic security and predictability of the maternal presence, that original and ultimate "system of equivalences." Moreover, in the special conventions of the love lyric, all six of Jakobson's functions of verbal communication can be set toward beloved as Source: the conative, in a poem addressed to her; the phatic, or the poem as effort to start and sustain communication with her; the referential, as she is the main referent described; the emotive, in the Poet-Lover's attitude toward the referent; the metalingual, insofar as "code terms" for *fin' amors* are glossed; and of course the poetic, as she is credited with inspiring the poem.[41] Thus through figures, tropes, phonic patterns, conventions of address, and perhaps every characteristic of the verbal texture, we can experience nonverbal Source pervading the wordwork, enabling the lyric text with affect and energy, its own presence and intentionality. Nancy Streuver stresses the importance of recovering the intention, coherence, and experience of the author "behind" the work, an experience transcending content or meaning: "Without its penumbra of affective form the doctrine is not fully intelligible; Plato was a personality as well as a mind."[42] And surely the penumbra of affective form belonging to Plato's texts arises ultimately from their sense of Source, Idea of the Good. Without some comparable intimation of Source, a dependable and nourishing still point around which a penumbra of affects can form, any text would lose its psychic life—it would be not *parole* as psychic gesture but dry and unnourished rhetoric.

Poet with Lover in Defensive Textures

Thus *Lover* and *Poet* can seem to move in conjunction throughout the wordwork, evoking Source, reaching toward Source. Yet in none of these Renaissance lyrics do these motions remain straightforward or uncomplicated; this conjunction is not always an easy one. Moreover, a given text will probably *also* reveal the directions *Lover* and *Poet* to be irrelevant, or even contradictory, to each other. To introduce these vicissitudes characteristic of our lyric text-milieu, we must begin by elaborating some of the equivalences we have proposed between self and lyric text.

We have been suggesting that during a lifetime of intrapsychic development and social interactions, the self remains centered by an intimation of Source, primally repressed and coenesthetically fantasized. Life becomes equivalent to a sense of being loved by this coenesthetic "figure" of a lady, amid all internal structuralizations and external contingencies. "Behind everyone there is a woman": real social and sexual developments must coexist with that permanent fantasy, that primal identification.[43] In the same way, the lyric text, amid a web of doctrinal, literary, social, biographical, even political references, can be sustained by the figure of a lady, the beloved evoked as the poem's sense of Source. Thus the beloved, with *Lover infans,* can become the unwordable dyadic "core identity" in the psycho-ontology of the text, allowing and enabling its coherences, its metaphors of fusion, its figures and phonetic patterns, its inexpressibility tropes, its affective energy and intentionality. To know her, we should recognize and respect her as central, unwordable fantasy: she cannot be documented historically or biographically, any more than the secret "core" of self, Source drawing *infans* in unspoken longing, can be matched literally with particular mothers or children. Thus the existing psychoanalytic studies of "courtly love" do not move from a central understanding of these lyrics, for they fix economic, political, and historical forces as the "matrix of the literature of love," citing medieval sex ratios and invoking the actual behavior of men and women in society.[44] Yet although the wordwork may indeed refer to historical realities, nevertheless the unspoken but evoked beloved as Source, she who is *arche* and *telos* of the lyric text, belongs to that vital fantasy that persists for self and text, despite doubt or even discovered reality. As Goldin puts it, "The most interesting lyric poets never forget that courtly love is a lie." William Paden is wise to point out that the social qualities of the troubadour's lady, which we have claimed to be "real" all these years—her marriage to another man, and her higher social rank—are, just as likely, metaphors that we have literalized in our interpretations, from our need to explain the difficult "inner feelings" and "mercurial emotions" she evokes.[45] With realities and despite realities, self and text are sustained by a lady of fantasy, vestigial Source.

Moreover, throughout all intrapsychic changes, this central fantasized "lady" must remain intact, unharmed "within" the self, all-loving and all-giving. While absence or rejection can indeed disturb this fantasy, the self's own aggressive impulses are also a catastrophic threat. Various mechanisms of "ego defense," like repression or projection, can work to deflect one's own rage from that sustaining center, and the deflected aggressions do not vanish but are caught and preserved in that "interstitial web," the intrapsychic texturing principle of the self. And in these Renaissance lyrics as well, the cherished beloved is not often the target of the speaker's direct aggression. The invoked cruel fair, who conventionally withholds her vital and nourishing presence, her flow of *joi,* also conventionally receives no retribution for this deadly neglect. Thus, perhaps, one can be both shocked and relieved by such anticonventional statements as Boccaccio's story of Nastagio degli Onesti and the Traversari lady (*Decameron* V. 8), or Raimbaut d'Aurenga's more comfortably amusing parody of advice to prospective lovers:

> Si voletz dompnas guazanhar,
> Quan querretz que·us fassan honors,
> Si·us fan avol respos avar
> Vos las prenetz a menassar;
> E si vos fan respos peiors
> Datz lor del ponh per mieg sas nars;
> E si son bravas siatz braus!
> Ab gran mal n'auretz gran repaus.

(If you want to win ladies and if, when you want them to do you honour, they make you a base, mean reply, begin to threaten them. And if they make you worse replies, give them some fist in the middle of their nose. And if they are uncouth, be uncouth! Through doing great evil you will have great repose.)[46]

But in most Renaissance love lyrics, one senses that the stakes are far too high to risk "giving them some fist": to de-idealize or otherwise threaten that crucial lady, to let the words focus anger directly upon her, would put the very being of the lyric in question. Thus the conventional laments express anger toward the lady only indirectly: *certain conventional representations of lover and beloved become analogues in the verbal texture for those familiar defensive mechanisms of projection, displacement, splitting, and turning against the self,* serving to deflect negative impulses away from the evoked lady. The lyric, like the intrapsychic self, becomes textured with deflected aggressions, deflected in order that *Lover infans* and beloved Source can survive unharmed at the felt center of the text. *Poet* and *Lover* move together in this texturing, but in no simple way; and the resulting wordwork may serve the interests of *Poet* more fully than those of *Lover.*

For example, often these lyrics represent the lady herself as directly angry with the speaker: she will indignantly reject him, or lecture him harshly, or even seem in fantasy to seek his death. Raimbaut's speaker, however bold with his threats in the above parody, in another poem calls his lady's eyes rods that chastise his heart, so that he dare not entertain a churlish desire toward her. The Cavalcantian lady can bring death with her glances, scattering the vital spirits; we see her successor in Dante's *rime petrose* and in such lyrics as "E'm'incresce de me sì duramente" and "Amor, da che convien."[47] The lady is more than deadly in one of Ronsard's versions: "He who follows love as I do," says the speaker, "will die from pining away, and his proud mistress, seeing him dead, will leap for joy upon his tomb, mocking his faith."[48] It is with this text-milieu as background that Spenser can playfully invoke the beloved as "Tyrannesse," making "huge massacres" with her eyes (*Amoretti,* 10). Within the equivalent self of the lyric, the Poet-Lover's potential frustration and anger can appear not as *his* but as *hers,* strengthened by the force of her presence and by her supposed wish for retribution against his insistent desires. Simply, the speaker's aggression is projected upon the lady herself: the representation of the harsh beloved thereby "places" the anger, protects the ideal beloved from the speaker's direct anger, and preserves that vital sense of Source for the poem. As Kernberg explains, the earliest superego structure, composed of projected and reintrojected "bad" self-object representations, reflects "primitive efforts of the infant to protect the good relationship with the idealized mother by turning the aggressively invested images of her (fused with the respective self-images) against himself."[49] Thus conscience is born, and thus an envisioned moral lecture by a disapproving lady can work as a purification, discharging one's own most dangerous aggressions. Dante is brought to repentant tears by an unyielding Beatrice in Purgatory; Laura tells Petrarch, as she visits him *in morte*, that she was harsh to him for the sake of his soul.

Thus the representation of the cruel beloved textures the conventional lyric with the Poet-Lover's anger, deflected from the beloved as Source. And the fierce lady often implies her counterpart, the representation of the suffering lover, *amant martyr*. For this lover, pleasure and pain become inextricable, and the conventional oxymorons are born; more than one scholar has remarked that this *amant martyr* seems to glory in his labyrinthine hardships, as though he set for himself obstacles to fulfillment. León Hebreo writes, "But as for pleasure, its delights consist not in possession nor enjoyment nor complete acquisition, but in a certain tension bound up with privation." In the texture of these lyrics, the Poet-Lover's frustrations with the aloof lady appear turned back upon himself, in the form of the various lover's torments he joyously undertakes. Freud suggests in "The Economic Problem of Masochism" that even morality, turned inward, can become sexualized.[50] In biological and social reality the *amant martyr* loses, in order to win that perfect image, a crucial intrapsychic reality.

The representation *amant martyr* is thus equivalent in the verbal texture to the familiar defense, turning against the self; furthermore, this representation can preserve both "ideal self" and "ideal object," as well as some hope for their eventual re-fusion. The self becomes its own scapegoat, a guiltless receptacle of its own negative or vengeful impulses—in the words of Giraut de Bornelh, "a vanquished sufferer who pays court, still suffering, because he is not recreant."[51] One finds analogous representations, of course, in Christian and ultimately in Platonic texts; as in Plato's *Gorgias,* it is less evil to be wronged than to wrong.[52] One forgives one's enemies seventy times seven. Thus the ideal state of self is secured, receiving aggression in order not to realize aggression. And *amant martyr* guards the ideal object as well: Raimbaut d'Aurenga protests to his lady, "it would be better for death to take me away, rather than that you should ever sin on my account."[53] All this pain is tolerated in order to cultivate that fantasy central both to selves and to these lyrics: "a wishful, ideal state of the self which would make the individual acceptable to, close to, and, in the last resort, symbolically refused with the ideal object (the unharmed, all-loving, all-forgiving early mother image)."[54] And as we have seen, this proposed "last resort," this hope of a future union earned by diligent suffering, belongs also to this text-milieu. "The lover's submission, his servitude, the long torment patiently endured ... all these were undertaken in joy and in the hope of greater joy to come."[55] One earns Paradise for the "Roman agony," and the expiations of the *amant martyr* are not without their echoes of Christ's passion: Petrarch and Boccaccio, for instance, each began their servitude to love during Holy Week.

Frequently in this lyric text-milieu, sexuality is devalued and displaced upon representations of false love and false lovers. Several scholars, among them Valency and Topsfield, have argued that *fin' amors* becomes increasingly spiritual as the tradition continues, through Guilhem de Montanhagol as a pivotal figure, to stilnovism and Dante. And Andreas, of course, calls sexual love "mixed," decidedly inferior to "pure love" (*amor purus*) in which the embrace of nude lovers without the "final solace" can "bind together the hearts of two lovers with every feeling of delight," and no one ever regrets practicing it. Whether or not Andreas is joking here, *amor purus* does have a certain suggestion of intrapsychic reality. For in the complex toils of Oedipal rivalries, and primal scenes real or imagined, sexuality may inevitably accumulate a charge of *thanatos:* savage, extreme, rude, cruel, not to trust. After all, sexuality is not just a biological matter, but is always joined to images: "nature is not exempt from its representation in mental life."[56] That is, sexuality in intrapsychic representations can become entangled with aggression, and thereby can become dangerous to that vital sense of Source in self and lyric text. In Cavalcanti's "Donna mi prega," when the lady becomes "aware of the fierce sensuality awakened in her lover, she is frightened and becomes hostile. The illusion of love is shattered."[57] Thus one invokes *amor purus*, or the like, and displaces full sexuality upon forms of love labeled as inferior. And characteristically, references to carnal love in the serious canso have an unimpeachable sensuality, purified of every hint of aggression or devaluation:

Dieus lo chauzitz,
per cui foron assoutas
las faillidas que fetz Longis lo cecs,
voilla, si·l platz, q'ieu e midonz iassam
en la chambra on amdui nos mandem
uns rics convens don tan gran ioi atendi,
qe·l seu bel cors baisan rizen descobra
e qe·l remir contra·l lum de la lampa.

(May God the wise, by Whom were absolved the sins committed by Longinus the blind, grant, if it please Him, that my lady and I lie together in the room where we both made a rich covenant from which I expect such great joy, and may he grant that I reveal, kissing and smiling, her lovely body, and behold it against the light of the lamp.)[58]

The representation of *lausengiers* (scandalmongers) in these lyrics can also work as a complicated defense, again on behalf of the central ideal lady. In troubadour lyrics that state of blameless carnal love, unharmed and causing no harm, is all too fragile; Andreas warns that "mixed love" may injure neighbors and offend God, implying that unlike "pure love" it can corrupt maidens and damage the reputations of widow or wife. And the tendency to devalue love is represented in the scandalmongers who would destroy love by destroying the perfect image of the lady; they would malign all these women as inconstant, effectively spoiling love by renaming it, by applying to it their cynical terms. These *lausengiers* have their analogues in the literature of psychic defenses: for example, Freud in three early essays, "Contributions to the Psychology of Love," explores the universal tendency to debase sexually desired women, to split affectionate feelings from sensual ones. Kernberg studies the purposes of such debasement in his work on "splitting" defenses: to state the matter perhaps too simply, the image of the "bad" or profligate woman (mother) draws all feared sexual impulses to itself, leaving the "good" image, the good dyadic internalization of self and object, uncontaminated by sexuality. Of course, we are familiar with this "splitting" defense on a cultural level, in the divided maternal image of whore and virgin. Sexually desirable women may be imagined as dark ladies in order to preserve the sense of some fair maiden or fair youth, perfect beloved

Source, center and hope of the soul. And sometimes the troubadour lyric does divide ladies into opposing categories, the treacherous and the true. But more often in this text-milieu the *lausengiers* effect this split, and thus these devaluers, rather than the devalued image of the lady, become the target of the Poet-Lover's invective. The *lausengiers* or *fals amadors* attract all the angry words of the poem: may they have their tongues cut out! Within the equivalent self of the lyric, the Poet-Lover rages at all efforts to devalue love, even if they be his own "lower impulses":[59] the defensive tendency to devalue is itself felt as dangerous, lest it truly de-idealize that crucial ideal object and ideal self, and thus endanger the evoked beloved as Source of the poem. The words of the *lausengiers* can threaten *joi* itself.

Thus in these representations equivalent to defensive mechanisms within the poem as self, *Poet* and *Lover* move together, but with no simple or harmonious result. For a lyric textured with deflected aggressions and thereby filled with negative energies cannot, as a whole, pretend to imitate its pure, sustaining beloved Source: the very efforts of *Lover* and *Poet* to secure that vital ideal image can seem paradoxically to distinguish and distance the resulting wordwork from its evoked Source. Contrasting the troubadour lyric with the hymn, James Wilhelm remarks, "the lyric ego destroys the basically idealized texture of the hymn, scattering negative statements . . . among the positive, and sundering the monistic song of praise into the brilliant shards of the lyric."[60] The poem becomes a self textured and characterized by its own defenses, its own brilliant negative statements. In the same way, when *Poet* and *Lover* move together to conceal that ideal lady or to possess her exclusively, the resulting wordwork may again become difficult: the very efforts to keep lady and love from common view may create a texture so dense and so strange as to veil entirely the poem's sense of Source. For such styles as *trobar clus* (closed style) can seem exercises in deviant language, with *senhals* (code names) and neologisms, *caras rimas* (rare rhymes), exotic proper names, and layered words that can thread more than one *razo* (theme) through a given poem. By these means *Poet* and *Lover* take care that love and the lady are not cheapened by being expressed too bluntly in an easy style "a toz comunal," common to all, as Raimbaut writes in his frequently cited tenso with Giraut de Bornelh,

"Ara·m platz."[61] Many have since complained that such poems can be dry, detached, and unintelligible—as though both lady and lover, both vital Source and core *infans,* had vanished within a *hortus conclusus* (enclosed garden) of words. One recalls the Stoics as described by Cicero, who write of their central good, *honestas,* in a style jarring and strange, incomprehensible in the marketplace.[62] When *Poet* and *Lover* both move to protect the ideal lady—to veil her with words or to deflect worded aggression from her—the result can be not a harmonious, idealized song but an intricate texture of negations and deviations.

Poet without *Lover*

It is through these negations and deviations, and many others like them, that we can begin to distinguish *Poet* as a separable impulse in these lyrics, not necessarily always in motion *with Lover.* The verbal texture can reveal *Poet* as an independent motion toward active self-texturing, a concern to weave a special being-in-words; *Poet* can be seen as equivalent to the *"drive for and toward individuation"* that is *"an innate,* powerful *given"* in all selves.[63] For negations surely can belong to the drive for individuation. E. Neumann states, "To become conscious of oneself, to be conscious at all, begins with saying 'no' to the uroboros, to the Great Mother, to the unconscious. And when we scrutinize the acts upon which consciousness and the ego are built up, we must admit that to begin with they are all negative acts. To discriminate, to distinguish, to mark off, to isolate oneself from the surrounding context—these are the basic acts of consciousness." Spitz proposes that the neurophysiological roots of negative head shaking, and thus the first abstract concept, "no," lie in the infant's typical movements in detaching his mouth from breast or bottle[64]—a more basic gesture of individuation would hardly be possible. Perhaps Burke's definition that language is the possibility of the negative would implicitly support Spitz's proposal. Moreover, the deviant words, phrases, and structures of a poem can also belong to the drive for individuation, to *Poet.* Thus the wordwork can show not only *Lover* and *Poet* moving together, imbuing the text with coherence, symmetries, even "coenesthetically fantasized" primal identification through word patterns, but also *Poet* as a motion in its own right, traveling *de via* or away from the established path, with a consequent aspect of the verbal activity that is not secure or predictable but strange, surprising, resistant to understanding. Here is a realm of the voluntary and the particular, where text and self are enabled by that crucial vestige of Source to create themselves, to become independent centers of initiative. For texture is the only real choice open to the contingent self, poised between the limits of Source and Void; self-texture is all that one can call one's own. Freud respected the texture of the dream-work, the irreducible mesh of detail that could be interpreted but not accounted for, that seemed to rise from some *omphalos,* some process primary or secondary, some willful and single chooser: why *these* particular displacements and condensations, and not others? The self weaves itself in symbols to itself, no two selves quite alike, and so with a lyric poem, where style can become, more than "sheer expression of self," the creation of an equivalent self.[65] No one can anticipate the results of the self-selecting *Poet* motion. As Wilhelm points out, given the traditional love symbolism of Ovid and the mystical symbolism of Christianity, one still cannot deduce Provençal poetry.[66]

The experience of a given poem will often include not only the coordinated efforts of *Poet* and *Lover,* but also their cross purposes. Thus we may be able to see in a certain lyric that *Poet* thwarts or contradicts *Lover* in any number of subtle ways. For instance, *Poet* may emerge as the care to violate expectations instead of fulfilling them, to cultivate differences instead of serving equivalences. On the simplest level, we may find rhyming words with opposite meanings, syllables set against the prevailing meter, or enjambement that arouses unfulfilled expectations of meaning or syntax. Phonically, we may hear *trobar braus* (rough style) as well as *trobar leu* (light style), or, in Dante's terms, *yrsuta* (shaggy) and *pexa* (combed) vocabularies may intermingle. For in a way, all nonequivalent contiguities, even if they do not signify precisely a "rage for chaos," can seem to impede *Lover* in motion toward monistic perfection. What is more, *Poet* can create a labyrinth of wordplay and ambiguity that seems to work against the interests of *Lover.* Words and phrases cleverly layered with multiple referents can seem to offer only their own strangeness; they can seem to move only toward other words

73

and other poems, in an entropic flow of intertextuality. The sense of central, wordless Source can seem lost in the eccentric wandering of words. The verbal texture can seem created to withhold its *razo* or meaning, and thereby its nourishment and rest. Language can be an opaque medium, like an uninterpreted dream, unable to move with *Lover* toward home. And finally, *Poet* can threaten *Lover* because a care for words can seem to be a care for a limited, circumscribed entity fixed upon a page. Valéry tells us that language is a resistant medium, and that in trying to build rhymes and conform to the rules of prosody, one meets words in their substantiality. The same secure poetic rhythms that can help to "coenesthetically fantasize" Source can seem, in another perspective, relentless bonds of time and space, meter and rhyme—as in many a sestina. The poem in its mutable speaking can seem to move not toward infinite Source, but simply toward the mortal end of space and time.

Thus *Poet* can endanger *Lover*. Yet with another small shift of perspective, we can discover that *Poet*, as a motion irrespective of *Lover*, can also offer some exhilarating compensations for these threats to core *infans* and sense of Source. One finds a certain freedom and confidence in vaunting independence from Source, especially if the boast is made playfully and in good humor. "Farai un vers de dreyt nien" (I am making a poem from nothing at all), begins Guillem de Peitau, as though announcing that he needs no love or lady to center his poem. Adventure can lie in negation and deviation simply for their own sake. Raimbaut d'Aurenga's "Escotatz, mas no say que s'es," with its stretched final verses, seems to grow not so much from a central ideal lady as from *Poet's* own inventive vitality. Here flaunting convention seems to be more fun than fulfilling expectations, as the words spill over unimpeded into the outrageously long final line of each stanza:

> Er fenisc mo no-say-que-s'es,
> c'aisi l'ay volgut batejar;
> pus mays d'aital non auzi jes
> be·l dey enaysi apelar;
> e diga·l, can l'aura apres,
> qui que s'en vuelha azautar.

E si hom li demanda qui l'a fag, pot dir que sel que sap be far totas
fazendas can se vol.

(Now I conclude my Whatdoyoucallit, for that is how I've had it
baptized; since I've never heard of a similar thing, I use the name
that I devised; whoever likes it, let him sing, once he has it
memorized, and if anyone asks him who made it, he can say: one
who can do anything, and do it well, when he wants to.)[67]

Wordplay away from Source can appear carried by its own
momentum, with no direction necessary. Brian Vickers believes
that the rhetorical figures "contain within themselves a whole
series of emotional and psychological effects, almost prior to the
presence of meaning." Robert Rogers concludes that the "modal
ambiguity" of poetic language, its simultaneous appeal to secondary and primary processes, makes enormous psychic resources
of unpredictable flexibility available to the poet.[68] *Poet* can direct
poem and reader away from unworded Source and into the
words themselves, into the poem where all elements are figures
of speech,[69] where, as in some of Dante's *petrose,* one metaphor
can seem to breed another. With seminal associations and antitheses, the poem can seem to generate its own energy: *contro-
pare,* "to speak in figures," may underlie the verb *trobar,* to "find"
or "invent" verses. The poem in *différance* from Source discovers
and creates its own new presence. According to Molinier's *Leys
d'Amors,* barbarisms and stylistic errors can themselves become
new rhetorical figures, if used well. The potential for growth in
words in inexhaustible: *Lover* moves toward eternal fusion with
Source, but *Poet* can move, in a way, toward another kind of
eternity. Richard Lanham remarks that "rhetorical man" will
often debate mainly for the pleasure it gives him, finding endless
"discussability" through the complex devices of rhetoric.[70] Perpetual differences in words can be curiously nourishing, a feast
of paradox, wit, irony, and ambiguity available in texts. Selves
and texts can apparently thrive on argument, renewing themselves with still more negations and deviations; they are enabled
thus to become situations of infinite discourse, to prolong themselves as though forever. Perhaps our current debates about
literature and language concern whether we can be willing to

trade our vital fantasy of Source, the eternity of our origins, for eternally resonating and self-generating play in language.

Poet-Lover

We have suggested that from the verbal texture of a given poem in this Renaissance love lyric text-milieu, we can often both intuit *Lover* and discover *Poet* in motion. In the conventional metaphoric language of fusion, as well as in the integrating measures of the wordwork, *Poet* and *Lover* can move in easy conjunction. *Poet* and *Lover* move together toward a more difficult result, a poem textured with negations and deviations, when they try to veil the beloved with words or to deflect aggressions from her with conventional defensive representations of lover and lady. Finally, *Poet* and *Lover* can seem to move at cross-purposes: *Poet* can prove a threat to *Lover,* but can also offer the exhilarating compensations of independent and potentially infinite wordplay. The result of this ongoing interplay between *Poet* and *Lover* motions is, by definition, the Poet-Lover, or the activity that is the lyric text, just as the result of our ontological motions toward and away from Source, through our continual self-texturing, is the ongoing self. The lyric text, like the self, can be an intricate chiasmus of *absent presence* and *present absence,* a construct woven with both the longing for fusion and the energy of individuation.

The text, like a self, is poised in contingent existence on the blank of the unsupportive page. The text or Poet-Lover pleases us when it appears to us as a being self-made, of identifications with Source and differences from Source, and thereby when it touches *Lover* and *Poet* "within" each of us. For all the knowledge and feeling, all the "cognition" and "affect" we can summon in response to the lyric text, arise from our ontological sense of being different from Maternal Source and yet somehow, centrally, the same. We build our multiple patterns of similitude and difference into texts and then find them there again, appealing to us with the combined strength of "cognition" and "affect," of primary and secondary processes. Gorgias believes that "through measure in rhythm and sound the artists convey measure or proportion in meaning according to patterns of thought which are primordial—the patterns of identity and antithesis—and therefore universally appealing."[71] Many centuries later, Wordsworth in the preface to *Lyrical Ballads* writes of the "pleasure which the mind derives from the perception of similitude in dissimilitude. This principle is the great spring of the activity of our minds, and their chief feeder." He continues by linking our sexual appetite, our ordinary conversation, our taste, and even our moral feelings with this "pleasure." The pleasures of the text are perhaps born here. For even the *registre*, as Zumthor shows in his chart, sketches a self woven in identity and difference, separate and yet with continual reference to *joie*.[72] It may be that the words of a text can only *seem* to wander, exactly *because* we must always understand Maternal Source as their ultimate referent. Thus when Eugene Vance calls the medieval erotic lyric "a kind of fetishism," or "a negative mediator that systematically displaces and defers the objectives of desiring man," he nevertheless knows that all these objectives, all meanings or referents that enliven and imbue with value the displacements and negations of these texts, are ultimately to be found in *joie*—that is, in fusion, in "the unmediated presence between two beings," in Source.[73]

The text or Poet-Lover can please, further, through our sense that he has emerged from the weaving of identities and differences as an intact new presence, illustrating for us at least the possibility of a new coherent self. But without enough incoherences as well, that self will not be equivalent to our selves. What we ask of art, Stephen Booth believes, is that it give us "comprehension of incomprehensible reality itself." We want and do not want oceanic fusion with all the world and all human existence, but we know as well that we cannot achieve it; thus we both distrust and scorn the work of art that grasps its ordering too easily. Artists "aim at replacing the complexities of reality with controlled complexities that will make the experience of the orderly work of art sufficiently similar to the experience of random nature, so that the comfort of artistic coherence will not be immediately dismissed as irrelevant to the intellectual discomfort of the human condition."[74] And not just intellectual pain is at issue here. For "random nature" tasks the self with the most profound affects of primal separation: thus we ask that the lyric within its wholeness still allow echoes of full absence commensurate with the unconscious threats belonging to our origin. We ask the possibility of self, not the guarantee of bliss, from the lyric. Freud names efforts toward happiness, not achievements: "Happiness . . . is a problem of the economics of the individual's libido."[75] Perhaps we seek flexible intrapsychic texturing from the text as equivalent self, rather than autonomous, gemlike beauty. And we ask that along with all its deviance and negative energy, the lyric text reserve somehow enough vestigial sense of Source to exist as a coherent entity, viable self. Thus beauty becomes a terror we are just able to bear, and we can sense that Shakespeare's sonnets, with their nuanced primal fears, their mazes of overlapping coherences, and their patterns of violated expectations, are true literary presences. If all art is distortion, we continue to make this last nourishing distortion, the possibility of self, for our selves.

Literary convention can itself work as an engulfing Maternal Source, posing an important threat to the possibility of the new text as equivalent self. That is, the Poet-Lover who waives his right to deviate from convention may yield his identity as well, essentially vanishing as a distinguishable texture. Thus the speaker of the *grand chant courtois, trouvère* poetry known for its uniformity, seems to many scholars hardly identifiable: "the writing appears to be divested completely of personal origin: only the text—neutral, composite, intransitive—seems to speak (or rather to sing)."[76] It is in working largely with *trouvère* poetry that Zumthor has evolved the concept of *registre* or *modèles d'écriture*, that is, systems of recurrences or coherences existing outside concrete realization in any given text—somewhat as though there were a continuous substratal text, entitled "The Convention." The *registre* is never found complete in written form (like the marvelous definitive library in Borges' story), so that it is itself finally unworded, in a way, as the ultimate referent of any specific lyric. Indeed, the *registre* seems to confer being upon the poem, just as Source confers being upon the self: "the unifying myth of the poem is the *registre*, a linguistic version of a neo-platonic form in which the individual participates and thereby draws ontological sustenance."[77] Thus the reader of numerous *trouvère* poems becomes blinded by recurrences, until the speaker is all but anonymous, fused with the convention. Thus in *trouvère* poetry even the lady fades as central infinite Presence, and the convention itself becomes effective Source, larger than life, setting and fulfilling expectations. Supposedly corporeal and material, the convention yet seems to supervene all substantial texts; as a realist truth inscribed in some background, it becomes a devouring maternal presence, assimilating and thereby annihilating its offspring.[78] The Poet-Lover disappears, subsumed by the charted "self" of the *registre.*

A poetry so rigidly conventional can seem appalling to us, for it speaks of our own engulfment and extinction: all selves and texts seem merged with the words of others, barely alive, in a poetry "as tenuously and thinly breathed as one can imagine poetry to be that still remains poetry."[79] But perhaps we need not believe with Haidu that medieval literature as a whole constitutes a *terra reservata,* indecently conventional, because history has determined a "medieval aesthetic" that runs counter to our "originalist aesthetic" and our recent talk of "modernity." Indeed, most scholars seem to insist, even more strongly than Haidu admits, that troubadour poets were well distinguishable from one another. Here is Guilhem de Montanhagol, for instance, advising poets to "make it new":

> Quar dir pot om so qu'estat dig no sia,
> qu'estiers non es trobaires bos ni fis
> Tro fai sos chans gais, nous e gent assis,
> Ab noels digz de nova maestria.

(One can say what has not been said, for otherwise a troubadour is neither good nor courteous if his songs are not new, gay and well composed on new ideas and according to a new theory of composition.)[80]

Perhaps we need only admit that, since every self moves from its "core" toward fusion with boundless Source, some selves in every historical period will try to fashion totally coherent and intrafused groups, literary movements, or religions, in order to tap the "immortality power" implicitly promised by the group as Source.

By contrast, the troubadour poets seemed to encourage separate poetic identities, Poet-Lovers as distinguishable selves. *Trobar:* to sing of love is to trope or deviate further than one's predecessors.[81] These poets named and praised themselves in their own poems, announcing their originality; they held contests, satirized each other, imitated each other, debated each other. They followed Aristotle's advice to deviate from common use for their own poetic dignity. They needed only a few terms for types of love, but they were prolific in their names for types of singing: *trobar clus, leu, ric, sotil, car, braus, plan, prim.* Styles and apologists seemed to generate each other, and discussions of style became textured with the poetry. Peire d'Alvernhe's satire, "Chantarai d'aquestz trobadors," marks differences not in "ideology of love" but in style and delivery. The *Poet* motion thrives in these texts. Artisan metaphors abound, as these craftsmen meet the substantiality of words: they polished, filed, sculpted, gilded, colored, burnished, bound, intertwined, and planed their verses. Many kept seeking new rhymes, new metrical patterns. As Smith summarizes, they "demonstrate a continuous esthetic attitude and an unbroken literary tradition which interpreted poetry as a highly conscious, careful, well-planned, and technically artful means of successful self-expression and ultimately of self-advancement in a society which to a large degree recognized, appreciated, and rewarded musical and poetic skills." And Paterson, after discussing several major troubadours, concludes that "each one has his own intentions, of arguing, persuading, entertaining, instructing, expressing his own feelings, or creating a new and perfect work of art."[82]

The Poet-Lover, the lyric text, can then resist engulfment by convention. Self and text are discovered in division: in a certain measure, the absence of Source enables self and text to be. And it is indeed the absence of the lady that, conventionally, allows the lyric text: the Poet-Lover, a being-in-words, testifies by his very presence that no wordless fusion with beloved as Source has been found. For "joy . . . must be vacant from the present if the poem itself is to progress," so that "the lyric text points to a state that the text itself precludes."[83] Just as full presence of Source would annihilate self, so full presence of the imagined beloved (never a true danger in this convention) would preempt the lyric. Judith Mitchell criticizes R. D. Laing for not stressing in his theories the presence of the symbolic father, to provide a possible breathing-space for maternal closeness that can be both nourishing and fatal: "In psychosis the mother and child remain a dyad, only the triadic structure of the Oedipus complex can

break up this 'symbiotic' predicament."[84] There must be some
saving measure of separation, before the self with its complex
yearnings can exist. Or in other words, in these lyrics "l'éloigne-
ment est paradoxalement consubstantial avec le désir de l'union."
Topsfield believes that Peire d'Alvernhe "demands distance in
love in order to preserve his mental, social, and spiritual self."[85]
And Arnaut Daniel implies that the poem that fails to win the
lady may therefore succeed in realizing itself:

> Ges pel maltraich q'ieu soferi
> de ben amar no·m destoli,
> si tot me ten en desert,
> c'aissi·n fatz los motz en rima.

(I don't even turn away from the suffering I endure through loving well, although it holds me in solitude, for thus from my solitude I put words in rhymes.)[86]

We have been questioning all along the significance of the
hyphen in Poet-Lover, as we have followed some of the pos-
sibilities of complex interplay between *Poet* and *Lover* motions in
the lyric. And by this route we have also been rediscovering that
old debate between Platonists and Rhetoricians, a debate that
persists today in our discussions about "centered" and "decentered" texts. For it is not difficult to sense *Poet,* the care for
the specific texturing of words, in the pre-Socratics or Rhetoricians; nor is it hard to find *Lover,* the desire to move through
words toward fusion with a central, wordless Idea, in the
Platonist and his successor, the Christian. And these love lyrics
can belong in turn to the arguments adduced by either side in
this continuing debate.

For the hyphen in Poet-Lover can signify that in some necessary measure, *Poet* must cooperate with *Lover* in the text. The
poem as new presence, "pensée dans la parole," will have a
vitality that seems inherited from that *absent presence*, beloved
an unwordable Source. Lest the words be faded rhetoric, they
must be luminous with this sense of Source. Although Edward
Condren argues that the vocabulary of love is sometimes used
metaphorically in these poems for the creation of poetry, he
nevertheless concludes that poetry fulfills the impulse to love:
"at once painful and beautiful for the poet, his creation of poetry

is his act of love."[87] *Lover* moves in these texts, toward a sense of Source however vestigial. Thus the Platonist's love for his *arrheton* is compatible with these lyrics, and they could be evidence today to support the arguments of the critics of presence. Indeed, the Rhetorician has often found that in debate with the Platonist he must give way a little to allow some minimal sense of Source, some "truth" or "center" to focus the language play: one recalls, for instance, Isocrates' "Panhellenic ideal," or Cicero's marriage of *sapientia* with *eloquentia,* or even today the "operative" or "functional" center of Derrida or Lévi-Strauss. It seems our texts are bound to shadow Source.

Yet the hyphen in Poet-Lover can also signify that, in some necessary measure, *Poet* must also move independently in the words, a direction tangential or even contradictory to the interests of *Lover.* There must be an awareness of Poet-Lover or poem as an entity separable from that evoked beloved Source: the poem achieves its own self-texturing at a certain "optimal distance" from that Source.[88] For *Poet* is care for the poem as present reality, with the acknowledgment that Source is either illusory (Goldin's "lie") or, if real, yet always stubbornly absent from the text, an *absent presence. Poet* attends the details of the poem's birth, "the transformation of preexisting potential signifiers into a real signifier, the poetry."[89] Thus the Rhetorician's love for words is compatible with these lyrics, too, and they could be evidence today for the advocates of decentered texts. For as the Rhetoricians have always known, there must be a certain energy of individuation to set the wordplay on its own: the text "means" itself, in this way, and the signifiers in this measure become the signified.

Of course, all these questions ultimately concern the nature of the self, for in the self the motions toward Source and toward individual self-texturing must meet. It takes *Lover* and *Poet* to make a Poet-Lover or self, just as it has taken Platonist and Rhetorician, centrist and decentrist, to constitute Western culture. *Lover* enables a text or self to be, by primal identification with a Source felt to be infinite, central, and therefore vital. *Poet* tries to insure that an individual self-texture be entirely unpredictable, *sui generis; Poet* cares for a particular, circumscribed, and distinct self among other selves. *Poet* and *Lover* meet at the enigmatic core of self, the hyphen of Poet-Lover.

3   Arnaut Daniel

e qe·l remir contra·l lum de la lampa.
                                            —[12. 32]

I

This line from "Doutz brais e critz" exemplifies a small group
of crucial passages throughout Arnaut's cansos where *Poet*
seems to move with *Lover*. For in such a line the poem can briefly
approach its *absent presence:* the reader intuits a vital dyad of
Poet-Lover and lady that sustains the poem, just as dyadic
Source sustains the textured self. And in most of Arnaut's poems
there are only a few such lines, phrases, or words where *Poet* and
Lover seem to meet in the metaphoric language of fusion—
where, through both conventional and strange uses of
metaphor, hyperbole, ellipsis, synesthesia, and other tropes, the
poem evokes a lifegiving dual unity that the language cannot
reach.

Some of the formulaic statements about love and *joi,* for instance, can belong to this language of fusion, *Poet* with *Lover.*
For when in metaphor *Amors* renews the Poet-Lover's heart,
"greens" him, "leafs" and "flowers" and "fruits" him (3. 11–12;
5. 5),[1] the Poet-Lover as plant depends symbiotically upon *Amors*
for his primary nourishment, his very life. Similarly, in another
set of conventional metaphors, the Poet-Lover must depend

Citations are from Arnaut Daniel, *Canzoni,* ed. Gianluigi Toja (Florence: Sansoni, 1961), by poem number and line number. The translations are mine, unless
otherwise noted. Epigraphs are translated as they are discussed in context.

83

upon the steady internal sight of the lady to keep him alive, so
that he introjects her presence, taking her within him to his
heart and mind (13. 18–19; 9. 104–7) where he can always gaze
at her:

> lo cors m'abranda
> e·ill huoill n'ant la vianda,
> car solamen
> vezen
> m'estai aizida:
> ve·us qe·m ten a vida!
>
> [7. 28–33]

(My heart sets me afire, and thence my eyes take food, for only
through seeing does pleasure stay with me: see what holds me to
life!)

In these lines the metaphor seems to work also as hyperbole,
with the emphatic "solamen" and the exclamatory "ve·us": how
can it be, this Poet-Lover seems to ask, that my eyes feed me, that
the sight of this lady is my lifeline? Such hyperboles of fusion
may suggest an equivalence between the poem's "core" and the
central *infans* of the self, where nourishing gazes continue, even
though primally repressed, to sustain the adult. For in the receptive motions of *infans,* gazing does indeed nourish: the infant's
gaze becomes the avenue for primal identifications, for internalizing Source with eyes and mouth.[2]

Thus in the metaphoric texture of Arnaut's poems, *iois (joi)*
becomes equivalent to the internalized presence of the lady,
brought "within" the Poet-Lover by his rapt gazing. *Iois* becomes
the seed ("grans") and effective center of his being; *iois* guards
him from madness, wrath, shame, sorrow (14. 17–22; 13. 5–7);
iois, like a firmly established maternal "good imago" within the
self, prevents the unmothered despair of *amor hereos* by allowing
the Poet-Lover rudimentary worth. And just as "core" *infans*
centers the adult self with maternal presence *only by incorporative
analogy,* so Arnaut's metaphors of *iois* and *Amors* teach us their
own insufficiency, teach us that the lady is "vianda" only by
analogy, that *Amors* is ever more forcefully alive than its
analogue, a real plant. In elaborated metaphors, the signifiers
pursue the elusive *Amors:* love is not a changeable violet but a

laurel or juniper that will last the winter, perhaps, of age and death (16. 12–14); love's fruit, immune to frost or mist, belongs to the loyal lover, who may heal with sacred balm any injuries to the plant by the treacherous or faithless (11. 9–16). And the *iois* of the lady's internalized presence is likewise evoked as unlimited, not a wordable object but a condition of infinite succour, both remembered and promised. The Poet-Lover works in religious terms here, thanking God as well as his eyes for that more than vital gift of *iois:*

> Dieu o grazisc e a mos huoills,
> que per lor conoissensa·m venc
> iois, q'adreich auci e fola
> l'ira q'ieu n'agui e l'anta.
>
> [8. 10–13]

(I thank God and my eyes that through them there came to me the knowledge of joy that kills and destroys the wrath and shame I received.)

The religious allusions help to demonstrate here the inadequacy of the basic metaphors, the comparisons with food and plants. For *Poet* and *Lover* reach together through such words toward an inexpressible and paradoxical fusion of finite self and infinite loving Presence: thus the Poet-Lover is more faithful to the lady than hermit or monk to God (14. 25–27). The lady, *iois* from within, is evoked through this language as eternal nourishment; the Poet-Lover, joined to the sacred tree *Amors,* implicitly shares its eternal life. The metaphors of *Amors* and *iois* seem consistently to be reaching past their own limits.

Poet and *Lover* can meet in erotic as well as spiritual metaphors of fusion; for instance, the speaker desires the lady more than the monks of Doma desire God (9. 82–85). And after all, *Lover infans* must be a somatopsychic longing, for in that first maternally presenced dyad we are polymorphous in sensuality and meditation.[3] The love lyric as equivalent self can move toward a nonverbal, nondiacritic goal with both religious and sensual words, just as the self is always set in inward motion toward its own coenesthetic, diffusely receptive infant identifications. Topsfield and Paterson, in two recent readings of the sestina "Lo ferm voler" (18), find there a harmony of carnal and religious loves within *fin' amors*. They agree, for instance, that the lines opening the final stanza express an intense desire for union that is not simply sexual:

> C'aissi s'enpren e s'enongla
> mos cors en lei cum l'escorss' en la verga;
> [18. 31–32]⁴

Topsfield, who translates "cors" as "my whole being," believes the lines exemplify the ideal harmony of the previous stanza, "the strength of *Fin' Amors* as the balance of desire in body, mind, and spirit." Topsfield and Paterson read a subsequent line, "q'en paradis n'aura doble ioi m'arma" (35), as consonant with the poem's harmonizing of loves, and with the Christian imagery of the last two stanzas. Sexual love is associated with the *summum bonum* or *mielhs* of *fin' amors,* "in which moral, spiritual, and Christian doubts are resolved" (Topsfield); Arnaut parallels the sexual union with the soul's entry into heaven, as did Bernard in his commentary on the *Song of Songs* (Paterson). In a contrasting reading, also recent, Charles Jernigan assembles a number of alternative sexual meanings for the rhyme words: "arma" as both soul and weapon (penis); "verga" as both rod and phallus; "cambra" as chamber or womb (vagina). He develops an alternative reading for the poem, literally sexual, and suggests that there is continual comic, associative language play between the literal and courtly meanings of these words, as well as between *cors* (heart with analogical −s) and *cors* (body). He concludes that Arnaut is "mocking formulaic troubadour sentiments by grinding them against the most disconcerting sexual reality." And the puzzling tornada, "key to the poem's true meaning," means simply that the lady has the lover's penis, *arma-verga* and *Desirat* (her Desired One), whose "pretz" or power enters her "cambra," vagina. To Jernigan the lines opening the final stanza (31–32, quoted above) are simply phallic, and "cors" is body; these and other matching lines of the poem (17, 21, 30) are "crude" or a "sexual dream wish." The double joy in Paradise (35) is sexual joy, and the double meanings of this line mock spiritual values.⁵

One wonders whether these literal sexual meanings need be so "disconcerting," and whether their discovery must define the poem as mockery, parody, irony, comic devaluation—a more elaborate joke, perhaps, than Arnaut's *servente* "Pois Raimons e·n Trucs Malecs." After all, to be closer to the lady than finger to nail, and to have double joy in Paradise—these are, no matter how sexually associative, not clinical and dispassionate sexual "facts" but tropes, passionate wishes in hyperbole. *Poet* and *Lover* move through these tropes toward a dual unity that the poem and Poet-Lover cannot reach, more sexual than the proximity of bodies and more nearly unified than words in their persistent *différance* can say. Of course, scholarship of troubadour poetry has been notoriously uncertain as to whether a given poem encodes *caritas* or *eros:* traditional wisdom is that the two types of meaning undermine each other, or that, in the Robertsonian perspective, praise in religious terms of profane love must be ironic. But perhaps "Lo ferm voler" with its array of sexual and religious potential meanings need not be a narcissistic, mocking game of "object-devaluation,"[6] but might be instead a richer, more comprehensive game of self, a Poet-Lover at work embracing a great range of such tones and affects as angry insistence, erotic boasting, anticipated ecstasy, even spiritual harmony. *Poet* and *Lover* move energetically here through a panorama of connotations, through such rhyme words as "arma," whose meaning cannot be limited, toward a thorough imagination of fusion that can sustain Poet-Lover and poem.

Thus we see that in the metaphoric language of fusion *Poet* and *Lover* can move to synthesize or integrate what some might consider conflicting "ideologies" or "perspectives" of love. This motion is even more clearly revealed in "Doutz brais e critz" (12), as for example in this climactic passage:

> Dieus lo chauzitz,
> per cui foron assoutas
> las faillidas que fetz Longis lo cecs,
> voilla, si·l platz, q'ieu e midonz iassam
> en la chambra on amdui nos mandem
> uns rics convens don tan gran ioi atendi,
> qe·l seu bel cors baisan rizen descobra
> e qe·l remir contra·l lum de la lampa.

Ges rams floritz
de floretas envoutas
cui fan tremblar auzelhon ab lurs becs
non es plus frescs . . .

[25-36]

(May God the wise, by Whom were absolved the sins committed by
Longinus the blind, grant, if it please Him, that my lady and I lie
together in the room where we both made a rich covenant from
which I expect such great joy, and may he grant that I reveal,
kissing and smiling, her lovely body, and behold it against the light
of the lamp.

The flowering branch, enveloped with blossoms that the little birds
set trembling with their beaks, is hardly more fresh . . .)

This scene is as clearly sensual as any passage of troubadour
literature, especially after the Poet-Lover's confessed "great
hunger" for the lady, his entrance into the castle, their kiss
under the blue mantle (12, 21). And some readers may be
alerted, as by Arnaut's *servente* or Jernigan's article, to possible
sexual connotations of *gran ioi, bec,* or *chambra,* of trembling and
flowering branches. Yet the language here and throughout the
poem is also religious and feudal: the birds sing "voutas" and
make pleas ("precs") in their own language, "en lur latin" (2, 3);
"lo nebotz Sain Guillem" (13) may refer to a questing knight,
perhaps in the *Chanson de Guillaume;*[7] "Ierusalem" is twice a
rhyme word (37, 45); the lady dwells in a castle (11) and covers
their kiss with the shield ("escut," 22) of her cloak. Here the
entire fourth stanza (25-32) is shaped in the hortative subjunc-
tive, so that the "qe" of line 32 introduces another wish for which
the speaker, effectively, is praying. The "convens" may have the
religious connotations of "covenant"; Longinus is the legendary
blind centurion who pierced Christ's side and was healed by his
blood; the word "lum" itself may be devotional—"e·n art lum de
cer' e d'oli / que Dieus m'en don bon issert" (10. 16-17).[8] And
finally the Poet-Lover is revealed before the lady, hands joined,
as *ordinandus* or as vassal before feudal lord: "totz fis, mas iuntas,
a li·m rendi" (all truly, hands joined, I give myself to her, 38).
  Thus within the Poet-Lover, or the poem as self, terms of

88

sexual rendezvous are worked with terms of religious or feudal ritual, as *Poet* and *Lover* reach through the words toward a sustaining Source. The language stretches past eroticism, Christian doctrine, and feudal custom as final realities or signifieds; rather, all these possible referents work instead as signifiers— metaphors and other tricks of language where *Poet* and *Lover* meet to move past language, poem, and self. For these interwoven terms help to suggest a direction away from terms, to an inexpressible dual unity: one recalls that in the "s'oblidar" of Bernart de Ventadorn's lark the self is forgotten, dissolved in *joi*, contemplating the sweetness of that presence at the heart. And indeed, in "Doutz brais e critz" the profound wish that two might become one seems to motivate the poem's verbal coherences, from the most prominent images to the most trivial points of grammar. Two are as one: the birds are paired, each with his mate (4); two lovers kiss under a single cloak (22); they lie together, make a covenant together (28, 29). The pronoun "nos," surely rare in this poetry, is repeated and even elaborated with "ieu e midonz" or "amdui," and the first person plural verb forms are centrally focused in the -*am* and -*em* rhymes, numbers 4 and 5 of an 8-line stanza: "cum nos fam ... en cui entendem ... ieu e midonz nos baisem ... ieu e midonz iassam ... amdui nos mandem." The form "uns rics convens" is "a case of plural-singular rather rare in Provençal";[9] the pair of gerunds "baisan rizen" is bound in asyndeton; the syllables of line 32 cohere in a flow of *l*'s. Two are as one: in the last metaphor, perhaps so common that it is invisible, "I give myself to her," hands joined in submission and in symbol—closer, no doubt, than finger is to nail.

In several other poems by Arnaut, *Poet* and *Lover* meet in hyperboles that evoke this dyadic state as pure, free of imperfections or threatening alloy; similarly, every infant psychically "purifies" its dyadic state, ejecting the "bad" self-object experience, the negative introjections, to the periphery, "not-me."[10] Thus Arnaut's *Poet* uses traditional metaphors of refining inherited from Peire d'Alvernhe and Raimbaut d'Aurenga.[11] In Raimbaut's "Cars, douz e feinz" the speaker tries to file the dross from his *Jois* (21–23). Arnaut's speaker declares, my heart is refined ("esmers") in her, and I will never desire another; she is gold and cannot be further refined (14. 31-2; 17. 13-16). The more he is refined to match her perfection, the more thoroughly the dyad of Poet-Lover and lady is concentrated, isolated, unique: two are as one, a dual unity in purified symbiosis. Thus in "Sols sui qui sai" (15) we find the term "sol" used focally, now for the speaker, now for lady: *only* I, who know the over-suffering that rises in my heart ... I find all good qualities in one "cors" *alone* ... this treasure is for me *only* (1, 13, 39). The "sol" is both one and two, a unit world like Donne's lovers, and separation would mean destruction: "I will not be hers or mine if she parts from me" (17. 27).

Finally, *Poet* and *Lover* meet in these poems in elliptical metaphors of light, which summon Source as a point of illumination within poem and self. It is as though, again, the transfixed and reverential Poet-Lover, through infant gazing ("remir"), introjects the presence illumined "contra·l lum de la lampa" until it centers Poet-Lover and poem. When Raimbaut's speaker rubs away the rust to brighten his gloomy heart, "mon escur cor esclaire" ("Cars, douz e feinz," 23), Paterson interprets that "the 'illumination' comes from within the poet's heart." Arnaut may well have been influenced by Peire's and Raimbaut's uses of light imagery: in Raimbaut's "Car vei qe clars," the leading rhyme-word "clars," according to Topsfield, describes in turn the sun, *Jois*, the lover's heart, and his desire.[12] And Jaufré Rudel's speaker intends to sustain himself with the memory of his lady's presence until chamber and garden always seem to him a palace—creating a "world illuminated by her memory."[13] Indeed, these metaphors of light are sometimes worked by Arnaut so that the radiance nourishing the poem seems to spread globally, within and without, an introjected and projected infinity of light and love, like Schreber's "rays of God" made purely benevolent.[14] Through that central *absent presence,* the lady and *iois,* the world of the poem is transfigured with light; the poem becomes a self suffused with that internalized Presence:

> Bertran, non cre de sai lo Nil
> mais tant de fin ioi m'apoigna
> de sai on lo soleils poigna
> tro lai on lo soleils plovil.
>
> [4. 49-52]

(Bertran, I do not believe here at the Nile that so much true joy will ever touch me again—from here where the sun struggles [to rise], to there where the sun rains down [light, as it sets].)

How Dante must have loved this closing metaphor that is no closure, but rather overflowing *iois* like the raining light of the *Paradiso*, God's glory that penetrates the universe, shining in one part more and another less (i. 1–3). Wilhelm concludes of the scene "contra·l lum de la lampa" that the reader "feels in Daniel's lines a rising of the physical into the metaphysical in a way that is consummated in Dante."[15] In psychoanalytic terms one might speak of the coenesthetic infant knowing no closure, suffused with the glow of a caring maternal presence, and receiving in ritual epiphany a lighted Presence in a darkened room. Arnaut's images of light are at once regressive and transcendent, for they deny or ignore the diacritic limitations of space, mass, and weight: all gaps are filled with a flowing light that violates the "reality principle" but respects our ontology. He addresses the poem as self, both vessel and mirror: "d'aussor sen li auri' ops espandres" (with the highest thought you will need to shine upon her, 13. 45).

The internalized dyadic presence of the lady is an ontological light, essential, indeterminate, even silent. In the following passage, elliptical light metaphors and other subtle devices of language evoke Source for the poem:

> L'aur' amara
> fa·ls bruoills brancutz
> clarzir
> qe·l dous'espeis'ab fuoills,
> e·ls letz
> becs
> dels auzels ramencs
> ten balps e mutz,
> pars
> e non pars;
>
> . . .
>
> Tant fo clara
> ma prima lutz
> d'eslir
> lieis don cre·l cors los huoills,
>
> [9. 1–10, 18–21]

(The bitter breeze makes the branching woods grow light, so that the sweetness from the leaves grows thick, and the joyful beaks of the fluttering birds, mated and not mated, are held stammering and mute; . . . So clear was my first light in choosing her whose eyes my heart fears.)

Three words for "light" are offered, as both metaphor and ellipsis; by their unexplained simplicity they seem both to reach past the lines and to stand, sufficient. Del Monte believes the single word-line "clarzir" is suggestive in its "luminous essentiality."[16] And the "lutz," intensified by "clara" and "prima," has no discernible referent: Toja cites suggested translations of "inspiration," "light," or "glance," but one feels a determinate meaning might dim this quintessential light, with that "prima" connoting "first" both in time and in value. Peire d'Alvernhe likewise in "Be m'es plazen" uses *amic* (lover) and *amiga* (mistress) as deliberately vague antonomasiae that call up an indeterminate group of meanings.[17] Moreover, these lines stutter, all but mute like the birds, as the Poet-Lover fearfully chooses in that first light: there is perhaps even an elliptical suggestion of regarding, silently, a lighted face. For the light flows, "clara," even if the words do not. Similarly, Raimbaut d'Aurenga in "Assatz m'es belh" contrasts his private understanding with his lady and the wordiness of supposedly more clever people; his *saber ver* or *cubert ver* is the true, nonverbal state of his feelings.[18] Finally, the passage from "L'aur'amara" is synesthetic: a bitter breeze lightens, sweetness thickens. The lines suggest a self at the dawn of being, in preverbal receptivity. These synesthetic and syntactic fragments seem illumined by some significant Presence that yet cannot be signified; like our "core" *infans,* perhaps, the lines can never be fully assembled to diacritic meaning, and yet they are vitally meaningful. Arnaut, "mystique de la rime,"[19] here works his mystical devices, evoking a lighted wellspring of poem and self, evoking Source.

II

q'ieu soi fis drutz,
cars
e non vars,
[9. 42–44]

Arnaut is no rebel. He does not parody courtly topoi and social convention as does the nonconformist Raimbaut d'Aurenga, and he is usually judged not "original" in content. Although he absorbs all the styles of his most influential predecessors, he does not take an explicit stand in the debate about styles, *leu* or *clus*. He is known for his use of *caras rimas,* and for a few unique stanzaic forms, such as "L'aur'amara" (9) and the sestina, "Lo ferm voler" (18); still, he does not devise new rhyme schemes or stanzaic forms as a matter of course, in the manner of Giraut de Bornelh.[20] To the contrary, Arnaut's Poet-Lover often appropriates conventional styles, as when he embraces lists of traditional "courtly" qualities:

> Ben ai estat a maintas bonas cortz
> mas sai ab lieis trob pro mais que lauzar:
> mesur' e sen et autres bos mestiers,
> beutat, ioven, bos faitz e bels demors,
> gen l'enseignet Cortesi e la duois;
> [15. 15-19]

(Indeed I have been in many good courts, but here in hers I find more advantages to praise: moderation and wisdom and other good qualities, beauty, youth, good deeds and fair pastimes; Courtesy taught and formed her graciously.)

> qu'ensenhamens e fizeutatz plevida
> jai per estar, c'a bon pretz s'i atorna.
> [5. 13-14]

(For courtly manners and pledged loyalty always stay here and turn into good reputation.)

> et ieu que soi dels leials amadors
> estau jauzens, c'Amors e Jois me guida
> lo cor en joi . . .
> [5. 40-42]

(And I, who belong to the loyal lovers, remain rejoicing, for Love and Joy guide my heart to joy [my lady] . . .)

> c'Amors enquier los sieus d'aital semblan,
> verais, francs, fis, merceians, parcedors,
> car a sa cort notz orguoills e val blandres.
> [13. 12-14]

(For love seeks his own to be of this appearance: sincere, open, noble, imploring, forgiving—for in his court pride is harmful and courtliness is worthy.)

These courtly nouns and adjectives serve as his *descriptio,* his *stilo del loda* (style of praise) of Love, lady, and poetic convention. This Poet-Lover cooperates more than fully with the "mothering" of convention, then, drinking in important topoi and reconstituting them in his being-of-words. He will stress particularly his perseverance, submission, fidelity, and single-mindedness, for he is unusually fervent in his obedience, always protesting his loyalty to traditional values and styles.

Poet and *Lover* thus join directions toward convention as Source, in such a way as to suggest, all the more securely, a loyal direction toward the lady as Source. Indeed, the very intensity of obedience to convention here distinguishes this Poet-Lover from others. For he is more conventional than convention: unlike several of his predecessors, he does not take continual pains to discriminate among *Amors, Fin' Amors,* and *Fals' Amors,* but follows nearly without question a single, "remarkably harmonious" *Amors.*[21] That is, he is obedient to a single *Amors* even as he is obedient toward a single lady:

> E pois tan val, no·us cuietz que s'esparga
> mos ferms volers ne qe·is forc ni qe·is branc,
> car no serai sieus ni mieus si m'en parc.
> [17. 25-27]

(And since she is worth so much, do not think that my firm desire is scattered, nor does it fork or branch, for I will be neither hers nor mine if she parts from me.)

He keeps a true course toward the union of "sieus" and "mieus" because he tries to make two into one, to belong to a single dyad. He will refine away disloyalties and other dross, direct himself toward a single bright intimacy; he is restrained, constricted, purified, governed by that single *Amors* that can assure his worth (3. 15-16). Love and the lady rule him absolutely.

Under this single rule, Arnaut's Poet-Lover is a creature of verbal compression. *Poet,* the drive for individuation, and *Lover,*

the persistent longing for Source, meet in a vigorously compressed poem, a self cultivated in mimesis of that controlling
wish, the dual unity of "ideal self" and "ideal object." As two must
be one, so the many signifiers of the poem must be one, intrafused, as close as finger is to nail. In Peire d'Alvernhe's ideal of
vers entiers, both "moral" and "aesthetic" integrity are implied by
well-linked verses; likewise, to Peire *motz romputz* (broken words,
expressions not well-bound-up) are morally corrupt.[22] And Arnaut's Poet-Lover seems to have taken Peire's theories to heart;
he seems to believe that his verbal coherences attest his moral
worth, his eligibility for *iois.* Thus he boasts of his zeal to make
necessary sacrifices, to make himself consummately obedient to
love and the lady—to work, compress, file, pare, and constrict
this self made of words, until poem and Poet-Lover show true
valor:

> obre e lim
> motz de valor
> ab art d'Amor
> [2. 12–14]

(I forge and file words of value with the art of Love.)

From many signifiers, one poem. To this end all the symmetries of a poem can work—the parallel structures of syntax, the
binomials and trinomials. And Provençal poetry is especially rich
in figures of repetition, or repeated words, morphemes, and
sounds.[23] In such devices *Poet* and *Lover* move together toward a
difficult result, encouraging the differentiated words to coalesce
into a unit, into a Poet-Lover who is "sol" like—and thereby
with—the lady, "ideal self" like "ideal object." The Poet-Lover
will pledge perfect service to Love in a line thoroughly alliter-
ative: "e pliu·t, Amors, si la·m conquers, / trevas totz temps ab
totas, fors del decs" (and I pledge to you, Love, if I conquer her
for myself, / truces all the time with all, except for your commands, 14. 15–16). And in "Sols sui qui sai" (15), the body of the
poem seems entirely saturated with alliteration, parallel phrases,
and equivocal rhymes. With this same energy of obedience the
Poet-Lover appears to file away his individual lines, making
them disyllabic or even unisyllabic. Indeed, the disyllabic lines of

"Anc ieu non l'aic" (7) themselves summarize the topoi of faithful love: *soffren, vezen, feignen, temen, li·m ren, si·t pren*. And all reach toward that single gift, the other rhyming word, *presen*. The unisyllabic lines of "L'aur'amara" (9) seem likewise planed in order to evoke an ideal of constancy: *pars* ("mated"), *rars, cars, clars, pars* (a verb, "tolerated"), *dars*. In this way, paradoxically, the quest for complete obedience to *Amors* and convention can work to strain or break the limits of convention: Arnaut's Poet-Lover is distinguished from his contemporaries by these short lines.[24]

Often, this felt strain is exactly the point. The verbal texture of the Poet-Lover proves that obedience to *Amors* can be painstaking and painful. Even in the frequent choice of *rimas dissolutas,* unity is made to sound labored: the ear has a long wait before a given rhyme is answered in the next stanza.[25] Often alliteration contends with dissonance, *braus* sounds or irregularly accented lines: "En breu brisara·l temps braus, / e·ill bisa busin'els brancs" (11. 1–2). And above all, the frequent *caras rimas* reveal the Poet-Lover at his toils: it is as though to answer *Lover,* the drive for absolute unity, *Poet* will move even *away* from convention in order to find matching rhymes. Indeed, with *caras rimas,* Arnaut's most prominent stylistic innovation,[26] his Poet-Lover sets up his own hurdles to show the grand energy of loyal love: he will distort syntax, alter forms of nouns and verbs, discover exotic proper names, and invent words, all for the rhyme—to make two one.[27]

> q'ieu soi fis drutz,
> cars
> e non vars.
> [9. 42–44]

(For I am a true lover, rare and unvarying.)

To be *non vars*—unchanging, faithful, purified, eligible for dyadic bliss—one must be *cars:* one must answer even the unanswerable rhymes, however deviant the result. *Poet* and *Lover* move together to answer all rhymes, but in the very answering, *Poet* is revealed as an independent motion: words born to match other words, words that seem to generate each other with a momentum all their own. Poet-Lover becomes textured with deviations, a self distinct from other selves, and the rhyming words themselves become precious, valuable as they are rare—*caras*, as the lady is *car*. It is a mimetic effort: Poet-Lover and lady meet in this word, *cars*.

By this route, perhaps, artistic form can be the expression of an exalted love; hermeticism can be the revelation of absolute sincerity; rare words can arise from rare *Jois*.[28] Consider this passage:

> e doncas ieu q'en la genssor entendi
> dei far chansson sobre totz de bell'obra
> que no·i aia mot fals ni rim'estrampa.
> [12. 6–8]

(And then I, who am intent upon the most noble lady, ought to make a song above the songs of all others, a song of lovely workmanship that might not have a false word in it, nor an unmatched rhyme.)

That word "estrampa," perfecting this dedication to poetic integrity in mimesis of "la genssor," is itself one of four original *caras rimas* in the poem,[29] and is not found again even in Arnaut's poetry. He had to wrench the word out of its usual sense just to place it here, unless he actually did misunderstand the conventional meaning, and thought *rima estrampa* meant *rims espars*, not *rima dissoluta*.[30] Thus with line 8 the poem not only asserts that all good poems have matched rhymes, but also contracts, simultaneously, to match that difficult term meaning "unmatched rhyme." We can see *Poet* here, in the evident care to find the requisite words: *rampa, escampa* (twice, in *rima equivoca*), *lampa, acampa*, and the extravagant proper names *Luna-pampa* and *Estampa*.[31] Such words individuate the poem, even while they move toward intrafusion: here rhyme-forcing is not an error or a barbarism, but the repeated cost of the Poet-Lover's devotion. Such words are the work of both *Poet* and *Lover*, in no easy conjunction.

Readers do agree that Arnaut's poetic voice is recognizably compressed and difficult. The author of his *vida* records a consensus that he is "not easy to understand or to learn" ("non son

leus ad entendre ni ad aprendre"); Petrarch found his poetry
"strano e bello," and commentators in this century have called
him brief, intense, compact, even cramped.[32] *Poet* responds to
Lover in these lines by trying to compress a long theme into a
short song, an infinite Source into a finite poem:

> farai, c'Amors m'o comanda,
> breu chansson de razon loigna,
> que gen m'a duoich de las artz de s'escola;

(I shall make, for Love thus commands me, a brief song about a
long theme, for he has trained me graciously in the arts of his
school.)[33]

Moving with *Lover* toward the lady's *absent presence, Poet* therefore attends the *present absence* of the poem: a laboring, constricted self, marked by the trials of obedience. If one can call the
languishing lover *amant martyr,* one may surely name the Ar-
nauldian poem *vers martyr.* In one interpretation of the following passage, love "attacks" both speaker and poem, in order to
harmonize the words with the melody—as though hatred of all
discord were here, typically, turned against the obedient self:

> pel ioi q'ai d'els e del tems
> chant, mas amors mi asauta,
> qui·ls motz ab lo son acorda.
> [8. 7–9]

(Through the joy I have in them [the birds] and in the season I
sing, but love attacks me, love that harmonizes the words with the
melody.)[34]

III

> e am ses faillida.
> [7. 44]

In Arnaut's poems, *Poet* and *Lover* move together not only to
compress and integrate diversity, in mimesis of that single dyad,
but also to deflect aggression from that sustaining *absent presence,*

the remembered and anticipated union of Poet-Lover and lady. Neither compression nor repression is made easy, and the poems are textured and distinguished by the pursuant difficulties.

Thus *Poet* and *Lover* enact the metaphor of "refining" in the texture of the poem, working steadily to banish all disloyalty, disobedience, unruly passion, lying or deceit, envy, slander, complaining, spying, disease or death, mockery, devaluation: all qualities or impulses that might endanger the sacred, safe, intimate fusion of selves, two as one, at the unwordable center of the poem. For *Lover,* like "core" *infans,* seeks to purify and protect without qualification the central fantasy of "ideal self" and "ideal object," the good dyad fundamental to poem and self. Thus Poet-Lover and poem may be filled with consonants that seem to spit (*br, b, t*), as though to expel winter from the poem, from that sacred, nourishing tree *Amors* (9–16):

> En breu brisara·l temps braus,
> e·ill bisa busin' els brancs
>
> [11. 1–2]

(Soon the fierce season will rage, and the wind already hisses in the branches.)

Here line 2 is further contorted with irregular accents, so that the Poet-Lover seems to reject the line even as he articulates it. In the same way, he will make a line of deceitful suitors break rhythm:

> D'aquest' amor son lunh forsdug
> dompneiador fenhen, fradel . . .
>
> [5. 36–37]

(From this love far away are banished hypocritical suitors, wretches . . .)

The ensuing lines about true love and "leials amadors" (loyal lovers) are by contrast regular, easily rhythmic, as though fully welcomed by the speaker (40–42). Sometimes, surely, the *caras rimas* may account for these irregular rhythms and harsh

LOVE WORDS

sounds, and they belong thus to the effort of compression. Yet more often they reveal traditional associations with *trobar braus*, a genre of blame. Marcabru, whose poems became models of *trobar braus*, used discordant and grating sounds, monosyllables, and violent rhythms in order to moralize, and thereby to "re-fine" away or exorcise all false social values that could threaten that centrally evoked *fin' amors*. Granted, later troubadours did use *braus* sounds for other purposes, Raimbaut d'Aurenga for humorous effect and Peire d'Alvernhe perhaps simply for eloquence, transferring Marcabru's vocabulary to love poetry in a mixture of rough and smooth that "suggests intellectual and moral effort."[35] But Arnaut's Poet-Lover seems again to moralize with harsh sounds, in the spirit of Marcabru. Here again he is even more conventional than convention, using harsh language more pervasively than tradition would require, as though his Poet-Lover were in continual vigilance against that false *Amors* that "turns and descends from so many sides" (4. 9–10), endangering that lifegiving *iois* central to the poem. Just so, perhaps, Dante used *rime aspre e chiocce* (harsh and raucous rhymes) for that most loveless of regions expelled from heaven—for Dante's category of *yrsuta* words may descend from the *braus* vocabulary of Arnaut and Marcabru.[36]

As *Poet* and *Lover* thus guard *iois*, sometimes aggressive threats to *iois* are concentrated upon the familiar *lausengiers*. Often, the fourth stanza or a later stanza will collect the relevant imprecations against them, after the cherished and vulnerable Source has been evoked earlier in the poem with lists of courtly qualities or with metaphors of fusion. For the *lausengiers* repre-sent the consummate, comprehensive threat: they are the spies, the callous mockers, those who murmur or shout in unadorned speech (2. 30–33; 17. 31–32; 15. 38–39; 7. 34–40). They seem to have the dangerous powers of Klein's "primal envy," the strength to jeopardize love by devaluing it, effectively spoiling the precious dyad that is crucial to the self, the central "me" of self-and-Source, without which life holds no value, no "sense." Physical strength is far from the issue here, for primal envy is a matter of psychic reality—of vision or imagination—and thus the *lausengiers'* words are their most feared weapon. With their words they can work a kind of black magic, a psychic reversal: in place of the reverent silence of that lighted dyad, "contra·l lum de la lampa," they offer noisy, deprecating speech. Talk can turn true love to folly, whether it is the "falsa paraulla loigna" (false, delaying words) of coy ladies (4. 14–16), or the careless words of those who dishonor themselves (8. 28–30). Thus all the more can the *lausengiers*, masters of evil speech, destroy reputations ("pretz") and even love itself (5. 38–39; 17. 44). *Iois*, intangible and wordless, can nonetheless be both conjured and destroyed by language.

Of course, the poem that actively banishes discord thereby makes itself discordant: *Il primo amore* establishes hell as one-third of the *Commedia*. As *Poet* and *Lover* move to protect *iois*, both threats and counterthreats are taken into the poem, in the same motion: the strain of this constant vigilance is realized in the verbal texture. For "not-me" is also me; the repressed and banished return, as the substance of the poem. The *autras*, excluded to prove the Poet-Lover's loyalty, accumulate to fill the stanzas even as they are "refined" away:

> De drudaria
> no·m sai de re blasmar,
> qu'autrui paria
> torn ieu en reirazar;
> ges ab sa par
> no sai doblar m'amia,
> qu'una non par
> que seconda no·ill sia.
> [3. 25–32]

(In love I know of nothing for which to blame myself, for I consider friendship with another lady to be a bad move; I do not know how to match my beloved with her equal, for not one lady appears that does not take second place to her.)

And "Sols sui qui sai" (15) seems a tissue of negated or omitted entities, even in its praise: "de lieis no cre rens de ben si' a dire" (I believe nothing good is lacking in her, 21). In this way the dross of aggression or sorrow becomes integral to a poem of *iois*, or as Raimbaut might phrase it, "Ira Joi entrebresca" (Sorrow entangles Joy).[37]

Thus this busy purification does not accomplish a purified poem. For even more than he fears the *lausengiers*, it seems, the speaker fears himself—his own failures in obedience or loyalty, his own attraction to those *autras* he resists with "frequent, vehement protests."[38] And most of all he fears his own tongue, for he can endanger true love even with unmatched rhymes, much less with vented impatience or anger, or with some lapse in reverence. Thus *Poet* and *Lover* meet again in the conventional representation of the timid speaker, his aggression tamed, trained in the arts of love but avowedly silent before his lady (15. 6–7), fearful, his tongue hesitant to express the thoughts of love in his heart (7. 12–16). After the "lum de la lampa" scene, he asks, "Bocca, que ditz?" (Mouth, what are you saying? 12. 41) as though amazed by his own boldness. He is always concerned lest his words become destructive, irreverent, inadequate— *lausengier* talk, in short. He therefore directs those *braus* curses, the vituperative language of distortion and disease, against himself and the *lausengiers* alike:

> Fals lausengier, fuocs las lengas vos arga,
> e que perdatz ams los huoills de mal cranc,
> [17. 41–42]

(False lausengier, may fire burn your tongue, and may you lose both your eyes through an evil cancer.)

> Pensar de lieis m'es repaus,
> e traga·m ams los huoills crancs
> s'a lieis vezer no·ls estuich;
> [11. 41–43]

(To think of her is rest to me, and may a cancer take out both my eyes if by seeing her I do not preserve them.)

> e pustell'ai en sa gauta
> cel c'ab lieis si desacorda.
> . . .
> e qui de parlar trassauta
> dreitz es q'en la lenga·is morda.
> . . .
> Arnautz am' e no di nems,
> c'Amors l'afrena la gauta
> que fols gabs no la·ill comorda.
> [8. 26–27, 35–36, 55–57]

(And may he have a pustule in his cheek, who quarrels with her. . . . And whoever grows mad with speaking, it is just that his tongue die. . . . Arnaut loves and does not speak too much, for Love reins in his throat, so that foolish boasting does not take it from him.)[39]

This language serves as both retribution for the *lausengiers* and prevention for himself, the most dangerous potential *lausengier*. For "fols gabs" can threaten to destroy the poem as self: just as maternal absence or disapproval instills a primal, life-or-death morality in the infant, so the lady's traditional implicit wishes— for restraint, caution, secrecy, even abstinence—are involved with the ontology of these poems. To risk her serious displeasure, her accusations, would be to risk the poem's heart, its central luminous metaphor evoking *absent presence*. For only from the memory and anticipation of Poet-Lover and lady, two as one, can the poem be spoken, just as all selves must spring from a mother-infant bond. The speaker who might offend the lady with *lausengier* talk might also render himself ineligible for that metaphor of dyadic fusion that allows the poem to be; the offending speaker courts full absence, the disintegration of the poem.[40] Consider this metaphor:

> que ies Rozers, per aiga qe l'engrois,
> non a tal briu c'al cor plus larga dotz
> no·m fassa estanc d'amor, qan la remire.
> [15. 26–28]

(For the Rhone, through the water that deepens it, has not such impetus that the lake of love does not make more generous currents in my heart, when I look upon her.)

Contained as it is, "estanc d'amor," the passage attests the strength and depth of the speaker's love; yet the lines also suggest a force, "briu," needing to be restrained, a perpetual chance of violent overflow. *Poet* and *Lover* check the words, then, and delay or deny expressions of desire. One pun (inherited from Raimbaut) epitomizes this chronic, supraconventional restraint taxing the lines: "ard' e rim" (burns and splits/rhymes, 2. 26). To practice the art of rhyming is, precisely, to burn and to split—to constrain the heart until it almost breaks, so as to preserve intact the vital promise of pure *iois*.

The energy of this restraint is made especially clear near the ends of the poems, where *Poet* and *Lover* often allow some expression of impatient desire, disrupting the carefully established verbal patterns. In "Sols sui qui sai" (15) for instance, the first four stanzas, even though technically "indivisible,"[41] seem built of evenly apportioned syntactic units—in a seven-line stanza, 2/3/2; 2/2/3; 2/3/2; and 2/2/3 for the first four stanzas. But in stanzas five and six, this regular pattern gives way, as though allowing the speaker's desires—like the invoked Rhone—to overflow the verbal "banks," violating the expectations set in the first four stanzas: 3/1/2/1; 4/1/2. Also breaking measure are the increased enjambement (22–23, 27–28, 38–39), exclamations, the question, "Dic trop?" (Do I say too much?), and the staccato line, "Hai! si no l'ai, las! tant mal m'a comors!" (Ah! If I don't have her, alas! So much ill has seized me! 32). In the poem "L'aur'amara," similarly, the speaker is timid for four stanzas, his silent pleas set in ranks within him (56–58), until he finally bursts forth in direct address: "Doussa car' . . ." (Sweet face . . . 69). In "En breu brisara·l temps braus" (11), another song about timidity which seems to bristle with harsh and constrained language, the speaker in the sixth stanza all but explodes, vowing and cursing himself, and breaks off, "C'ai dig?" (What have I said?), ending in both prayer and frustration. In "Er vei vermeills" (13) the speaker elaborates for five stanzas upon his loyalty and patience, and in the sixth erupts in complaints: moon and sun, you make your course too long! (41). By such qualified outbursts as these, we can measure the energy it takes for *Poet* and *Lover* to restrain anger and desire in the more measured passages, just as the *caras rimas* demonstrate the effort of compression. And again, paradoxically, these efforts work ultimately to reveal *Poet,* the effort of individuation, as a motion all its own. For as the poem becomes textured with deflected aggressions and restrained desires, we come to know the Poet-Lover as a self particularized by these lapses in coherence, these violated proportions. The negative energies of *Poet* help to characterize the Poet-Lover.

Thus in his reach toward the unattainable lady, "ideal object," the speaker tries to become the flawless counterpart, "ideal self"—he means to justify the claim, "am ses faillida," that is, "I

love without fault." *Poet* and *Lover* move to expel those im-
purities and dangers necessary to poem and self, and as well to
cover and conceal them, diminishing their threat to that perfect
dyad, Poet-Lover and lady:

> ma·l cors ferms fortz
> mi fai cobrir
> mains vers;
> [9. 45–47]

(But my firm, strong heart makes me cover many truths.)

Many a *ver* is covered in such a *vers.* The lady's name is well
protected, *cobert* or *clus* in a code, like "lebre" for "l'Ebre," and
secured from the sandalmongerers. What is more, through dis-
creet *double entendres* the Poet-Lover and lady can meet in *absent
presence,* in that *ver* that is the alternative sexual meaning of
words, safe from the devaluation of common view. Here in *double entendre,* carnality can be intensified without threatening the
desired intimacy. Of course, *Poet* and *Lover* allow only a few
direct expressions of sexual hunger, like "lecs e glotz" (greedy
and gluttonous, 15. 34), great love "n'ams los flancs" (in both my
flanks, 11. 18), or "gran fam" (great hunger, 12. 12) for the lady.
But consider also the following:

> c'ab lieis c'al cor plus m'azauta
> sui liatz ab ferma corda
> [8. 17–18]

(For to her who most delights my heart I am bound with a strong
cord.)

> q'er sui letz, er m'o trastorna,
> car a son vol me liama.
> [7. 59–60]

(For now I am happy, now it is lost to me, for she chains me to her
will.)

> l'espers
> qe·ill prec qe·m brei
> [9. 64–65]

(the hope that I pray her to shorten for me)

er iauzimens breuia·m temps lonc
[11. 30]

(Now my joy shortens the long time.)

In Marcabru's usage, "Qu'ela·m lass' e·m lia" refers to sexually entwined bodies, and "se breia" means "he is (sexually) shortened."[42] Through such coverings, *Poet* creates poems as castles of safe, accepted words, "paraulas coutas" (12. 18), castles of self which will not admit devaluers.

Indeed, poems as castles—both to protect *iois* and to possess it exclusively—are entirely traditional; *Poet* and *Lover* join to make the language enigmatic, and therefore possessive. Marcabru seems to have started this custom with "D'aisso lau Dieu," a gap with a double *razo,* both an erotic boast and a claim of supreme rhetorical skill. One stanza reads:

> Mos alos es
> en tal deves
> res mas ieu non s'eu pot jauzir:
> aissi l'ai claus
> de pens venaus
> que nuills no lo·m pot envazir.

(My private property is in such a prohibited enclosure that no one but I can take pleasure in it: I have so closed it round with deceiving thoughts that no one can invade it.)[43]

Paterson believes that here the speaker claims both to lock up the lady as sexual property and to lock up "pens venaus," deceitful little thoughts, or "gignos sens" (13), cunning meanings, from easy interpretation. Topsfield, allowing the "alos" to be of more serious value, believes the stanza refers to a refuge for a form of higher love. Peire d'Alvernhe in "En estiu" writes of a castle, "caslar," built upon a high rock, "auta roch," perhaps a sacred or illusory love, defended against reality.[44] And in "Be m'es plazen" Peire writes:

> Mais am un ort
> serrat e fort
> qu'hom ren no m'en puesca emblar

(I prefer a locked, strong garden, from which nothing can be stolen from me.)[45]

Paterson concludes that the "ort / serrat e fort" is his poetry, perfectly well bound up so that no one "can steal anything from it," so that meanings cannot too easily be unlocked. Indeed, the verb *lassar* itself, quoted above by Marcabru in the sexual meaning, can also refer to a troubadour *topos*, the binding up or integration of a theme for one's song—as though the binding of words itself imitated the joining of bodies.[46]

For like the self, the poem as castle both protects and possesses an exclusive dyad, a single *hortus conclusus* of fused selves. The *iois* guarded by those *arma eloquentiae* is like the primally repressed identification guarded by the "interstitial web" of self—a dyad and not a triad, an intense intimacy that cannot be shared. *Poet* and *Lover* multiply "gignos sens" in order to possess Source completely. And yet again, paradoxically, the interests of *Poet* are served: for the design of the castle appears all the more distinguishable and special, a hermetic and therefore recognizable Poet-Lover. Finally, it may be that such a Poet-Lover, through the deviation of those dark, protecting words, and through those negative encrustations of restrained desire and banished discord, manages to keep clear a free area or courtyard within the castle of the poem, where space and time belong to *Lover* in "ioi desliure" (unbounded joy, 4. 9). Words closed to others help poem or self to open inwardly to an infinite center, a *Seelenzustand;*[47] the heart shut to others is free to leap inward, in hyperbole or elliptical metaphor, toward its own private *absent presence,* "sol" toward "sola":

> Pretz e Valors, vostre capduoills
> es la bella c'ab si·m retenc,
> qui m'a sol et ieu liei sola,
> c'autr' el mon no m'atalanta;
> anz sui brus

et estrus
ad autras e·l cor teing prems,
mas pel sieu ioi trep' e sauta:
no vuoill c'autra m'o comorda.
                                    [8. 46–54]

(Pretz and Valors, your stronghold is the fair one who retained me,
who has me alone and I her alone, for no other in the world
pleases me; rather I am dark and brusque toward others, and hold
my heart shut, but through joy it dances and leaps: nor do I want
another woman to take this from me.)

IV

We can find these various workings of Arnaut's Poet-Lover
focused and integrated in an individual poem like this one:

1

En cest sonet coind' e leri
fauc motz e capuig e doli,
que serant verai e cert
qan n'aurai passat la lima;
q'Amors marves plan' e daura
mon chantar, que de liei mou
qui pretz manten e governa.

2

Tot iorn meillur et esmeri
car la gensor serv e coli
el mon, so·us dic en apert.
Sieus sui del pe tro q'en cima,
e si tot venta·ill freid'aura,
l'amors q'inz el cor mi plou
mi ten chaut on plus iverna.

3

Mil messas n'aug e·n proferi
e·n art lum de cer' e d'oli
que Dieus m'en don bon issert
de lieis on no·m val escrima;
e qan remir sa crin saura

e·l cors q'es grailet e nou
mais l'am que qi·m des Luserna.
[10. 1–21]

(1 In this charming and gay tune, I make and plane and polish
words so that they will be true and certain when I have passed the
file over them; for Love at once smooths and gilds my song, that
moves from her who guards and rules merit.

2 Every day I am better and more pure, for I serve and honor the
fairest lady in the world, this I tell you frankly. I am hers from my
foot up to my head, and although the cold wind blows, the love
that rains in my heart keeps me warm where it winters the most.

3 I hear and offer a thousand masses, and I burn lights of wax
and oil so that God might give me good luck with her where no
defense avails; and when I behold her blonde hair and her slender
and young body, I love her more than I would love him who might
give me Luserna.)

In these first three stanzas, *Poet* and *Lover* move in evocative
terms toward a radiant Presence. We can sense this language of
fusion especially in the rhyming words "daura" and "mou," and
other words linked to them by sound or connotation. Associated
with "daura," for instance, we may notice the "lum" of wax and
oil that the Poet-Lover reverentially burns; the golden hair, "sa
crin saura," that holds him rapt in the familiar incorporative
gaze, "remir"; the metaphor of refining, "meillur et esmeri";
perhaps even the "chaut," strange warmth in winter. And the
-*aura* rhyme itself seems to belong to words that cherish a
suggestion of this *absent presence*—besides "saura," the "restaura" reaches toward the healing powers of her favor, and
"aura" belongs with the later "laura" and "l'aura" which may
encode the lady's name, Laura.[48] The phrase "que de liei mou"
invokes the mystery of Source, since "mou" means not only
"moves" but also "begins" or "originates." And the other phrases
forming the -*ou* rhyme seem to intensify this question of ontology: "q'inz el cor mi plou" suggests an unlimited rain of love
arising paradoxically from the closed space of the heart; her
admired body seems wondrously "grailet e nou"; and further
echoes of renewal and origin appear in "renou" and "annou."
And there are even more subtle phonic devices, such as the

lingering *r*'s and *s*'s of line 19, or, perhaps, the receptivity of the -*aura* and -*ou* sounds. This language texture is merely the glimmer, the vital shadow of a lady who was once there before the Poet-Lover, and whose lighted *absent presence* enables the poem.

And in these first three stanzas, love not only gilds but also planes. *Poet* and *Lover* here move obediently to compress the words, in mimesis of that envisioned dual unity. A *vers martyr* takes shape, *cars* like the lady. For we notice at once the seven *caras rimas* (four of them original) which seem to curtail the lines a bit more than usual.[49] We find the diminutives "sonet" and "grailet" (a neologism), precious and small like the lines themselves. And the unusual match "doli" and "d'oli," the neologism "issert," and the legendary Spanish city "Luserna" all seem born from the exigencies of rhyme: wealth discovered in compression, *Poet* revealed as non-deducible. Furthermore, in ten of the first twenty-one lines, words are paired: one noun pair, three adjective pairs, six verb pairs (including a triplet, in line 2). This almost obsessive pairing happens to suggest the obsession necessary to the *Lover* motion: the faith that two may be construed as one, pressed and compressed to one.

4

Tant l'am de cor e la queri
c'ab trop voler cug la·m toli
s'om ren per ben amar pert.
Q'el sieus cor sobretracima
lo mieu tot e non s'eisaura;
tant a de ver fait renou
c'obrador n'a e taverna.

5

No vuoill de Roma l'emperi
ni c'om m'en fassa apostoli,
q'en lieis non aia revert
per cui m'art lo cors e·m rima;
e si·l maltraich no·m restaura
ab un baisar anz d'annou
mi auci e si enferna.

[22-35]

(4   So much do I love her and seek her with my heart, that with too much desire, I think, I steal her from myself, if a man can lose something by loving well. For her heart submerges all my heart, and does not evaporate; so much in truth has she practised usury that she has by it both the workman and the shop.

5   I do not want the empire of Rome, nor do I want anyone to make me pope of it, if I could not then return to her for whom my heart burns and splits; and if she does not cure my suffering with a kiss before the new year, she kills me and damns herself.)

In these next two stanzas, *Poet* and *Lover* move to tame words of desire. For the conjured *iois* of the first three stanzas is now called vulnerable to "trop voler," and Rudel's lines echo behind these lines to amplify the threat: "E cre que volers m'enguana / Si cobezeza la·m tol" (and I fear lest my will should cheat me / if urgent desire robs me of her).[50] As though partly to confirm this threat, the careful array of pairs seems now disrupted; the joined efforts of *Poet* and *Lover* cannot yield harmony and balance now, in these defensive texturings. Significantly, the pair "art" and "rima" remains: the heart rhymes and splits in the same word, for it is in the word that *Poet* and *Lover* are always on guard against *lausengier* talk, in order to constrain and control. Yet even so, the flood of words here is not quite contained: the neologism "sobretracima" becomes its own referent, as the line "flows over the top" in enjambement and carries the wave of desire through the next line, unevaporated: "non s'eisaura." We sense *Poet* and *Lover* tasked by outbursts of desire, and by anger as well. For in the explosive phrases of stanza 5, revenge is at once expressed and paid for, so that aggression toward the lady is in part deflected, turned back upon the speaker himself. He is killed ("mi auci") even as she is damned ("si enferna"). Threat and counterthreat appear in a balanced line, checking aggression even while giving voice to threats and accusations. Poet-Lover and poem grow to be textured with these negative energies, these defensive representations.

6

Ges pel maltraich q'ieu soferi
de ben amar no·m destoli,

si tot me ten en desert,
c'aissi·n fatz los motz en rima.
Pieitz trac aman c'om que laura
c'anc plus non amet un ou
cel de Moncli n'Audierna.

7

Ieu sui Arnautz q'amas l'aura,
e chatz la lebre ab lo bou
e nadi contra suberna.

[36–45]

(6   I don't even turn away from the suffering I endure through
loving well, although it holds me in solitude, for thus from my
solitude I put words in rhymes. I work harder in loving than a man
who tills the soil, for he of Moncli loved the lady Audierna not a bit
more.

7   I am Arnaut, who gathers the wind, and chases the hare with
the ox, and swims against the tide.)

The problematical relationship of *Poet* and *Lover* still does not
come to rest in these final stanzas. "En cest sonet" is in this
regard not so conventional as some of Arnaut's other poems,
which close, by contrast, with such lines as these:

Arnautz dreich cor
lai o·us honor
car vostre pretz *capduoilla.*

[2. 56–58]

(Arnaut runs straight there where he honors you, because your
worth reaches a peak.)

que s'ill no fos
no·i meir'Arnautz s'ententa.

[3. 59–60]

(If it were not for her, Arnaut would not have put his mind on the
song.)

Vai t'en, chansos, a la bela de cors
e diguas li c'Arnautz met en oblida
tot'autr' amor per lieis vas cui s'adorna.
[5. 43-45]

(Go, song, to the one with a lovely body, and tell her that Arnaut
forgets every other love and adorns himself for her.)

q'el cor remir
totz sers
lieis cui dompnei
ses parsonier, Arnaut,
q'en autr'albir
n'es fort m'entent'a soma.
[9. 104-9]

(For in my heart I behold every evening her whom I court without
part owner, I Arnaut, for in another thought my effort is not
brought to an end.)

Ma chanssos prec que no·us sia enois,
car si voltez grazir lo son e·ls motz
pauc prez' Arnautz cui que plass' o que tire.
[15. 43 45]

(I pray that my song not be an annoyance to you, for if you wish to
welcome the melody and the words, Arnaut cares little who else it
pleases or annoys.)

Sieus es Arnautz del cim tro en la sola.
[16.43]

(Arnaut is hers from head to toe.)

In these tornadas, the name "Arnautz" is nothing more than a
label of supraconventional loyalty and obedience. These closing
lines testify that a song draws all its value from the unproblematic cooperation of *Poet* and *Lover* toward that *absent present* lady.
Iois, song, and thought are here in accord: they are together *a
soma*, at an end, and *a cima*, at a peak, and the lady fits both
readings, as goal and height of the song. Good songs move from

her (14. 43-44; 7. 56-58) and return to her in constant tribute, and in tribute as well to the Poet-Lover's constancy and thorough dedication, from the toe to the *cima* of his song.

In the last stanzas of "En cest sonet," on the other hand, *Poet* and *Lover* are not harmoniously intent upon Source, the lady who moves the song. Rather, the stanzas seem to emphasize the song itself, and the Poet-Lover "Arnautz" as the particular, curiously textured voice, by synecdoche. Now this Poet-Lover accepts the solitary occupation of putting words into poems, and the angry outburst of line 35 becomes a calm statement. *Poet* dominates now, as a self-texturing motion tangential to *Lover,* so that the stanzaic form itself can offer implicit direction: we are back to the cooler business of the first few lines, making comely verses, compressing many *motz* into one *rima* (39). Appropriate here are the equivocal rhyme *rima* itself, less anguished this time; the constructed rhymes *laura* and *l'aura;* and the exotic *n'Audierna* and *cel de Moncli,* a pair of legendary lovers whom no one has so far been able to identify.[51] Words like these seem generated by the demands of prosody, providing their own momentum. And the impatient Poet-Lover does not finally overflow his banks, after all; desire even seems newly restrained, as though suborned to this effort of compression.

These last lines of "En cest sonet" discover the poem in division and absence. For the lines give only the most spare evocation of the absent lady, an elusive Laura who is both loved and gathered, both gold and insubstantial breeze, a presence dispersed in the wide assonance of -*a: Arnaut, amas, aura.* This Source barely evoked in line 43 may indeed *sustain* the poem, a vestigial presence that enables the "Ieu sui Arnautz" to be said, but it does not *texture* the poem or characterize the Poet-Lover. This tornada, and not any of the conventional ones, has become Arnaut's signature exactly because it does emphasize and define Poet-Lover instead of Source, *present absence* instead of *absent presence*—just as most of Arnaut's poems do, ultimately. For the tornada announces a self, a new being-in-words discovered in solitude and separation, "en desert," in spite of all desires and beliefs that move with *Lover.* This Poet-Lover is defined in struggle: *amas, chatz, nadi.* He never weeps, like the Arnaut of Dante's *Purgatorio,* but doggedly strokes against the tides of her submerging heart and his overflowing impatience (25-26). His efforts may be futile and disproportionate, but as Poet-Lover he preserves his own texture, his *vers martyr* of compression and repression, his "contra." Even in "Ans qe·l cim" (16), when he seems to have stopped a certain tide and caught a certain hare, he still appears in character, "contra," warding off threats to loyalty and constancy. The particular texture of the words themselves seems more important than the object of the chase: *Poet* offers compensation for the uncertain goals of *Lover*.

This Poet-Lover of the tornada is also idiosyncratic, a wanderer in words, introducing such curiosities as "lebre" and "bou" which may even encode proper names. While he embraces the wind, he creates the *parlar materno*. In the *aura* he gathers there may also be *aur, trobar ric* (rich style). Thus in "Si·m fos amors" (17) we might read the tornada as an implicit claim that the song itself has become a "rica conquesta" (8), with its store of *caras rimas* and derivative rhymes, both compensation and result of the speaker's "lonc esper" (long wait, 9):

> Arnautz a faitz e fara loncs atens,
> q'atenden fai pros homs rica conquesta.
>
> [17. 49–50]

> (Arnaut has endured and will endure a long wait, for waiting brings to a worthy man a rich conquest.)

"Er vei vermeills" (13) is also a song made *ric* by waiting, adorned with *amplificatio* and other rhetorical colors, with such rhymes as *Alixandres* and *Mandres*, until in the tornada the song takes the lady's place as luminary, shining upon her—"for Arnaut does not know how to count his great riches" (44).

The idiosyncratic Poet-Lover may have planned lines 43 and 44 of "En cest sonet" as *senhals*, and may have invested line 40 with an alternative sexual meaning: even if the verb "trac" has no sexual connotation, the verb "laura," to plow or work the earth, certainly does. Thus although the fusion of Poet-Lover and lady remains unlived, and unworded in the poem, the speaker can at least appropriate the language of sexual intimacy and bind it up, *cobert* and *clus;* with *double entendres* and *senhals* he can joyously possess the lady in the verbal texture, as close as finger is to nail. The *gap*, as rhetorical and erotic triumph, must have been born thus from the troubadour poet's strange victory in absence. Often the alternative sexual meanings will occur in the last few stanzas of Arnaut's poems, perhaps as a reward for the Poet-Lover's patience heretofore, and a demonstration of the limits of that patience:

> mais volgr'ieu trair pen'els desertz
> on anc non ac d'auzels agre.
>   .   .   .
> per q'ieu sui d'est prec tant espertz
> non ai d'als talen neis magre.
>   [11. 23-24, 39-40]

> Contra mon vauc e no m'encreis,
> car gent mi fai pensar mos cucs.
> Cor, vai sus: ben sai, si·t suffers,
> sec tant q'en lieis, c'ai encubit, no·t pecs.
>   [14. 45-48][52]

Such games of verbal innuendo might help to draw the self from that unworded Source back into the linguistic texture of the poem—back to the self. There may be joy in these detours of words, if not *iois:* they become a "sonet coind' e leri," exuberant, graceful, affirmative. In Arnaut's poems, the culmination of *ric* or *car trobar*,[53] *Poet* creates its own goal, the fabric of self. *Poet* and *Lover* move together in these poems, yet *Poet* also moves in contradistinction to *Lover,* as the words draw their own momentum and goal from the energy of separation, "en desert." The confluent and contradictory motions of *Poet* and *Lover* enable a distinct new presence: "Ieu sui Arnautz," Poet-Lover.

4 Dante

Però, là onde vegna lo intelletto
delle prime notizie, omo non sape,
e de' primi appetibili l'affetto,
che sono in voi, sì come studio in ape
di far lo mele; e questa prima voglia
merto di lode o di biasmo non cape

—*Purg.* xviii. 55–60

Central to Dante's *Vita Nuova* and *Commedia* are scenes of a
virtual birth that follows and completes physical birth: a *presencing event,* in which an overwhelming Presence awakens the new
soul to love. Such an event centers the *Vita Nuova,* in the two
sonnets of chapters xx and xxi. For in "Amore e 'l cor gentil"
(34) the "saggia donna" (woman worthy of love) changes *potentia*
to *actus,* awakening the sleeping spirit of love in the noble heart,
effectively delivering the Poet-Lover into life.[1] This sonnet turns
upon the verb "nasce" (is born), as does the next sonnet, "Ne li
occhi" (35), where the lady can even bestow *potentia* upon those
who behold her, making them "gentil"—that is, capable of loving. And we find a similar presencing event in the middle of the
Commedia, where the joyful Maker himself directly turns potential to act, "animal" to "fante" (child), endowing the articulated
fetus with possible intellect:

Epigraph   "Therefore, whence come the knowledge of primary ideas and the
bent to the primary objects of desire, no man knows; they are in you just as in
bees zeal to make honey and this primal will admits no deserving of praise or
blame."

Citations and translations of Dante's *Inferno, Purgatorio,* and *Paradiso* are from
The Divine Comedy of Dante Alighieri, with translation and comment by John D.
Sinclair (London: The Bodley Head, 1961) 3 vols.: *Inferno, Purgatorio* and
Paradiso.

> ... sì tosto come al feto
> l'articular del cerebro è perfetto,
> lo motor primo a lui si volge lieto
> sovra tant'arte di natura, e spira
> spirito novo di vertù repleto.
> [*Purg.* xxv. 68–72]

(... as soon as the articulation of the brain is perfected in the embryo the First Mover turns to it, rejoicing over such handiwork of nature, and breathes into it a new spirit full of power.)

This passage elaborates Virgil's explanations to the pilgrim in those earlier, more precisely central cantos (*Purg.* xvi–xviii): it is the nature of the Creator's creatures to love, for this Creator breathes his own love and immortality into each human soul.

In these centered accounts of presencing, we recognize *Lover* and *Poet* joined in the familiar language of fusion, original spell-casting: in one mysterious gesture, Source infuses the new self with being, awakens it to life and love. For object-relations theorists today hypothesize a presencing event, too: like the Poet-Lover of the *Vita Nuova* or the articulated fetus of the *Commedia,* the self in object-relations theory is not fully born until birth by Maternal Source completes biological birth. Spitz explains that "although the innate equipment is available to the baby from the first minute of life, it has to be quickened; the vital spark has to be conferred on the equipment through exchanges with another human being, with a partner, with the mother. Nothing less than a reciprocal relation will do."[2] The "equipment" here is for the establishment of the mother as original "libidinal object," enabling the development of affect and cognition that leads to selfhood. More precisely, the affects of the mother-infant bond themselves enable cognition: "affects organize internalized object relations into the overall structures of the mind," and again, "cognition and affect are thus two aspects of the same primary experience."[3] That is to say, perhaps, that Source changes *potentia* to *actus,* too, and that for us as for Dante, cognitive ability (his "possible intellect") is inseparably wound with this mysterious scene of awakening love. Quickening, awakening, breathing in a new spirit, conferring a vital spark: Spitz and Dante share the same cluster of metaphors, for at this difficult ground of being, the Source of the loving soul can at best be evoked, not analyzed.

These central evocations of Presence in the *Vita Nuova* and *Commedia,* where *Lover* and *Poet* meet, may be understood as belonging to the "core" *infans,* the node that imbues these texts with coherence, affective energy, and intentionality, just as the primally repressed scenes of maternal presence enable the intrapsychic texturing, the "interstitial web" of the adult self. One might even say that by these central scenes the *Vita Nuova* and *Commedia* define themselves as innately receptive to love, worthy of *gentilezza,* divinely marked new presences.[4] But at the least, Source becomes goal in these texts: that central presencing event provides intuitive direction for the words, just as adult selves are centered and ultimately led by that primally repressed, everlasting longing for absolute primal identification. At the close of the *Vita Nuova,* the Poet-Lover still sighs after that presencing lady, and the quest continues in the *Commedia,* whose pilgrim is again drawn since the moment of engendering presence by that *prima voglia* that is normative and supreme.[5] In neither the adult self nor in Dante's poem is this a rational matter: Virgil must finally refer the pilgrim to Beatrice, who teaches him that the joyful Maker sets each soul in love toward Himself at the moment of creation:

> ma vostra vita sanza mezzo spira
> la somma beninanza, e la innamora
> di sè sì che poi sempre la disira.
> [*Par.* vii. 142–44]

(But your life the Supreme Beneficence breathes forth immediately, and He so enamours it of Himself that it desires Him ever after.)

That is, the pilgrim, like every human soul, is created always already in love with the Creator, and must emerge from the false paths of hell in order to move again toward that love, to reexperience and confirm that engendering moment forever. Dante's *Commedia* as equivalent self is textured between twin infinite moments: the *spira / spirito novo* of the new soul and the consummate "fulgore" (flash, *Par.* xxxiii. 141) of the pilgrim, the original and definitive scenes of Presence.

Often Dante's individual lyrics may be understood as equivalent selves on the model of the *Vita Nuova* and *Commedia:* centered, defined, and ultimately directed by that overwhelming event of Presence, that birth to love. Just as the *Commedia* is a cosmic detour in language from its own central moment of Presence, so a single lyric can be a distinct, more limited detour in language from that moment: each lyric weaves its own texture, acknowledging its own special distance from a central birth and moving, by its particular measures, to reconsummate that birth. We must include the *Commedia,* equivalent cosmic Dantean self, as inescapable context in our hermeneutics for the lyrics.

I

"Ne li occhi" (35) and other similar lyrics in the *dolce stil nuovo* (sweet new style) are in this context equivalent to newly born selves, still hovering close to that first moment of Presence and taking their being from that moment.[6] Strangely, what distinguishes these poems is that *Poet* seems in them barely distinguished as a separate impulse: instead, here *Poet* and *Lover* seem joined in a single motion toward the Source of the poem, toward the wordless presencing event from which the poem itself is the slightest possible detour in language. That is, these lyrics can seem almost all node, all center, all *infans:* their coherence, affective energy, and intentionality can seem dominated by the presencing moment.

> Ne li occhi porta la mia donna Amore,
> per che si fa gentil ciò ch'ella mira;
> ov'ella passa, ogn'om ver lei si gira,
> e cui saluta fa tremar lo core,
>
> sì che, bassando il viso, tutto smore,
> e d'ogni suo difetto allor sospira:
> fugge dinanzi a lei superbia ed ira.
> Aiutatemi, donne, farle onore.

Ogne dolcezza, ogne pensero umile
nasce nel core a chi parlar la sente,
ond'è laudato chi prima la vide.

Quel ch'ella par quando un poco sorride,
non si pò dicer né tenere a mente,
sì è novo miracolo e gentile.

(My lady bears Love in her eyes, so that she ennobles all she looks
at. Wherever she goes everyone turns towards her, and when she
greets someone she makes his heart tremble, so that, lowering his
eyes, he turns all pale and sighs over all his faults. Pride and ill
humour fly before her. Help me, ladies, to do her honour.

All gentleness, every humble thought is born in the heart of all
who hear her speak; and so he who first sees her is praised. What
she seems when she smiles a little can neither be described nor held
before the mind; it is a marvel so rare and perfect.)

Here *Lover* and *Poet* move together to evoke an omnipresence
that instantly commands the being of the poem. With the rare
inversion "Ne li occhi" and the parallel "ov'ella passa," the lady
usurps the sense of place here, just as in the crystalline sphere,
"where" exists only in relation to the divine mind (*Par.* xxvii.
109–10). Her "where" is everywhere here—she simply *is*, an
ontological gift, a vision appearing from no background, as with
"Bieltate appare" (beauty appears, 34. 9) or "Tanto gentile e
tanto onesta pare / la donna mia" (So gentle and so full of dignity
my lady appears, 43. 1–2). She is a diffused, global presence,
much as one would suppose our internalized Source to be at
that primally repressed "core" *infans:* the infant first receives
(rather than perceives) the mother through an extensive coenesthetic organization, so that she is experienced as everywhere, an all-or-none affective phenomenon defining reality.
And in this poem the impersonal, "pure" stilnovist pronouns
such as "ogne" and "tutto" extend her presence so that, as Love
of the *Vita Nuova (VN)* might say, she is the center of a circle
whose circumference is the indefinite "everywhere" of the
poem; and all beholders share "core" and "viso" in their
spellbound, all-or-none response. "Ella si va, sentendosi lau-

dare" (She goes on her way, hearing herself praised, 43. 5). Exacting love and reverence, she controls all the verbs in the poem, whether or not she is their grammatical subject—except when the overpresenced octave, out of words, must call for help with its final line.

The lady evoked here is simply, profoundly, tenderly maternal. Dante has created her by winnowing out his earlier Cavalcantian terms such as *paura, morto, trono,* and *percosse,* and retaining only those stilnovist terms that, among all their more intricate connotations, suggest quintessential and peaceful sensitivity: *soave, dolce, umile, piano,* even *gentile.* And he adds a smile, emphatic in the final tercet here, that distinguishes this lady of the poem from her stilnovist contemporaries and her troubadour and Sicilian predecessors. This unnamed *donna,* who commands the poem's being, gazes and smiles in mysterious simplicity, like that nameless, crucial face that smiles at our central *infans,* repressed out of memory. For we need not perceive or remember this *occulta virtù* in order to recognize the Presence in us as central and profound (42. 1-4; *Purg.* xxx. 34-39).

Lover and *Poet* thus move together here to enact the original scene of spell-casting, in its simple depths. Through this language of fusion the poem moves to *be* that original Presence, past language and metaphors. For there is no metaphor about it, scholars insist; we have the opposite of allegorism, in Gianfranco Contini's words the "objective presentation of internal facts."[7] The poem, or Poet-Lover, works to interpose no words between itself and the Presence that is its meaning; it works to be all *verace* and no *vesta di figura* (*VN* xxv. 107-11), to be at once literal and spiritual. Or, in other words, this lady's presence is both immediate and otherworldly, her passing an event both on earth and "in the empyrean realm of the ultimate and absolute."[8] The poem seeks to be transparent to its Source, imitating her so perfectly that it is defined by her, its being as language all but effaced before her. For here is no accumulation of similes as in Guinizelli's "Al cor gentil," but, instead, a simple event without ambiguity, antithesis, paradox, or irony, and with barely a concrete term or a proper name. The few antonomasiae such as "la mia donna" or "chi parlar la sente" seem to simplify rather than to complicate the language, and such a phrase as "Ogne dolcezza, ogne pensero umile," in its motion toward direct, global, *infans* experience, is to Boyde not really a trope but "intimate hyperbole," inaccessible to normal rhetorical analysis. And the esoteric concepts of the *cor gentil*, the complex movements of *spiriti*, are re-presented in these poems so unobtrusively that Boyde takes them as a *proprium* base for his analysis of Dante's lyric style—not metaphor, that is, but psychophysical reality.[9] Moreover, except for the inversion of the first phrase, the words fall easily into their natural order; the periods are clarified with all causals and consecutives decisively placed; meaning is matched with syntax, metrics, and rhyme; the octave is even syntactically linked between quatrains.[10] The words do their best to recede before that lucid and unhindered first presence, "novo miracolo e gentile." The poem seems a newly born self, hugging its Source symbiotically, not yet distanced or detoured from that universal moment of maternal presence.

And just as "Ne li occhi" and other similar lyrics are defined by this commanding and tender lady, so they are directed, structurally, by her presence. *Poet* and *Lover* let her set the word patterns and fulfill the expectations here, while the Poet-Lover introjects her presence as a psychophysical reality. This "taking in" of the lady is the "event" (Auerbach's word) that makes each of the poems coherent; this introjection, simply, is that *happens* in the poems. In "Ne li occhi" the presencing face approaches, speaks, and reveals that smile ("un poco") that eludes the memory. Indeed, her features compel the metrical and sentence divisions (except for line 8, the helpless "particella"): octave, tercet, tercet; eyes, speaking, smile. Similar motions and structures inform related sonnets: the omnipresent lady of the octave will grow closer or more distinctly tender in the sestet, as though the poem were "taking in" this Source to its heart, or core, or conclusion. In some, for instance, Love's awesome figure fills the octave, while in the sestet the actual lady comes into view: "Bieltate appare in saggia donna pui" (Then beauty appears in a woman worthy of love, 34. 9), or "Io vidi monna Vanna e monna Bice" (I saw my lady Vanna and my lady Bice, 42. 9). Or the octave will suggest grandeur, a lady "tanto onesta" (so full of dignity, 43. 1), clothed with *gentilezza* or *fede*, a miracle descended from heaven, while the sestet collects the more warmly maternal adjectives and substantives (*dolcezza*, *umile*), the closer presencing with eyes and smile, as here in the sestet of "Tanto gentile":

Mostrasi sì piacente a chi la mira,
che dà per li occhi una dolcezza al core,
che 'ntender no la può chi no la prova:

e par che de la sua labbia si mova
un spirito soave pien d'amore,
che va dicendo a l'anima: "Sospira."
[43. 9-14]

(She appears so beautiful to those who gaze at her that through the eyes she sends a sweetness into the heart such as none can understand but he who experiences it; and from her lips seems to come a spirit, gentle and full of love, that says to the soul: 'Sigh.')

And when she approaches, the Poet-Lover will introject the present lady as a psychophysical reality, as those "spiriti d'amore inflammati" (33. 52) that emanate from eyes and mouth. In this sestet the *spiriti* are explicit, while in other poems they are still implied in more muted terms: "La vista sua fa onne cosa umile" (The sight of her makes every creature humble, 44. 9), or "Bieltate . . . piace a li occhi sì, che dentro al core / nasce un disio . . ." (Beauty . . . so pleases the eyes that in the heart is born a desire . . . 34. 9-11). These incorporated *spiriti* usually establish themselves, somehow, "within," in the heart or elsewhere: for these incorporative metaphors belong to the stilnovist tradition, and they appear in comparable passages by Cino da Pistoia, Cavalcanti, and Guinizelli. Often the incoming *spiriti* will disturb the resident *spiriti,* as in the Cavalcantian second chapter of the *Vita Nuova.* Of course, these stilnovist metaphors are not so "uncanny" as they may seem: they belong to our central being, *infans,* out of memory. For psychophysical, or somatopsychic, is a term appropriate to our commingled perception and reception of Source. As Spitz observes, the nursing infant, in a "unified situational experience with the character of 'taking in' or incorporating," crosses the bridge from coenesthetic reception to diacritic perception, drinking from the mother (coenesthetic) while gazing unswervingly at her face (diacritic).[11] At the origin of each self, incorporative metaphor *becomes* psychophysical reality: one *drinks in* Source with eyes and mouth. Effectively, *spiriti* flow from maternal eyes, through receptive infant eyes, into the central self.

The goal here, as these poems tell us structurally, is to make this incorporation a consummate birth, to receive one's very being with these *spiriti:* Source becomes self. In the sestet of "Tanto gentile," we see *Lover* and *Poet* joining to imply that the Poet-Lover *becomes* the lady, centrally: the *spiriti* that flow into the self seem almost to become the *sospiri* that flow outward toward the lady. Certainly the two terms are close enough in stilnovist convention to suggest a continuum, an intermingling of being.[12] Dante's terms are easier than Freud's—Schreber's "rays of God," which surely resemble these *spiriti,* were to Freud "a concrete representation and projection outward of libidinal cathexes."[13] But in the sweet new style, more simply, *sospiri* answer *spiriti:* the presencing breath becomes, as though with a single motion, the new soul's responsive breath. After all, as Virgil has shown us in the *Purgatorio* (xxv. 68–72), no more than a line ending and a derivational suffix separate God's breath from the new soul, *spira* from *spirito novo:* the self is but a new line in God's book, a line pulled by enjambement. The new soul senses that it belongs with, longs to be with, its engendering Source: thus the responsive *sospiri.* This ultimate longing for re-fusion is precisely Beatrice's argument in the *Paradiso* for immortality and resurrection: the soul believes that it belongs with its infinite Creator (vii. 145–48). And in the terms of the sweet new style,

> . . . nessun la si può recare a mente,
> che non sospiri in dolcezza d'amore.
> [44. 13–14]

(. . . no one can call her to mind without sighing with the sweetness of love.)

The "sospira" of "Ne li occhi," then, is a wish to be perfect like the lady, to belong with the lady—the Poet-Lover longs to imitate his Source. Indeed, the last word of the poem is a gesture of mimesis: as though in answer to line 2, "fa gentil," the poem words itself, at last, "gentile." *Proodos* summons *epistrophe:* the lady as Source grants being to poem and Poet-Lover, who in turn goes signifying her, forming himself as her, symbiotically, mimetically.

This responsiveness to an engendering breath becomes,

exactly, Dante's theory of the sweet new style: the *nove rime* are in theory primally receptive to a creative Presence, in theory unrestrained by any stylistic "nodo" (knot):

> E io a lui: 'I' mi son un che, quando
> Amor mi spira, noto, e a quel modo
> ch'e' ditta dentro vo significando.'
> [*Purg.* xxiv. 52–54]

(And I said to him: 'I am one who, when love breathes in me, take note, and in that manner which he dictates within go on to set it forth.')

Yet the continuing present tense here shows that this responsive signifying, this sighing in words, can never be adequately completed. *Amor, la mia donna,* or God presence the central self, "write" the self—but this "ditta" is a metaphor. The *spira* and *spiriti* are preverbal and supralingual, accompanied by responsive words but not *of* words. The zealous self, living and signifying, can be awakened, centered, defined, and directed by Source, but the self can never be completely textured by that Source. And thus the sonnets of the sweet new style must acknowledge that even their symbiotic language cannot re-present that present lady:

> e sì come la mente mi ridice,
> [42. 12]

(and as memory now retells it . . .)

> e sì è cosa umil, che nol si crede.
> [46. 14]

(And it is a thing so humble it passes belief.)

> che 'ntender no la può chi no la prova
> [43. 11]

(such as none can understand but he who experiences it . . .)

These minimal negations and deviations, these threads of primal absence as the poems draw to a close, reveal *Poet* there as a separable motion, *de via*, deviating from the lady in language. The Poet-Lover cannot be made of words transparent to the lady, as he works to be; in "Ne li occhi," finally, that smile cannot be told or remembered. "If the wax were moulded perfectly and the heavens were at the height of their power, all the brightness of the seal would be seen," as at the incarnation of Christ (*Par.* xiii. 73–75), but in Dante's universe men do not fuse with this original brightness. Source may belong in self, infinite may belong in finite, but the finite cannot, except in Christ the Word, become entirely transparent to the infinite: His Word remains in infinite excess (*Par.* xix. 44–45). And the sonnets of the sweet new style, beings-in-words, must exist in some necessary measure apart from their lady and Source, as short detours from her presence, as their own finite texturing, distinct selves. *Poet* and *Lover* move toward Source, but cannot finally arrive there.

II

Donne ch'avete intelletto d'amore,
i' vo' con voi de la mia donna dire,
non perch'io creda sua laude finire,
ma ragionar per isfogar la mente.
    Io dico che pensando il suo valore,   5
Amor sì dolce mi si fa sentire,
che s'io allora non perdessi ardire,
farei parlando innamorar la gente.
    E io non vo'parlar sì altamente,
ch'io divenisse per temenza vile;   10
ma tratterò del suo stato gentile
a respetto di lei leggeramente,
donne e donzelle amorose, con vui,
ché non è cosa da parlarne altrui.

    Angelo clama in divino intelletto   15
e dice: 'Sire, nel mondo si vede
maraviglia ne l'atto che procede
d'un'anima che 'nfin qua su risplende.'

Lo cielo, che non have altro difetto
che d'aver lei, al suo segnor la chiede,   20
e ciascun santo ne grida merzede.
Sola Pietà nostra parte difende,
   che parla Dio, che di madonna intende:
'Diletti miei, or sofferite in pace
che vostra spene sia quanto me piace   25
là 've alcun che perder lei s'attende,
e che dirà ne lo inferno: "O mal nati,
io vidi la speranza de' beati".'

Madonna è disïata in sommo cielo:
or vòi di sua virtù farvi savere.   30
Dico, qual vuol gentil donna parere
vada con lei, che quando va per via,
   gitta nei cor villani Amore un gelo,
per che onne lor pensero agghiaccia e pere;
e qual soffrisse di starla a vedere   35
diverria nobil cosa, o si morria.
   E quando trova alcun che degno sia
di veder lei, quei prova sua vertute,
ché li avvien, ciò che li dona, in salute,
e sì l'umilia, ch'ogni offesa oblia.   40
Ancor l'ha Dio per maggior grazia dato
che non pò mal finir chi l'ha parlato.

Dice di lei Amor: 'Cosa mortale
come esser pò sì adorna e sì pura?'
Poi la reguarda, e fra se stesso giura   45
che Dio ne 'ntenda di far cosa nova.
   Color di perle ha quasi, in forma quale
convene a donna aver, non for misura:
ella è quanto de ben pò far natura;
per essemplo di lei bieltà si prova.   50
   De li occhi suoi, come ch'ella li mova,
escono spiriti d'amore inflammati,
che feron li occhi a qual che allor la guati,
e passan sì che 'l cor ciascun retrova:
voi le vedete Amor pinto nel viso,   55
là 've non pote alcun mirarla fiso.

Canzone, io so che tu girai parlando
a donne assai, quand'io t'avrò avanzata.

Or t'ammonisco, perch'io t'ho allevata
per figliuola d'Amor giovane e piana,   60
  che là 've giugni tu diche pregando:
'Insegnatemi gir, ch'io son mandata
a quella di cui laude so' adornata.'
E se non vuoli andar sì come vana,
  non restare ove sia gente villana: 65
ingegnati, se puoi, d'esser palese
solo con donne o con omo cortese,
che ti merranno là per via tostana.
Tu troverai Amor con esso lei;
raccomandami a lui come tu dei.   70

[Poem 33]

(1 Ladies who have understanding of love, I wish to speak with you of my lady; not that I think I can exhaust her praises, but I want to speak to unburden my mind. I say that when I consider her perfection Love makes himself felt in me so sweetly that, did I not then lose courage, I would make people in love with her by speech alone. However, I will not attempt a style so lofty as to make me faint-hearted through fear; rather, I will speak of her excellence in a meagre style—compared with what she is—and to you, ladies and girls who know love; for it is not a thing to speak of to others.

2 An angel cries in the divine intellect, saying: 'Lord, in the world there appears a marvel in act, proceeding from a soul whose splendour reaches even here on high!' Heaven, whose only lack is the lack of her, begs her from its Lord, and every saint cries out for this favour. Pity alone defends our cause, so that God, his mind on my lady, says: 'My loved ones, bear it patiently that your hope remains as long as I please in the place where there is one who knows he will lose her, and who in hell will declare: "O ill-fated ones, I have seen the hope of the blessed"'.

3 My lady is desired in highest heaven: and now I wish to show you something of her excellence. I say that any lady who would show she is noble should go in her company; for when she passes on her way Love casts a chill on base hearts, so that every thought in them freezes and dies; and were any such person able to stay and regard her, he would either become noble or die. And when she finds someone worthy to see her, he receives the full effect of her power; for what she then gives him turns to his good and happiness, and renders him so humble that he forgets every in-

jury. Again, God has given her this greater grace, that no one who has spoken with her can come to an evil end.

4   Love says of her: 'How can a mortal creature be so lovely and so pure?' Then he looks at her and swears within himself that in making her God intends to make a marvel. Her colour is pearl-like, in a way befitting a lady, not to excess. She is the most perfect thing that Nature can produce: beauty is known as imaged in her. From her eyes, wherever she turns them, come fiery spirits of love that strike the eyes of whoever may be regarding her, and pass inward so that each one reaches the heart: you see Love depicted in her face, there where no one can fix his gaze.

Congedo   Song, I know that when I've sent you forth you will go about speaking to many ladies. Now I charge you—having brought you up to be a modest young daughter of Love—that wherever you come you make this request: 'Tell me where I am to go, for I have been sent to her with whose praises I am adorned.' And if you don't wish to travel in vain, don't stop where there are base people; contrive, if you can, to show yourself only to ladies or men of courteous mind, who will lead you quickly to your destination. With her you will find Love; commend me to him, as is your duty.)

Many critics after Bonagiunta have selected the canzone "Donne ch'avete" as the epitome of the *dolce stil nuovo*. And this canzone does appear, like "Ne li occhi," both *nuovo* and *dolce*, a poem where *Lover* and *Poet* move together in easy harmony. It seems *nuovo*, first, because like "Ne li occhi" it tries to be newly born, transparent to its Source and close to its birth: all "Guitto-nian" elements, such as reflective *sententiae* or concrete items of *descriptio* ("color di perle" a notably purist exception), are gone, yielding to the immediate and present lady. Moreover, like "Ne li occhi" the poem is directed structurally by her presence, so that the *event* here is the Poet-Lover's introjection of her as a psychophysical reality. For stanzas two through four move from heaven, to earth, to her direct appearance—from *valore, virtu, vertute* to *adorna, pura, cosa nova, bieltà*—and when she appears, she is incorporated as *spiriti:* "e passan sì che 'l cor ciascun re-trova" (54). And the poem seems *dolce,* too, in mimesis of that presencing lady whose perfection is felt "sì dolce" (6) here; the poem is a *cor gentil,* taking to heart "suo stato gentile" (11), forming itself in imitation of her. Even *necessaria* monosyllables have been winnowed from that first gently compelling line, "Donne ch'avete intelletto d'amore," and for the rest, *pexa* words sustain and integrate the poem with their soft vowels, their rather muted dentals and labials.[14] If happiness can be found in "quelle parole che lodano la donna mia" (those words that praise my lady, *VN* xviii. 50–51), it would be in a texturing of these *pexa* words that Dante loved so well, that linger with a certain "suavitate" (*DVE* II. vii. 31), like that presence after whom the Poet-Lover sighs. The poem even personifies itself as a true daughter, "figliuola d'Amor giovane e piana" (60), thereby appropriating those tender stilnovist adjectives that usually belong to the presencing lady. Even though this Poet-Lover allows that he cannot "sua laude finire" (3), imitate her completely through his being-in-words, he still belongs without question to the *nove rime*, to poems made in response to a commanding presence: "la mia lingua parlò quasi come per sè stessa mossa" (my tongue spoke as though moved by its own power, *VN* xix. 10–11).

"Donne ch'avete" is not only defined, like "Ne li occhi," by that presencing lady, but is also clearly directed toward an elite and caring group of ladies. These "donne e donzelle amorose" are distinguished from the uncomprehending "altrui" as "gentile" from "vile" (10–14): the poem belongs not with "gente villana" but with "donne o con omo cortese" (65–67). Of course, Dante's lyrics often presuppose a selected audience of ladies; he even tells us once that love poetry was conceived in the vernacular for the ladies' benefit (*VN* xxv). And through these understanding ladies, *Poet* and *Lover* move the poem again toward Source, reinforcing the presencing lady with the mothering presence of stilnovist tradition. For these elite ladies and their suitors constituted the special stilnovist group; the stilnovists cultivated fidelity to one another *and* to the inspiriting ladies, as shown in the sonnet "Guido, i' vorrei" (15). Stilnovism encouraged a social, literary, and spiritual bonding as strong as any *alma mater*. The ideals of stilnovism reveal that the individual could find and cherish Source in that intrafused group (see above, Chap. 1): the primal wish to re-fuse identities even determines stilnovist policy, with their theoretical and often practical interchangeability of manuscripts, and their "tendentious refusal to differentiate themselves."[15] In "Poscia ch'Amor" (70), moreover, those who possess the alogical *leggiadria* can nourish each other, mutually giving and receiving benefits, like the sun and stars. The pilgrim in Purgatory knows the nourishing presence of a literary tradition as he feeds his sight ("di riguardar pasciuto") upon "padre" and "madre" Guinizelli, lingering for a long moment without hearing or speaking; to him Guinizelli's poems are gentle presences, "rime d'amore . . . dolci e leggiadre" (sweet and graceful rhymes of love), or "dolci detti" (sweet lines) whose very ink will be dear to future generations of vernacular poets.[16] In this language *Poet* and *Lover* are joined, and poetic tradition gives maternal sustenance.

What is more, these literary men and ladies who have "intelletto d'amore" are bound together precisely through that central presencing event, that incorporation of *spiriti* that must be experienced to be understood (*VN* xiv). This event is the root of their "esoteric" knowledge, this event that enables love, poetry, and even (in "intimate hyperbole") life itself. We have seen the current object-relations theory stating that affects—which cannot be translated for everyone into numbers—structure cognition: the initiates of the *cor gentil*, one might say, are those men and women whose cognition ("intelletto") has been engendered by the intense, unwordable affects of the presencing event. For ladies, too, can be presenced, awakened to love by "omo valente" (a worthy man), as the sonnet "Amore e 'l cor gentil" (34) takes care to stipulate in its final tercet.

Like other initiation rites, the presencing event carries a definite risk. For as we learn at the mathematical center of "Donne ch'avete," one can fail the test:

> e qual soffrisse di starla a vedere
> diverria nobil cosa, o si morria.
> [35–36]

(And were any such person able to stay and regard her, he would either become noble or die.)

Of course, one might pass the test, too, as perhaps one cannot in those poems by Cavalcanti where love is death—still, the lady of "Donne ch'avete" is no easy comfort, not *muliebria propter sui mollitiem* (womanly because of her softness, *DVE* ii. vii. 22). For in this language the issue is life or death, Source or Void: in this ordeal, one who cannot dare to drink in those *spiriti* cannot be made "nobil" or, equivalently, "gentil," cannot be awakened to love, cannot complete his birth. As her presence winnows out the *cor villani* from the *cor gentili*, she grants life or death, heaven or hell. He who proves worthy to see her is effectively drawn through Lethe, forgetting every offense (38–40), and her speech is as good as illuminating grace: "non pò mal finir chi l'ha parlato" (42). Her face can be a bliss so intense that it exceeds one's capacity to contain it (*VN* xi, xvi), just as in Paradise Beatrice's sweet smile deprives the pilgrim's mind of its very self (*Par.* xxx. 26–27). But she can damn as well, leaving the frozen regions of hell in her wake:

> ... che quando va per via,
> gitta nei cor villani Amore un gelo,
> per che onne lor pensero agghiaccia e pere;
>
> [32–34]

(... for when she passes on her way Love casts a chill on base hearts, so that every thought in them freezes and dies.)

And whatever the debated allusions of lines 26 and 27, "perder lei" reads syntactically as a possible cause of "ne lo inferno"— that is, to lose her is equivalent to being in hell among the "mal nati," those who failed the test of her presence, for whom her memory in hell is the only antidote. Indeed, her absence is a primal deprivation, qualifying even the bliss of the saints: "sofferite in pace" (24). One must "suffer" both the presence and the absence of this lady, then; birth and initiation become a single rite, a single moment.

Thus with the very risk of the presencing event, certain hellish strands are textured into this *nuovo* and *dolce* poem: *inferno, mal nati, villani, gelo, agghiaccia, pere, si morria, offesa, mal finir*. With these worded negations and deviations from the lady, this canzone does not hover so close to the presencing event as "Ne li occhi"; it is more obviously and more substantially a detour in language from her presence. In the conventional representations here of unworthy lovers, *Poet* and *Lover* do not move in easy harmony; rather, they move toward a more difficult and negative texture, distancing poem from Source and perhaps also distinguishing *Poet* in some of these unpredictable phrases.[17] Furthermore, these conventional representations work as defensive mechanisms for the poem as self, deflecting the risk of Presence onto the *villani* while preserving unharmed the sustaining event of Presence central to the poem. That is, because the lovers are categorized here, the problematic YES or NO of the central presencing event becomes a sure YES—at least for the worthy ones. It is in the interests of such ontological security, perhaps, that *il primo amore* has created hell.

Still, in "Donne ch'avete" such defensive representations are minimal, and not after all very effective. For the Poet-Lover must take further care that he not fall among the unworthy. He fears lest, speaking "sì altamente" of his lady, he implicitly fail his initiation, "ch'io divenisse per temenza vile" (10). Thus the poem speaks only to the selected group of ladies, and it moves in the *congedo* not to "la mia donna" but to Amor, who is "with" the lady. That is, the Poet-Lover or poem itself will not risk the presencing event: it avoids the lady's gaze and puts her smile in a revealing periphrasis, "là 've non pote alcun mirarla fiso" (56). The poem is like a shy and inexperienced young girl, safely modest, as dutiful and obedient as its final phrase, "come tu dei." It is a safely indirect poem, "cortese."[18] As another sweet new poem says, *superbia* and *ira* have now fled (35. 7)—and *cupiditas* is nowhere to be seen, either. We find no aggression, no rage or fierce desire toward this lady upon whom the Poet-Lover's life and death depend: all such dangerous emotions have left no trace in the language of "Donne ch'avete."

III

Così nel mio parlar voglio esser aspro
com'è ne li atti questa bella petra,
la quale ognora impetra
maggior durezza e più natura cruda,
  e veste sua persona d'un dïaspro   5
tal, che per lui, o perch'ella s'arretra,
non esce di faretra
saetta che già mai la colga ignuda:
  ed ella ancide, e non val ch'om si chiuda

né si dilunghi da' colpi mortali,   10
che, con'avesser ali,
giungono altrui e spezzan ciascun'arme;
sì ch'io non so da lei né posso atarme.

   Non trovo scudo ch'ella non mi spezzi
né loco che dal suo viso m'asconda;   15
ché, come fior di fronda,
così de la mia mente tien la cima.
Cotanto del mio mal par che si prezzi
quanto legno di mar che non lieva onda;
e 'l peso che m'affonda   20
è tal che non potrebbe adequar rima.
Ahi angosciosa e dispietata lima
che sordamente la mia vita scemi,
perché non ti ritemi
sì di rodermi il core a scorza a scorza,   25
com'io di dire altrui chi ti dà forza?

   Ché più mi triema il cor qualora io penso
di lei in parte ov'altri li occhi induca,
per tema non traluca
lo mio penser di fuor sì che si scopra,   30
   ch'io non fo de la morte, che ogni senso
co li denti d'Amor già mi manduca;
ciò è che 'l pensier bruca
la lor vertù, sì che n'allenta l'opra.
   E' m'ha percosso in terra, e stammi sopra   35
con quella spada ond'elli ancise Dido,
Amore, a cui io grido
merzé chiamando, e umilmente il priego;
ed el d'ogni merzé par messo al niego.

   Egli alza ad ora ad or la mano, e sfida   40
la debole mia vita, esto perverso,
che disteso a riverso
mi tiene in terra d'ogni guizzo stanco:
   allor mi surgon ne la mente strida;
e 'l sangue, ch'è per le vene disperso,   45
fuggendo corre verso
lo cor, che 'l chiama; ond'io rimango bianco.
   Elli mi fiede sotto il braccio manco
sì forte, che 'l dolor nel cor rimbalza:

allor dico: 'S'elli alza   50
un'altra volta, Morte m'avrà chiuso
prima che 'l colpo sia disceso giuso.'

 Così vedess'io lui fender per mezzo
lo core a la crudele che 'l mio squatra!
poi non mi sarebb'atra   55
la morte, ov'io per sua bellezza corro:
 ché tanto dà nel sol quanto nel rezzo
questa scherana micidiale e latra.
Omè, perché non latra
per me, com'io per lei, nel caldo borro? 60
 ché tosto griderei: 'Io vi soccorro';
e fare' l volentier, sì come quelli
che ne' biondi capelli
ch'Amor per consumarmi increspa e dora
metterei mano, e piacere'le allora. 65
 S'io avessi le belle trecce prese,
che fatte son per me scudiscio e ferza,
pigliandole anzi terza,
con esse passerei vespero e squille:
 e non sarei pietoso né cortese, 70
anzi farei com'orso quando scherza;
e se Amor me ne sferza,
io mi vendicherei di più di mille.
 Ancor ne li occhi, ond'escon le faville
che m'infiammano il cor, ch'io porto anciso, 75
guarderei presso e fiso,
per vendicar lo fuggir che mi face;
e poi le renderei con amor pace.

 Canzon, vattene dritto a quella donna
che m'ha ferito il core e che m'invola 80
quello ond'io ho più gola,
e dàlle per lo cor d'una saetta:
ché bell'onor s'acquista in far vendetta.
      [Poem 80]

(1 I want to be as harsh in my speech as this fair stone is in her behavior—she who at every moment acquires greater hardness and a crueller nature, and arms her body with jasper such that, because of it, or because she retreats, no arrow ever came from quiver that could catch her unprotected. But she is a killer, and it is

no use putting on armour or fleeing from her deadly blows, which find their target as though they had wings and shatter one's every weapon; so that I've neither the skill nor the strength to defend myself from her.

2   I cannot find a shield that she does not shatter, nor a place to hide from her face; for like a flower on its stalk so she holds the crest of my mind. She heeds my misery no more than a ship heeds a sea that lifts no wave; and the weight that sinks me is such that no verse would suffice to describe it. Ah, agonizing merciless file that hiddenly rasps my life away! Why do you not refrain from so gnawing my heart through layer by layer, as I do from revealing who she is who gives you strength?

3   For whenever I think of her in a place where another may turn his eyes, my heart trembles more with fear lest my thought shine out and be discovered, than I tremble at that death which already is devouring all my senses with the teeth of Love; that is, my torment is gnawing away their strength and slowing down their action. Love has struck me to the ground and stands over me with the sword with which he slew Dido, and I cry to him calling for mercy, and humbly I implore him, but he shows himself set against all mercy.

4   Again and again he raises his hand threatening my weakened life, this evil one who pins me to the ground, flat on my back, and too exhausted to move. Then shrieks arise in my mind, and the blood that was dispersed through my veins runs fleeing back to the heart that summons it, so that I am left white. He strikes me under the left arm so violently that the pain rebounds through my heart. Then I say: 'If he lifts his hand again, death will have locked me in before the blow descends.'

5   Would that I could see him split the heart of the cruel woman who cuts mine to pieces! For then that death would not seem black to me, to which her beauty drives me—striking as she does with equal force in sunlight and in shade, this murderous assassin and robber. Alas, why does she not howl for me in the hot gorge, as I do for her? For at once I'd cry: 'I'll help you': and gladly would I do so, for in the yellow hair that Love curls and gilds for my destruction I'd put my hand, and then she would begin to love me.

6   Once I'd taken in my hand the fair locks which have become my whip and lash, seizing them before terce I'd pass through vespers with them and the evening bell: and I'd not show pity or courtesy, O no, I'd be like a bear at play. And though Love whips

me with them now, I would take my revenge more than a thousandfold. Still more, I'd gaze into those eyes whence come the sparks that inflame my heart which is dead within me; I'd gaze into them close and fixedly, to revenge myself on her for fleeing from me as she does: and then with love I would make our peace.

Congedo Song, go straight to that woman who has wounded my heart and robs me of what I most hunger for, and drive an arrow through her heart: for great honour is gained through taking revenge.)

"Così nel mio parlar" is not nearly so restrained a poem. Here the lady effectively denies that lifegiving presencing event to the Poet-Lover, and the poem is defined by that denial. For that denial proves a central threat to which the poem responds variously—through conventional *amant martyr* representations, through deliberate rage and *cupiditas,* through angry mimesis of the lady. And in the complex texture of these responses, *Poet* and *Lover* move toward difficult, violent compensations for that denial; by such means, *Poet* becomes more clearly distinguishable here, and in other *petrose,* than in the poems of the sweet new style.

For in "Così nel mio parlar" the feared crisis of "Donne ch'avete" is at hand; the alternative "o si morria" (33. 36) is being realized. Here we are given no explanatory categories of *villani* and *gentili:* we are told simply that the lady is harsh, no longer *soave* or *dolce.* She deals out hell instead of heaven, death instead of life. The *bella petra* of "Così" and other *petrose* is the negative face of the *donna* of "Ne li occhi" and other *nove rime;* moreover, in the lyrics of Dante's "Cavalcantian phase" (25 through 32, according to Foster and Boyde), we can at times glimpse both faces of this crucial figure, both lifegiving and death-dealing, kind and hostile:

> . . . la mia nemica,
> madonna la Pietà, che mi difenda,
> [26. 13–14]

(. . . my enemy, lady Pity, to take my side)

> 'Per quella moro c'ha nome Beatrice.'
> [25. 14]

DANTE

('Through her I die, whose name is Beatrice.')

When good, she makes Paradise seem trivial, and she cures the
punishments of hell (33. 25, 28, 38–40); yet when she mocks, she
can create a hell, scattering the Poet-Lover's spirits until they
wail in terrified exile (27. 14). To risk the presencing event is to
risk this lady, at once dangerous and radiant (30. 2, 6). Her eyes
seem "piani, / soavi, e dolci," seem to promise "pace" (32. 10–11,
14), but once they capture the Poet-Lover they leave forever,
and he does not see that victorious face again (32. 22–23). And
her departure spells his death: the lady kills by withholding herself, by her stony rejection, just as surely as she can grant life
when she is tender, "soave" (46. 4). Thus in "Così," perhaps, her
retreat is combined with her murderous offensive (lines 6, 9).
For in Dante's Cavalcantian lyrics, in his *petrose*, and in certain
other poems such as "Io sono stato con Amore insieme" (86) and
"Amor, da che convien" (89), the lady can be a murderess. Her
image of stone turns him to marble (77. 13, 71). In a moment
you will see him die! she calls, a hostile figure (89. 42). Die! Die!
cry the stones (*pietre*) that support him in her presence (28. 8).
By such means the lady can be, virtually, his fate: we may see the
Poet-Lover doomed by the intensity of his own gaze (32. 74–78),
or religiously submissive in his melancholy: Into your hands,
my gentle lady, I commend my dying spirit (31. 1–2). Through
this lady, the presencing event can bring death or life, "Donna
mi prega" or "Ne li occhi."[19]

That is, we might understand Dante's lyrics to be generated by
a single, crucial figure of a lady, who effectively changes toward
the Poet-Lover as she is suffused, by turns, with *dolcezza* or
durezza. This central figure becomes an ontological promise or
threat, to which the poem grows its texture in response. In this
way, the lyrics become equivalent to selves—for we are all generated, like these lyrics, by two contrasting ladies, or more nearly,
by two contrasting images of the same lady. Object-relations
theory suggests two *a priori* images for the self: the "good" or
gratifying mother and the "bad" or frustrating mother (or, in
Kernberg's more precise language, opposite "good" and "bad"
dyadic self-and-object representations). These images or dyads
linger, primally repressed at our core *infans*, as those two fundamental motions of every self, the longing for Source and the

dread of Void. These images become the vestigial promise and threat, the "fate" woven within the interstitial web of the psyche. We may question these images if we like, perceived and half created as they are by the vulnerable self, but it seems more rewarding and more various a task to question just how the new self is shaped from these images, with what distinctiveness and individuality. And so with Dante's lyrics, it seems less important to recover their changeable ladies as realities, than to determine just how the new poem is woven in response to that given measure of *dolcezza* or *durezza*.

And "Così nel mio parlar" is textured in response to ultimate *durezza*, to the catastrophic denial of Presence, against which the poem as self must work somehow to survive. Among the responses of *Poet* and *Lover* are, first, those conventional defensive representations of cruel lady and *amant martyr*. That is, the lady of the first two stanzas attacks by rejecting the Poet-Lover, delivering killing blows with her merciless face, and the poem seems in consequence to swallow the attack: for a scene of imminent murder appears, as it were, in the poem's belly, in the two central stanzas. The poem or Poet-Lover turns against himself, in a primitive and agonizing defense that recalls Kernberg's analysis of early superego structures, created to protect the good relationship with the idealized mother; here the effort would be, for a few stanzas at least, to deflect aggression from the *bella petra*. The Poet-Lover attacks himself here through Love, his own masculine rage who is more than a match for him, and who holds appropriately "quella spada ond'elli ancise Dido" (36), that suicidal instrument. Central to this poem, then, is the *lack* of the presencing event. For Death comes now through the absence of the lady's eyes and smile and voice: as though the Poet-Lover were among those in Cocytus locked from all human affection, Love removes his faith or hope ("sfida") and pins him down "a reverso" (See *Inf.* xxxiii. 93), so that shrieks arise "ne la mente," demonic in their silence. To lose her is to be in hell (33. 26–27).

Yet at the close of the fourth stanza, before the Poet-Lover can be "closed" by death, the poem reaches the nadir of his turning-against-the-self and shifts his response to direct, controlled rage. Now the fleeing *superbia* and *ira* return: the rage that the Poet-Lover has been inflicting upon himself is now dealt out toward the lady, as he repays the first four stanzas count for count. Just as Love has been set against all mercy, so the Poet-Lover's mercy would be ironic, for "'Io vi soccoro'" denies all succour: he grasps her by the hair as the pilgrim grasps Bocca degli Abbati, in that lake void of all warmth. He promises, "non sarei pietoso né cortese" (70), just as he supposes in "Amor, da che convien" that Florence, another rejecting mother, might be "vota d'amore e nuda di pietate" (void of love and stripped of compassion, 89. 79). He would split her heart, as she has quartered his. In return for Love's enduring threat, "ad ora ad or" (40), he would exact a long revenge through *terza, vespero, squille*. Finally, one killing glance deserves another: he will put himself as murderer at her center, just as she has, through her rejection, placed the murdering Love at his center. To drive the arrow through her heart is to drive his own hostile presence into her, just as she has, in effect, attacked him centrally:

> Ancor ne li occhi, ond'escon le faville
> che m'infiammano il cor, ch'io porto anciso,
> guarderei presso e fiso,
> per vendicar lo fuggir che mi face;
> e poi le renderei con amor pace.
>
> [74–78]

(Still more, I'd gaze into those eyes whence come the sparks that inflame my heart which is dead within me; I'd gaze into them close and fixedly, to revenge myself on her for fleeing from me as she does: and then with love I would make our peace.)

Through this focused rage his own death becomes "less black" (55–56), and the poem reaches its own kind of *pace*.

In the poem's effort toward this *pace, superbia* and *ira* are joined with *cupiditas*. The poem moves to recapture that denied presencing event as it moves to its final scene: the Poet-Lover angrily consumes the lady in ultimate, definitive sexual union. If the poem is erotic, it is so on a violent, primal level of devouring and being devoured. We can understand this motion as belonging to the darker side of our core *infans*, a fierce hunger for presence in aggravated response to the "bad" or rejecting *a priori* figure. For Dantean *cupiditas* recalls Melanie Klein's "greed," as a primal reaction-formation toward Source felt to be inadequate or hostile, a primal defense against the pull of Void. In the language of the *Inferno* (iii. 123), fear turns to desire. Thus the souls in hell, severed from their original presencing event (*Inf.* iii. 103-5) are beset by *cupiditas*, quintessential sin. With the loss of that primal warmth and light and love, the loss of "il ben dell' intelletto" (the good of the intellect, *Inf.* iii. 18), their ontological hunger rises: hell becomes a throat, *gola* (*Inf.* xxiv. 123; *Purg.* xxi. 31-32; xxxi. 94), filled with shades who consume others in ravenous rage, and at its base Satan, with three mouths, "dirompea coi denti" (crushed . . . with his teeth, *Inf.* xxxiv. 55) three of those who betrayed the bond, more than filial, between self and master.[20] These nightmarish scenes express the profound, thwarted original wish for Eternal Love: even in Paradise we read of Love's teeth (*Par.* xxvi. 51), and in the puzzling early lyric "A ciascun'alma presa" (6), Love gently feeds *madonna* the Poet-Lover's burning heart.

Thus through grotesque oral metaphors, the language of the *Inferno* permeates "Così nel mio parlar," following upon the lady's rejection of the Poet-Lover. Love files and gnaws him "a scorza a scorza," and Death devours his senses: *bruca, denti, manduca*—the last a Latinism perhaps chosen for its emphatic energy, and used again to describe Ugolino chewing Ruggieri (*Inf.* xxxii. 127). For this *aspro* language bites and chews, its harsh labials and dentals and fricatives involving contortions of teeth, lips, and tongue. The *caras rimas* ("scorza, / . . . forza," 25-26) often add to the discordant sounds. Stressed syllables clash: "è tal che non potrebbe adequar rima."[21] The poem even screams, like a hungry infant or a damned soul: *grido, strida, latra, griderei.* Finally the lady, a vehicle for the prevailing wish, becomes a figure of sexual hunger: "Omè, perché non latra / per me, com'io per lei, nel caldo borro?" (59-60). For only the forced satisfaction of hunger brings this poem its *pace:* she has taken from him her desired presence, "quello ond'io ho più gola" (81), but he will reclaim it, grasping the hair that has consumed him ("consumarmi," 64), compelling her now to give him sexual food. Perhaps these terms *do* belong to that "lingua che chiami mamma e babbo" (tongue that cries *mamma* and *babbo, Inf.* xxxii. 9).

For these fierce desires do bring about a facsimile of that original scene, where self *drinks in* Source; at the close, Poet-

Lover and lady mutually incorporate each other. Still, this is only a facsimile, not the ontological gift of Source to self; this is, one might say, the incorporative scene with a vengeance. For here no measure of separation is tolerated, no thread of absence admitted, no "depressive position" undergone: no answering *sospiri* follow the implied *spiriti* of the Poet-Lover's long gaze, for no new self is born from this merging of selves. After all, any longing for individuation would be overwhelmed in such a raging, reactionary desire for fusion. In other words, love has gone astray, in *amor torto,* so that the pair at the end of "Così nel mio parlar" resembles to some degree those unholy dyads in the *Inferno,* doomed to be joined forever. One recalls Francesca and Paolo, "che mai da me non fia diviso" (he who never shall be parted from me, *Inf.* v. 135); or Ugolino and Ruggieri, "due ghiacciati in una buca" (two frozen in one hole, xxxii. 125); or the thieves, "Due e nessun l'imagine perversa / parea" (the perverted shape seemed both and neither, xxv. 77–78)—however various these characters, they have in common those features of boundary dissolution and mutual engulfment that we find at the close of "Così." To such a compensatory *pace,* which is hardly peaceful, the self can be seized and driven, as Francesca indicates when in her story she stresses the verbs *s'apprende, condusse,* and *prese (Inf.* v. 100–107). But this is a dead end, not a lifegiving event: two become as one, or as none.

Thus we find the rich linguistic texture of the *Inferno* in this lyric's several responses to the lady's denial of the presencing event: in the *amant martyr* representations, and in the more direct language of *superbia, ira, cupiditas.* That is, *Poet* is revealed in the negative energies of these words, in all the *petrose* but especially in "Così," just as *Poet* has been widely recognized and praised in the distinctive style of the *Inferno.* For in the *petrose* and in the *Inferno, Poet* moves with *Lover* in difficult, unpredictable, even contradictory ways, in order to preserve some version, even a demonic parody, of the original scene of Presence. And in "Così nel mio parlar," the individuating *Poet* is revealed all the more in the poem's other response to the lady's harshness: for the poem imitates the harsh lady.

The poem announces with its opening lines that it will move to create itself in the lady's image:

Così nel mio parlar voglio esser aspro
com'è ne li atti questa bella petra.

(I want to be as harsh in my speech as this fair stone is in her
behavior—)

In this mimesis, as in the other textured responses, *Poet* and
Lover move together to make the poem one with the lady. But
since the lady has removed herself, *Poet* and *Lover* do not work
here as in "Ne li occhi" to efface all words between poem and
Source; instead, the poem tries to be one with the lady by dup-
licating her, by contriving a distanced, worded imitation of her
in harsh, unyielding, coldly beautiful language. This mimetic
impulse seems to direct the tortured coherence of the *petrose*.
Here, perhaps, is the psycho-ontological joy in the stimulus of
supposedly "pure form" or technical virtuosity: the craftsman
conquers that resistant maternal presence, lady and language, by
reconstructing her. Thus, however distantly, he finally catches
the ear of that unresponsive, deaf medium, that "parlar
materno." Similarly, the souls in hell, each in his own particular
ditch, can only cultivate their own difficult speeches, for they
have failed the presencing event, rejecting "il seme / di lor
semenza e di lor nascimenti" (the seed of their begetting and of
their birth, *Inf.* iii. 104–5), and each is thereby convinced that
the King of Heaven has shut him out.[22] And thus the *petrose*
become equivalent selves responding to the lady's denial of Presence by imitating her: the song will be marble, if the lady keeps
her heart like marble.

Walled off from its Source, the language freezes itself into
walls. Thus we find in the *petrose* the locked winter world of the
lower *Inferno,* deprived of that *prima voglia.* In "Io son venuto"
that image of stone brings universal cold, so that even the ani-
mals are kept from loving; the climactic fifth stanza is rigid with
the images of Cocytus—*smalto, acqua morta, vetro, freddura, serra.*
"Così nel mio parlar" also presents images of *durezza,* the "dïaspro" or green stone of chastity, the file that works "sordamente"
(like the unresponsive lady), Death who kills by shutting, "chiuso,"
as though closing the Poet-Lover off from nourishment or affection, just as Ugolino and his sons are imprisoned, "si chiuda"
(*Inf.* xxxiii. 24), and starved. And the *petrose* barricade them-

selves with concrete nouns, *cose in rima*,[23] making themselves opaque to the gentle presencing event of "Ne li occhi." Metaphors seem to generate each other in dense clusters, neither *dolce* nor *nuovo*. Pronounced symmetries of syntax, meter, and rhyme wall off the inner portions of the poems from each other, as in the ever more frequent partitions of lower hell; rhymes are forced, meanings impeded. In "Io son venuto" lines 4, 7, and 10 of the first three stanzas begin with "e," and an ingenious and restricting *rima equivoca* closes each stanza; in the sestina "Al poco giorno" (78), on the other hand, the *parole-rima* (word-rhymes) constrict and demand because they are used in the *same* sense, not *equivoche* or *composte* as in Daniel's sestina. In "Così nel mio parlar" the final eight lines of the thirteen-line stanza are rhyming pairs, if not couplets; nouns, verbs, and adjectives are often paired; periods are constructed symmetrically; enjambement is frequent. There are *caras rimas,* words chosen for unusual rhyme, such as the "cima," "lima," and "rima" surely inherited from Arnaut's "En cest sonet"; there are such ostentatious *rime equivoche* as "latra"; there is in the first stanza the *rima composta* "petra, / . . . impetra," with "impetra" extended from its usual meaning, "obtains by asking," to mean "takes on," and perhaps also in paronomasia "becomes like stone," with a superfluous object for the verb offered in enjambement.

Meanings do not flow easily from this language. As in hell, perhaps, language is shown losing its power to communicate, to move, to bind in love, to "innamorar la gente" (33. 8).[24] As in hell, language is a medium of fraud, resentment, and isolation. In response to the lady's denial of her presence, "Così nel mio parlar" becomes a formidable, cold, painfully symmetrical equivalent self. Still, these opaque words, though they may seem contrary to *Lover,* do move at last in co-operation with *Lover:* the poem duplicates the lady.

Finally, since the *petrose* as a group seem to condense strangely the desire and aggression spared the *nove rime,* one wonders whether to some degree these poems can work also as a "splitting" defense enacted against that primal denial of Source, the given *durezza.* That is, perhaps through the rigid poetic forms, the rejected and rejector, the self and object and negative affect, are walled off together and experienced purely, in isolation, in the hope that there will remain, as though saved or reserved past the walls, an accepting, "good" Maternal Source.[25] Thus in "Io son venuto" the love frozen in the Poet-Lover's heart finally emerges from the wintry stanzas when love flows again in the metaphor of the *congedo:*[26]

> Canzone, or che sarà di me ne l'altro
> dolce tempo novello, quando piove
> amore in terra da tutti li cieli
> [77. 66–68]

> (My song, what will become of me in that other, that sweet young season when love pours down to the earth from all the heavens)

And in "Amor, tu vedi ben" the speaker tells his song, "I dare to create for this cold object the novelty that is alight through your form" (79. 64–65). For the novelty of form, perhaps, structures the cold within, allowing Love's warming light to emerge as the poem draws to a close.

By analogy, the hellish texturing of the *Inferno* might be understood to serve this "splitting" purpose, among others, for the *Commedia* as equivalent self. In the *Inferno* all aggression and reactionary desire are concentrated within secure structural and ideological walls, as though one could experience them separately and then, as it were, climb away from them once and for all by reversing one's gravitational center—from *durezza* to *dolcezza,* say, or from a state of sin to a state of grace. For even though the road out of hell may seem labyrinthine, it is ultimately the simple reversal of the road in: Love is the seed both of every virtue and of every action deserving punishment (*Purg.* xvii. 104–5). That is, if the dread of primal absence provokes primal negative reactions, fear turning to desire, then perhaps somehow to take back or to undo those drives, that *ira* and that *cupiditas,* would be to remove the ontological threat and thereby to reinvoke Source forever. In other words, if one might somehow give up the insistent, devouring, reactionary infant hunger for survival, the P's (for "peccatum," sin) would be erased from one's brow, the "nodo" loosened, the walls dissolved: to leave hell, one must seem to die. Thus Virgil cajoles Dante the pilgrim through the biting ("morde"), thirst-making fire, assuring him that it is not death, as it seems: now see, my son, this wall lies between Beatrice and you (*Purg.* xxvii. 35–36). And beyond the wall is the original face, emanating those vital *spiriti:* I seem already to see her eyes (xxvii. 54). And face to face, when the heavenly singing confronts him with his present wish for her present compassion, the pilgrim melts the wall of ice around his heart, with responsive tears and breath ("spirito e acqua," *Purg.* xxx. 97–98). It takes tears of re-fusion, "colpa e duol d'una misura" (sin and sorrow . . . of one measure, xxx. 108) to undo the disloyalty, to heal the separation from original Source; only confession enables the pilgrim to trace his "via non vera" (way not true) back through "cose fallaci" (deceptive things) to the presencing event (xxx. 130; xxxi. 56). Only tears can remove the threat of that other sword ("altra spada," xxx. 57), an intolerable and suicidal barrier between self and Maternal Source—both the quintessential engraved P and the self-directed "spada" of "Così nel mio parlar." Tears and penitence wash all frightening aggressions and negative impulses into Lethe and down to Cocytus where they are locked in and essentially forgotten, split off by *divine ordine* (142–45), in eternal division. Here it is through a stern maternal figure, a "madre . . . superba" (harsh mother) with "pietade acerba" (stern pity) that these tears are accomplished, those unspoken wanderings and rages and desires solved forever (xxx. 79, 81).[27] " 'Guardaci ben!' " (Look at me well!, xxx. 73). She keeps the pilgrim before her like a guilty child, mute, reflective, eyes down (xxxi. 64–66), in marked contrast to the Poet-Lover of "Così nel mio parlar" with his relentless fixed gaze. Moreover, the tears enable a renewed hunger and thirst for infinite Source. For Lethe cleanses the throat: Matelda draws the pilgrim "infin la gola" (up to the throat), and, as he tells it, "mi sommerse / ove convenne ch'io l'acqua inghiottissi" (plunged me under, where I must swallow the water, xxxi. 94, 101–2). With his soul's throat now *umile,* the pilgrim can consume the "eucharistic presence of Christ," with the "symbolical representation of the consecrated host in the person of Beatrice":[28]

> l'anima mia gustava di quel cibo
> che, saziando di sè, di sè asseta,
> [xxxi. 128–29]

(My soul ... tasted of that food which, satisfying with itself, for itself makes appetite.)

An original hunger continues to drive the self, but now the pilgrim can fill that dreaded Void with just penalties (*Par.* vii. 83–84). He is restored ("rifatto," *Purg.* xxxiii. 143) to an imagined state before primal envy and greed, and he can drink forever those *spiriti,* in the approving regard of that crucial face. The *cor gentil* rejoins the Source that first awakened him: his brow cleared of P's, he walks with her while she speaks "con tranquillo aspetto" (with tranquil look) and tells her, I do not recall ever having been estranged from you (xxxiii. 19, 91–92).

IV

Donna pietosa e di novella etate,
adorna assai di gentilezze umane,
ch'era là 'v'io chiamava spesso Morte,
　　veggendo li occhi miei pien di pietate,
e ascoltando le parole vane,   5
si mosse con paura a pianger forte.
　　E altre donne, che si fuoro accorte
di me per quella che meco piangia,
fecer lei partir via,
e appressarsi per farmi sentire.   10
Qual dicea: 'Non dormire',
e qual dicea: 'Perché sì ti sconforte?'
Allor lassai la nova fantasia,
chiamando il nome de la donna mia.

　　Era la voce mia sì dolorosa   15
e rotta sì da l'angoscia del pianto,
ch'io solo intesi il nome nel mio core;
　　e con tutta la vista vergognosa
ch'era nel viso mio giunta cotanto,
mi fece verso lor volgere Amore.   20
　　Elli era tale a veder mio colore,
che facea ragionar di morte altrui:
'Deh, consoliam costui',
pregava l'una l'altra umilemente;
e dicevan sovente: 25

'Che vedestù, che tu non hai valore?'
E quando un poco confortato fui,
io dissi: 'Donne, dicerollo a vui.

    Mentr'io pensava la mia frale vita,
e vedea 'l suo durar com'è leggiero,   30
piansemi Amor nel core, ove dimora;
    per che l'anima mia fu sì smarrita,
che sospirando dicea nel pensero:
"Ben converrà che la mia donna mora."
    Io presi tanto smarrimento allora,   35
ch'io chiusi li occhi vilmente gravati,
e furon sì smagati
li spirti miei, che ciascun giva errando;
e poscia imaginando,
di caunoscenza e di verità fora,   40
visi di donne m'apparver crucciati,
che mi dicean pur: "Morra'ti, morra'ti."

    Poi vidi cose dubitose molte,
nel vano imaginare ov'io entrai;
ed esser mi parea non so in qual loco,   45
    e veder donne andar per via disciolte,
qual lagrimando, e qual traendo guai,
che di tristizia saettavan foco.
    Poi mi parve vedere a poco a poco
turbar lo sole e apparir la stella,   50
e pianger elli ed ella;
cader li augelli volando per l'are,
e la terra tremare;
ed omo apparve scolorito e fioco,
dicendomi: "Che fai? non sai novella?   55
Morta è la donna tua, ch'era sì bella."

    Levava li occhi miei bagnati in pianti,
e vedea, che parean pioggia di manna,
li angeli che tornavan suso in cielo,
    e una nuvoletta avean davanti,   60
dopo la qual gridavan tutti: *Osanna;*
e s'altro avesser detto, a voi dire'lo.
    Allor diceva Amor: "Più nol ti celo;
vieni a veder nostra donna che giace."
Lo imaginar fallace   65

mi condusse a veder madonna morta;
e quand'io l'avea scorta,
vedea che donne la covrian d'un velo;
e avea seco umiltà verace,
che parea che dicesse: "Io sono in pace."   70

Io divenia nel dolor sì umile,
veggendo in lei tanta umiltà formata,
ch'io dicea: "Morte, assai dolce ti tegno;
   tu dei omai esser cosa gentile,
poi che tu se' ne la mia donna stata,   75
e dei aver pietate e non disdegno.
   Vedi che sì desideroso vegno
d'esser de' tuoi, ch'io ti somiglio in fede.
Vieni, ché 'l cor te chiede."
Poi mi partia, consumato ogne duolo;   80
e quand'io era solo,
dicea, guardando verso l'alto regno:
"Beato, anima bella, chi te vede!"
Voi mi chiamaste allor, vostra merzede.'

                             [Poem 40]

(1   A lady, tender in heart and young, much graced with gentle qualities, who was by me when I was often calling on Death, seeing my eyes full of grief and hearing my wild words, began to weep violently out of fear. And other women, made aware of me by her who was weeping beside me, led her away and themselves drew near to recall me to myself. One said: 'Sleep no more'; another: 'Why are you so distressed?' Then I came out of the strange vision, calling on my lady's name.

2   So grief-stricken was my voice, so broken with the stress of sobbing, that I alone heard that name in my heart; and, notwithstanding the shame that had come over my face, Love turned me towards them. Such was my colour, it made them speak of death. 'Ah, let us comfort him', they gently begged one another; and repeatedly they said: 'What was it you saw that you are left so faint?' And I, when I had recovered a little, said: 'Ladies, I'll tell you.

3   'While I was thinking of the frailty of my life, and seeing how slight is its power to endure, Love wept in my heart, where he dwells; at which my soul became so dismayed that with sighs I said in my thoughts: "It's true, my lady will have to die." Then such

dismay took hold of me that I closed my eyes that were weighed down with despondency; and so distracted were my spirits that each went his way, not knowing where; and then in my fantasy, all lost to knowledge and truth, women's faces loomed angrily at me, repeating these words: "You will die! You will die!"

4   'Then, in the delusive vision I came into I saw many fearful things; and I seemed to find myself in a strange place and to see dishevelled women going by, some weeping, some uttering laments that were as fiery arrows of sorrow. Then I seemed to see little by little the sun grow dark and the stars come out, both he and they weeping; the birds in full flight fall to the ground and the earth tremble; and a man appeared, pale and faint, who said to me: "What are you doing? Don't you know what has happened? Your lady, who was so beautiful, is dead."

5   'I raised my eyes, wet with tears, and saw the angels like a shower of manna returning on high to heaven; and a small cloud went before them, and following it they all cried, "Hosannah!"— and if they had said more I would tell you. Then Love said: "I will hide it from you no longer; come and see our lady where she lies." So the false vision led me to see my lady dead; and when I came in sight of her I saw ladies covering her with a veil; and with her was true humility, such that she seemed to say: "I am in peace."

6   'In my grief I became so humble, seeing such great humility take form in her, that I said: "Death, I hold you very dear: now you are surely ennobled, since you have been with my lady; you are surely merciful and not harsh. I have become, you see, so full of desire to be yours that truly I have taken on your very likeness. Come, for my heart calls you." Then, all mourning done, I went away; and when I was alone I said, looking up towards the high kingdom: "Blessed is he who sees you, fair soul!" It was then that, in your kindness, you called me.')

"Donna pietosa," the central of three canzoni in the *Vita Nuova,* is itself centered like "Così nel mio parlar," with a radical threat: the lady's departure may spell the Poet-Lover's death. Yet there the resemblance ends. For with "Donna pietosa" *Poet* and *Lover* move to texture an equivalent self in primal mourning, a poem created in imitation of the tender, *umile,* benevolent (but admittedly absent) lady. Unlike "Ne li occhi," this poem does not hover close to the presencing event; instead, it forms itself at an acknowledged, bereaved distance from its Source, as a separate being-in-words. From this distance, *Poet* and *Lover* move to texture the poem through continual "represencing": that is, they move to reconsummate the central presencing event through all worded detours. The poem's intentionality and coherence are still rooted in that event: all *Poet* efforts, however widely ranging, are brought at last to serve *Lover*.

Almost precisely in the center of "Donna pietosa" appears the cry, "'Morra'ti, morra'ti'" (42). Most scholars read these words as the prophecy, "you will die," and are mildly puzzled about the relevance of the speaker's own death to the theme of Beatrice's forecast death. J. E. Shaw, in response to this felt incongruity, interprets, "she will be taken from you by death." Perhaps *Poet* and *Lover* here deliberately contrive a double statement: with the ingenious, centrally placed *rima composta,* the Poet-Lover's death and Beatrice's death seem existentially bound, two deaths in one. For in this third stanza their deaths are mutually associative: when the Poet-Lover ponders *his* frail life, he concludes that "la mia donna" will die; when he closes his eyes in despondency over *this* conclusion, he envisions the women who call, "morra'ti." (We never see Beatrice's eyes closed in death here; perhaps the association of line 36 is meant to suffice.) Moreover, it is the Poet-Lover with his pale "colore" who reminds the attendant ladies of death. Thus the poem suggests a central fear and wish: that Poet-Lover and Beatrice live and die in symbiosis. For at central *infans,* death of Maternal Source can mean final disapproval, abandonment: just as the removal of Beatrice's "salute" made the Poet-Lover weep like a beaten child, her death, or her implied rejection of him and departure forever, might kill him. Thus the central cry, "morra'ti," rhymes with "donne cruc-·ciati," an epithet connoting anger, or indignant reaction to some offense. These women not only lament the death of Beatrice, diffuser of virtues, but also stand as figurae of displaced maternal anger, uncaused and thus always a present danger, like the *durezza* of the *bella petra:* "crucciati" and "morra'ti" are a pair, cause and effect. This poem as self centrally fears the loss of its Source and its own consequent death, prophesied by angry women: one recalls the allegory of despair in the *Inferno* at the walls of Dis, with only caring "mamma" Virgil (*Purg.* xxx. 44) between the pilgrim and the fatal sight of that other *petra,* Medusa.

Still, in "Donna pietosa" *Poet* and *Lover* do not move to represent the departing lady as cruel, angry, a *bella petra*. It is as though such defensive representations, along with all rage and desire, have been washed away with the abundant weeping, somewhat as in the *Purgatorio* scene. Thus Beatrice, even though absent, can remain a lifegiving Source for the poem because her image is still intact, her goodness still viable. *Poet* and *Lover* move to qualify and soften her death even as it is foretold, so that her *absent presence* can continue to direct the poem. For instance, the Poet-Lover may be hinting that he feared her death mistakenly, because he was in confusion, dismay, error: *smarrita, smarrimento, smagati, errando*. He even introduces the central cry, "morra'ti," with the description of himself as "imaginando, / di caunoscenza e di verità fora" (39–40). As the vision continues to the announcement of her death and the sight of *madonna morta*, it is called "vano imaginare" and finally "imaginar fallace," with the pointedly contrasting rhyme, "umiltà verace." Foster and Boyde wonder why the speaker here should keep insisting that his vision is false, since in a few more chapters of the *Vita Nuova* the prophecy will be "verified," and Beatrice will die. But after all, Beatrice is *not* dead, truly, and this vision *is* a falsehood: she departs only *this* life (*VN* xxix), and she reappears at the Earthly Paradise, "sovra candido vel cinta d'uliva" (girt with olive over a white veil, *Purg.* xxx. 31), recalling here the line "donne la covrian d'un velo" (68) and, earlier in the book, the adjective "cinta" (*VN* ii. 17). Whoever believes in Beatrice's death forgets the theology of presence without *carne:* memory, intelligence, and will, drawn together at the presencing event by that "spirito novo" God breathes into us, even become more acute after death—the "alma sola" survives intact as a presence, with formative virtue, to take on more glorious flesh at the resurrection (*Purg.* xxv. 79–108). Beatrice "nel vano imaginare" (44) may seem dead, but she remains in bliss, and anyone turning over the pages of the philosophers could reach no other endurable conclusion (*Con.* II. ix. 49–100). As the Poet-Lover of "Li occhi dolenti" concludes, "whatever my state may be, my lady sees it, and I still hope for recompense from her" (47. 69–70). For we die here to live above, in the refreshment of the eternal showers (*Par.* xiv. 25–27), just as Beatrice and the angels return to heaven like a shower of manna (40. 58). The vision of *madonna*

LOVE WORDS

morta is essentially false, then, and Beatrice as Source is preserved, absent to the Poet-Lover but still intact, cosmically Present.

Moreover, *Poet* and *Lover* join to word Beatrice's death so that through these very words the poem seems to take to itself her lifegiving Presence, *umile* and *gentile*. Likewise, when the self grows able to perceive the maternal figure as a separable, differentiable and therefore losable whole, the newborn guilt and sorrow of this primal mourning or "depressive position" enable the self to reinternalize an image of the good mother, ideal object; then through mimesis and identification the self can symbolically and deliberately fuse with her again, can recover that first vital state of nondifferentiation. Just so, the Poet-Lover in "Donna pietosa" sees Beatrice in death as an infinitely valuable whole, a lost Presence, maternal *umiltà* that he learns to imitate in his mourning:

> Io divenia nel dolor sì umile,
> veggendo in lei tanta umiltà formata
> [71-72]

(In my grief I became so humble, seeing such great humility take form in her ...)

This Poet-Lover's tears do not signify his self-indulgence, comic breakdown, or spiritual sterility;[29] the tears belong to the full perception of loss, and thus to the effort of recovery. He does not strive to rejoin the departing lady at all costs, as in the tearless "Così"; he allows absence, separation. The Poet-Lover feels the most pain when he thinks most intently of the departed lady, and by contrast the "cor villan" (mean heart) who can form no image of Beatrice likewise cannot mourn (47. 49, 35-37). It is the grieving heart, "cor dolente," with whom the pilgrim spirit, having seen the lady, talks so subtly (57. 11). The Poet-Lover who clearly perceives the lady, and thus fully and securely internalizes her image, "la gloriosa donna della mia mente" (the glorious lady in my mind, *VN* ii. 5-6), *must* weep with the simultaneous realization of potential loss. Beatrice admonishes the pilgrim, "pianger ti conven per altra spada" (thou must weep for another sword, *Purg.* xxx. 57), *recommending* tears to dissolve the last impediment between them. Arnaut Daniel, dry-eyed in his

154

own poetry, weeps in Dante's poetry. And in "Donna pietosa" the grieving Poet-Lover can re-fuse with that Source through the implied mimesis woven into the personifications of the final stanza: for when Death becomes like Beatrice, the Poet-Lover, in turn, becomes like Death. Into this condensation are drawn those maternal stilnovist words: *dolce, gentile, umile, pietate.* In death and through death the Poet-Lover recovers her presence by mimesis: in truth I resemble you, he tells Death, you who are (as I wish my lady to be) merciful and not harsh, not one of the "crucciati." This may seem like death, as at Christ's death the world seemed to end. But just as Christ's death will enable eternal greeting, "l'ultima salute" (*Par.* xxxiii. 27), so the Poet-Lover can find again Beatrice's lost greeting by becoming as she is, in a consummating flow of *umiltà* (69, 71, 72). Beatrice and Death are maternal, "soave e dolce" (49. 11), and the Poet-Lover is one with them. He speaks with her, for her, the line "'Io sono in pace,'" and with this mimetic "pace" the poem eludes the central threatening Void of her departure.

This re-fusion through Death becomes in "Donna pietosa" a virtual rebirth; by contrast to "Così nel mio parlar," a new self *is* born from *this* union. Similarly, the self who, through primal mourning, preserves that image of ideal self and ideal object, union of self and Source, can begin to move through the solitude of separation to the exhilaration of freedom, a freedom directed to refinding that Source in a world of other presences—continuing to "represence" himself, to be reborn. For freedom is always maternally qualified: the self, ontologically belonging to its Source, will always need represencing, strengthening of that central good dyad.[30] The self must spin upon a solid imagination of fusion. It is the secure oneness of self and Source at the presencing event (*spira / spirito novo*) that enables the new and distinct soul—the "alma sola" that seems, alone, to spin upon its own center, "sè in sè regira" (*Purg.* xxv. 71–75). Indeed, the *Purgatorio* is heavily textured with scenes of bereavement, loss, solitude, freedom, and represencing, whence may arise its nostalgic tone, its landscape "suffused with mist."[31] We notice, for example, Cato as "un veglio solo" (an old man alone), eternally bereft of Marcia's love; Virgil and Dante as travelers on "lo solingo piano" (the lonely plain, i. 31, 118); Dante held distant from "padre" Guinizelli by the fire, and at last calling in vain for "dolcissimo patre" Virgil. For through this loneliness and loss lies freedom: the pilgrim, like Cato, "libertà va cercando" (goes seeking liberty, i. 71); the pilgrim that Virgil coaxes through the libidinal fire emerges with mitre and crown over himself. And even in freedom the self is never without renewed Source: on the lonely shore Virgil bathes the pilgrim's face, completing his birth from hell, and finds with him that "umile pianta" (lowly plant, i. 135), inexhaustible *umiltà*, the sensed grace of eternal represencing. Cato himself, unmoved by Marcia, will answer to the love of the "donna al ciel"; the pilgrim held away from Guinizelli still feeds long upon his sight. Even in Paradise, when Beatrice, having drawn the pilgrim "di servo . . . a libertate" (from bondage into liberty, xxxi. 85), must leave him to take her seat in the Empyrean, there is no lack of caring presences to take her place: Bernard, "tenero padre" (tender father," xxxi. 63); Mary, "Vergine madre" (xxxiii. 1); and even, in the final internalizing gaze, "la luce etterna" (the Eternal Light, xxxiii. 83). For Poet-Lover, pilgrim, and self at core *infans*, the original Source is never truly lost, but more firmly internalized, clarified, strengthened: to look from Beatrice to God is to look the more closely to Beatrice, as Ciardi notes of *Paradiso* xiv. Placed in the Rose, Beatrice is as far from the Pilgrim's eyes as the sky from the depths of the sea, but he can still see her, drink in her last smile and gaze in a final evocation of that first presencing event as though she were near:

> . . . chè sua effige
> non discendea a me per mezzo mista.
> [xxxi. 77–78]

(. . . for her image came down to me undimmed by aught between.]

The canzone "Donna pietosa" shares with the *Commedia* these motions of bereavement, separation, solitude, freedom, represencing. Several of these rich developments are concentrated in the final stanza, where the mimetic call to Death allows the mourning to come to an end, and the virtual rebirth to begin. For all along, this rebirth has been heralded by the obvious care to include variants of "novo" and "gentile": *novella etate, gentilezze umane, la nova fantasia.* The man who announces Beatrice's death asks, "non sai novella?" Beatrice, in ascent to heaven, is "una nuvoletta." Even Death is "cosa gentile," the word recalling those newborn sonnets like "Ne li occhi." And finally the speaker, *umile,* filled by mimesis with *umiltà formata,* her ideal image, can separate himself from the scene of grief:

> Poi mi partia, consumato ogne duolo;
> e quand'io era solo,
> dicea, guardando verso l'alto regno:
> "Beato, anima bella, chi te vede!"
> [80–83]

(Then, all mourning done, I went away; and when I was alone I said, looking up towards the high kingdom: "Blessed is he who sees you, fair soul!")

He is "solo" like Cato, or like the newly made "alma sola," because he has taken to heart a vision of that "anima bella" that he can now pursue. He leaves her, and she leaves him, only for a while; the cry "morra'ti" has been transformed into a pilgrimage.

In "Donna pietosa" the pilgrimage has in a sense already begun, as the Poet-Lover finds his Source to recur in other presences. For *Poet* and *Lover* move to represence the poem, so that the entire canzone is embraced by the consolation of sympathetic ladies who speak "umilemente," matching that consummating *umiltà* of the last two stanzas. And *Poet* is here brought further to serve *Lover* with the final line, which redirects the four last stanzas to these ladies, deliberately juxtaposing the "Voi" with the "te" of the preceding line. The bereaved self reads the world using "la gloriosa donna ne la mente" as guide and standard: "te" becomes "Voi." Thus the self moves from its own maternal center outward, to group, community, patria, world, cosmos; the self moves from "mia" to "nostra" (49. 18, 21), as the eagle of Justice says "I" and "mine" meaning "we" and "ours" (*Par.* xix. 11–12). In the *Vita Nuova* the speaker increasingly perceives Beatrice's qualities extending miraculously to the ladies in her company. And "Donna pietosa" itself is a community of varied presences: the attendant ladies, one of whom must be led away;

the disheveled and weeping *donne;* the pale and weak man who announces Beatrice's death; the angels who return with her to the heavens; the ladies who cover her corpse with a veil; the personifications of Death and (absent in the prose) Love; even the unusually frequent *conversiones,* like *gentilezze umane* or *umilità verace,* that are nearly personifications themselves. Each stanza includes dialogue at or near its close; "donna" (once "madonna") or "donne" occurs a dozen times. That "solo" in the last stanza (81) comes as a marked change, and the return to "vostra merzede" is no surprise. The poem as self, as new presence, may be "solo," sustained by the lady present within it, but it is far from solitary, for it exists in presentation to the listening ladies. Words and language indeed may mark the Poet-Lover's separation from Beatrice, yet words are also his means of re-presencing, of beginning his pilgrimage toward her through other presences, of directing *Poet* to move with *Lover.*

> ch'io solo intesi il nome nel mio core
> [40. 17]

(. . . that I alone heard that name in my heart)

> So io che parla di quella gentile,
> però che spesso ricorda Beatrice,
> sì ch'io lo 'ntendo ben, donne mie care.
> [57. 12–14]

(I know he speaks of that noble one, for he often mentions Beatrice; so that I understand him well, my dear ladies.)

V

> Amor che ne la mente mi ragiona
> de la mia donna disïosamente,
> move cose di lei meco sovente,
> che lo 'ntelletto sovr'esse disvia.
>   Lo suo parlar sì dolcemente sona,   5
> che l'anima ch'ascolta e che lo sente
> dice: 'Oh me lassa, ch'io non son possente
> di dir quel ch'odo de la donna mia!'

E certo e' mi conven lasciare in pria,
s'io vo' trattar di quel ch'odo di lei,　　　　　10
ciò che lo mio intelletto non comprende;
e di quel che s'intende
gran parte, perché dirlo non savrei.
Però, se le mie rime avran difetto
ch'entreran ne la loda di costei,　　　　　15
di ciò si biasmi il debole intelletto
e 'l parlar nostro, che non ha valore
di ritrar tutto ciò che dice Amore.

Non vede il sol, che tutto 'l mondo gira,
cosa tanto gentil, quanto in quell'ora　　　　　20
che luce ne la parte ove dimora
la donna, di cui dire Amor mi face.
　Ogni Intelletto di là su la mira,
e quella gente che qui s'innamora
ne' lor pensieri la truovano ancora,　　　　　25
quando Amor fa sentir de la sua pace.
　Suo esser tanto a Quei che lel dà piace,
che 'nfonde sempre in lei la sua vertute
oltre 'l dimando di nostra natura.
La sua anima pura.　　　　　30
che riceve da lui questa salute,
lo manifesta in quel ch'ella conduce:
ché 'n sue bellezze son cose vedute
che li occhi di color dov'ella luce
ne mandan messi al cor pien di desiri,　　　　　35
che prendon aire e diventan sospiri.

　In lei discende la virtù divina
sì come face in angelo che 'l vede;
e qual donna gentil questo non crede,
vada con lei e miri li atti sui.　　　　　40
　Quivi dov'ella parla, si dichina
un spirito da ciel, che reca fede
come l'alto valor ch'ella possiede
è oltre quel che si conviene a nui.
　Li atti soavi ch'ella mostra altrui　　　　　45
vanno chiamando Amor ciascuno a prova
in quella voce che lo fa sentire.
Di costei si può dire:
gentile è in donna ciò che in lei si trova,

e bello è tanto quanto lei simiglia.   50
E puossi dir che 'l suo aspetto giova
a consentir ciò che par maraviglia;
onde la nostra fede è aiutata:
però fu tal da etterno ordinata.

Cose appariscon ne lo suo aspetto   55
che mostran de' piacer di Paradiso,
dico ne li occhi e nel suo dolce riso,
che le vi reca Amor com'a suo loco.
Elle soverchian lo nostro intelletto,
come raggio di sole un frale viso: 60
e perch'io non le posso mirar fiso,
mi conven contentar di dirne poco.
Sua bieltà piove fiammelle di foco,
animate d'un spirito gentile
ch'è creatore d'ogni pensier bono;   65
e rompon come trono
l'innati vizii che fanno altrui vile.
Però qual donna sente sua bieltate
biasmar per non parer queta e umile,
miri costei ch'è essemplo d'umiltate!   70
Questa è colei ch'umilia ogni perverso:
costei pensò chi mosse l'universo.

Canzone, e' par che tu parli contraro
al dir d'una sorella che tu hai;
ché questa donna, che tanto umil fai,   75
ella la chiama fera e disdegnosa.
Tu sai che 'l ciel sempr'è lucente e chiaro,
e quanto in sé non si turba già mai;
ma li nostri occhi per cagioni assai
chiaman la stella talor tenebrosa.   80
Così, quand'ella la chiama orgogliosa,
non considera lei secondo il vero,
ma pur secondo quel ch'a lei parea:
ché l'anima temea,
e teme ancora, sì che mi par fero   85
quantunqu'io veggio là 'v'ella mi senta.
Così ti scusa, se ti fa mestero;
e quando pòi, a lei ti rappresenta:
dirai: 'Madonna, s'ello v'è a grato,
io parlerò di voi in ciascun lato.'   90

        [Poem 61]

(1   Love, speaking fervently in my mind of my lady, often utters such things concerning her that my intellect is bewildered by them. His speech sounds so sweetly that the soul, as she attends and hears, says: 'Alas that I am unable to express what I hear of my lady!' And certainly, if I wish to treat of what I hear of her, I must first leave aside what my intellect does not grasp; and then, too, much of what it does understand, for I should not be able to express it. If then these words of mine which undertake her praise be found wanting, let the blame fall on the weak intellect, and on our faculty of speech which lacks the power to record all that Love says.

2   The sun that circles the whole world never sees anything so noble as when its light falls there where dwells the lady of whom Love makes me speak. All Intelligences on high gaze at her, and those who here below are in love still find her in their thoughts, when Love brings them to partake of his peace. So much does her being please Him who gives it her that He continually pours His power into her beyond the requirement of our nature. Her pure soul makes it clear through what she governs that she receives this perfection from Him; for among her beauties such things are seen that the eyes of those on whom her light falls send to the heart messengers full of longing, which gather air and turn into sighs.

3   The divine goodness descends into her in the same way as into an angel that sees Him; and let any noble lady who does not believe this keep her company and contemplate her bearing. Whenever she speaks a spirit comes down from heaven to testify that the high perfection she possesses transcends our measure. The gracious actions that she displays vie with each other in calling on Love with such a voice as must awaken him. Of her it can be said: nobility in woman is what is found in her, and beauty is all that resembles her. Further, it can be said that her aspect helps to induce belief in what seems miraculous; and so our faith is strengthened: and it was for this that she was established from eternity.

4   In her aspect things appear that show the joys of Paradise—I mean in her eyes and her lovely smile; for it is there, as to the place which belongs to him, that Love leads them. And they overpower our intellect as a ray of sunlight overpowers a weak sight; and since I cannot look steadily at them I must be content to write but little of them. Her beauty showers down flames of fire alive with a lofty spirit, the creator of all good thoughts; and like a lightning flash they shatter the inborn vices that debase one. Therefore let every woman who hears her beauty slighted for seeming to lack gentle-

ness and humility, gaze at this lady, the very model of humility! She it is who brings back to humility whoever strays from it. She was in the mind of Him who set the universe in motion.

Congedo My song, it seems you speak in a sense contrary to one of your sisters, seeing that this lady, whom you declare so humble, she calls harsh and scornful. You know that the sky is always shining and clear and never itself grows dark; and yet our eyes, for a number of reasons, sometimes say the stars are dimmed. Similarly, when your sister calls this lady 'proud', she does not consider her as she really is, but only as the lady seemed to her. For my soul was afraid, and indeed it is still afraid, so that whatever I see, when this lady perceives me, seems harsh. Make your excuses thus, should the need arise; and when you can, present yourself to her and say: 'Lady, if it be your wish, I will speak of you everywhere.')

The canzone "Amor che ne la mente" seems at first to resemble "Ne li occhi" and "Donne ch'avete" as a poem both *nuovo* and *dolce* in purified stilnovist texture. It seems *nuovo* because it is defined by its means of birth, receptive without "nodo" to Love's engendering breath; it goes obediently signifying. For love both speaks to this poem and makes it speak (1, 22); Love moves ("move," 3) the discussion of *la mia donna*, who in turn was in the mind of Him who set the universe in motion ("mosse," 72). The poem as equivalent self receives its motion from God and the lady, then, these Sources of the loving soul; moreover, the soul with its noblest part, that "mente" where Love speaks, moves to be united with its Source (*Con.* III. ii. 57-59). Thus Casella with this canzone may console the company in ante-Purgatory; no "nuovo legge" (new law) takes its memory from him (ii. 106-11). The repetition of "gentil" (20, 39, 49, 64) also marks this canzone as *nuovo*, in primal receptivity to Love; the *donna* herself is the essence of *gentilezza*. And the central lines tell of the awakening familiar in "Ne li occhi," the self at that universal moment of maternal presencing:[32] her gracious actions call on Love "with such a voice as must awaken him" (45-47). At first it seems that the poem tries to be responsively transparent to that presencing Source, in exalted simplicity: we notice again the impersonal and universal pronouns, the abstractions, antonomasiae, mild periphrases, the "intimate hyperbole," the clear periods, easy correspondence of meter and syntax, the renunciation of almost all metaphor. And with this cultivated purity the poem becomes also *dolce,* in imitation of its Source, its own speech merely the continuation of Love's inspiring breath: "Lo suo parlar sì dolcemente sona" (5). Indeed, when Casella performs this song, the pilgrim introjects it, keeping it "within" him:

> cominciò elli allor sì dolcemente
> che la dolcezza ancor dentro mi sona.
> [*Purg.* ii. 113-14]

(. . . he began then, so sweetly that the sweetness sounds within me still.)

The sweetness lingers even in the retrospective narrator, evoking a contentment (116) in the listener that suggests perhaps the goal of the newly born self, fusion with its Source. Like any song to Beatrice, then, the poem seems consummately *nuovo* and *dolce*—and one may learn first with some surprise that *la mia donna* here is Lady Philosophy, and that Dante allows this canzone a lengthy decoding, as allegory, in *Convivio* III. Perhaps the poem is a self reborn, then, represented in Beatrice's absence or death, with Lady Philosophy as the new consoling presence, even more powerful than those sympathetic ladies of "Donna pietosa."

Perhaps so—but if we were to understand "Amor che ne la mente" so easily, Cato might well chase us away as "spiriti lenti" (laggard spirits, *Purg.* ii. 120). We need more zeal to know a poem in love with Philosophy, for the path of reasoning love is laborious, leading through a universe full of texts. All possible deviations through *Poet* and words are entirely necessary, and must be fully experienced. The *Commedia* is an odyssey through these scattered pages; the pilgrim must *earn* the final intuition, that all these leaves belong in a single volume bound with Love. Because he must detour with *Poet* in order to return with *Lover,* the pilgrim is not allowed to rest in this metaphoric perception:

> 'Lo ben che fa contenta questa corte,
> Alfa ed O è di quanta scrittura
> mi legge amore o lievemente o forte.'
> [*Par.* xxvi. 16-18]

('The good that satisfies this court is alpha and omega of all the scripture that love reads to me in tones loud or low.')

Here the pilgrim answers John's first question in the examination of love ("say on what aim thy soul is set") with a circular metaphor: Love, the good that satisfies this court, is the alpha and omega of all scripture that Love reads to me. Of course, this answer is perfectly correct in the consistent terms of the *Paradiso:* Love moves and completes the study of philosophy, indeed all texts. It is the loving mind ("mente, amando") that can discern that *vero* or *ben* at the foundation of a philosophical proof (*Par.* xxvi. 28–39); the divine bow shoots those creatures who have "intelletto ed amore" (*Par.* i. 120); it is when the soul is in love that it works most profoundly (*Con.* III. iv. 41–43). Thus Love moves the canzone "Amor che ne la mente." Nevertheless, John is not satisfied with this answer: the pilgrim must sift with a finer sieve, he replies; he must discuss the *auctores* who have led him to this conclusion (22–24). The mind in love moves to rejoin its Source—but to know one's Source, it seems, it helps to know thoroughly one's literary, philosophical, theological sources. *Lover* must be known through the lengthy creations of *Poet.* The pilgrim has already cited his texts of faith and hope (*Par.* xxiv, xxv), and he has listened lovingly to Beatrice's discourses. To live is both to love and to reason, and the mind in love works hard. The student's power of study is not always commensurate with his desire (68. 12); the gentle maternal qualities of Lady Philosophy are conflated with her more imposing *grandezza* (59. 46–47).

Thus "Amor che ne la mente" shows the effort of its love. The would-be philosophers do not enjoy full *pace,* but sigh longingly when they take Lady Philosophy's light to their heart; and as the *congedo* concludes, it is difficult to know "'l ciel . . . lucente e chiaro" (77) when one's own eyes are dimmed. Indeed, the very sentences of this canzone, for all their apparent grace, are involved in the strenuous repetitive effort of apprehending this light, of *proodos* and *epistrophe.* The verb "luce" (21, 34) is only one of many verbs of descent here, as divine qualities move from God to the Lady, or from the Lady to Poet-Lover; numerous other verbs, in turn, show the receiver trying to respond to this pouring light. The presencing event in this song is not single but multiple, not quickly completed but a continual trial. The extended *sirima* of each stanza does not merely conclude or exemplify the *frons,* but often introduces new arguments, new elaborations. Moreover, the lengthy and digressive commentaries on this canzone and "Voi che 'ntendendo" (59), *Convivio* II and III, further complicate the texts of the poems. The signifers are not so *dolce* or *nuovo* as they seem at first, and those ingenious allegories make them all the more opaque—the eyes as wisdom's demonstrations, the smile as its persuasions, the *atti soavi* as the virtuous conduct of philosophers when not philosophizing.[33] Even if these poems did seem "bella," such commentary would make them "faticosa e forte" ("intricate and difficult," 59. 61, 55). *Poet* seems to thwart *Lover* here, losing wordless Source in this dense network of referents that show *Poet* in eccentric motion, *de via.* And if one wanted to make matters even more complex, one could ask what happened to Beatrice, that "gloriosa donna ne la mente" where Love now reasons so zealously, "disïosamente" (2).[34] Such insistent questions provoked by texts can indeed make Lady Philosophy "fera e disdegnosa" (76), and he who finds her in his mind has only partitive peace, "de la sua pace" (26)—like the souls who hear Casella sing this canzone, he still has a long way to go. Finally, to demonstrate that love of Lady Philosophy makes one diligent and humble, this canzone closes with a number of references to humility (69, 70, 71, 75). From the long journey through multiple texts, "Questa è colei ch'umilia ogni perverso" (71).

This humbling, though, is also a represencing, as we see if we look once more at line 71 in its context. The complications of *Poet* never become their own reward; they always move with *Lover* to reconsummate that central presencing event. For in the fourth stanza, before this line, appear the familiar "occhi" and "dolce riso" and "bieltate" of the presencing face—this canzone, then, also moves in introjection, like "Ne li occhi," "Tanto gentile," and "Donne ch'avete." That is, to humble the aspirant philosopher who has grown too proud is also to bring back the wanderer in texts to that fundamental *umile* Source, to take the "perverso"—he who has turned away or strayed—and represence him, as this stanza does, with the original maternal features, "queta e umile." To make humble is then to bring back to the path, to the origin. Appropriately, the next and final line of the stanza does indeed return to the cosmic event of Presence: "costei pensò chi mosse l'universo" (72). After repeated efforts to know Philosophy's light, the eyes and smile bring this poem home. Perhaps Dante does here attribute to Philosophy powers the theologians reserved for divine grace, as Foster and Boyde think; still, the situation in stanza four finds significant parallels in Dante's other works.

For however the traveler of Dante's poems may be lost and bewildered, "perverso," he can always be led back to the "diritta via" by some caring maternal presence. One might call this "coherence by grace," the coherence of intermittent and unstructured—yet dependable—representing, where *Poet* joins *Lover* again to evoke the original presencing scene. Thus the anguished Poet-Lover of "Donna pietosa," describing himself as "smarrita," envisions "madonna morta" but is comforted by a maternal Death, like Beatrice: blessed be he who sees her! Thus in the *Vita Nuova* the Poet-Lover refers to his bereavement as "mia vita oscura" (this sad life of mine, 51. 6), and he is terrified ("spaventami sì," 53. 10) lest he lose the sustaining image of the departed Beatrice; yet the new lady's consolations are effective (54). And thus in "Voi che 'ntendendo" Lady Philosophy is concerned about the Poet-Lover's conflict of loyalties, and sets him straight: " 'Tu non se' morta, ma se' ismarrita' " (You are not dead but only bewildered, 59. 40). Of course, all these passages are consummated in the opening of the *Inferno,* with the pilgrim "smarrita" and lost in that "selva oscura" (i. 2-3). Representing saves him here, too: mother Mary, "gentil nel ciel" (ii. 94), and Beatrice, who leaves her "vestige" (footprints) for him to follow (*Par.* xxxi. 81). With such figures as Mary, Lucia, Beatrice, Virgil, Matelda, and Bernard, heavenly grace keeps reappearing as a simple and profound maternal face, offering words *soave* or, when necessary, *acerba:* this grace guides the traveler through a bewildering array of texts while it remains "un semplice lume" (a simple light, *Par.* xxxiii. 90), like the "beacon of orientation" that mother remains for infant (Mahler's term). This face is irreducible and unanalyzable, "come letizia per pupilla viva" (as joy through the living pupil, *Par.* ii, 144), the introjected maternal face that, evoked as Lady Philosophy, enlightens the student of the world's texts, reroutes his uncertainties and digressions toward *primo vero.*

Since love "ragiona," or talks reasonably within the mind, one might suppose that Lady Philosophy draws the student back to humility by reason, or that she directs the philosopher by reason to labor through the world's texts. Certainly the pilgrim's path in the *Commedia* seems in large measure to have been charted by Aristotle's analytical rationality, a landscape laid out in categories. One follows Aristole and truth, not the emperor, in finding the right paths (*Con.* IV. vii); if one renounces reason, "è morte e va per terra" (he's a dead man walking! 69. 40). Nevertheless, these texts are not carried forward by *Poet*, by the momentum of their own logical consistencies: they have instead coherence by grace, *Poet* with *Lover*. For instance, the clauses of "Amor che ne la mente" are not woven together themselves by reason. The few causals and conditionals that do appear are not logically compelling: for instance, "if I wish to treat of what I hear of her, I must first leave aside what my intellect does not grasp" (9–11), a statement of praise arranged as an "if . . . then" sequence; or, again, "So much does her being please Him who gives it her that He continually pours his power into her" (27–28), a statement of divine will presented as cause and effect. And indeed, most of the statements in this canzone are not even qualified like these by reason, by "if" or "because," but appear plainly as categorical, absolute: divine goodness descends into her . . . her beauty showers down flames of fire. Reason does not hold this language together, as it does by contrast in "Le dolci rime d'amor" (69), the canzone defining *gentilezza*. As Foster and Boyde comment here, the beauty of philosophy is an order grounded on moral virtues not particularly logical in themselves.

> Matto è chi spera che nostra ragione
> possa trascorrer la infinita via
> che tiene una sustanza in tre persone.
> [*Purg.* iii. 34–36]

(Foolish is he who hopes that our reason can trace the infinite ways taken by one Substance in three Persons.)

Instead, in the texture of "Amor che ne la mente," goodness, truth, and beauty are measured by Source, by the presencing face of Lady Philosophy herself. *Poet* meets *Lover* in the texture of a moral represencing. Flames of fire, alive with "un spirito gentile," create good thoughts and shatter like lightning inborn vices: her eyes and smile show the joys of Paradise. As with Beatrice's speeches in the *Paradiso*, Poet-Lover here "sets out . . . to make even proof and refutation winsome,"[35] perhaps, but he achieves a more radical goal. By thus texturing Philosophy as a presencing lady, he makes her demonstrations and persuasions more than, almost other than rational. Beatrice is not just another well-informed resident of heaven, but the original Present beloved, through whom the pilgrim asks and receives answers. Just so, Lady Philosophy here encourages virtue and destroys vice not by reasons, in this text, but by the same language used in "Ne li occhi" or "Donne ch'avete"—there anagogy, perhaps, and here allegory, but always evocations of Source. What is more, the awesome Lady herself is in this poem the measure and standard for individual virtues: nobility ("gentile è . . . ," 49), beauty ("bella è . . . ," 50) and humility ("essemplo d'umiltate!", 70). One measures virtues by their degree of resemblance to her; thus morality is presenced, in this texture, rather than reasoned. Similarly, in the *Purgatorio* the individual soul has an innate freedom to separate good loves from bad ones by a faculty, "la virtù che consiglia," that acts like reason; but that counseling virtue consults mainly that "prima voglia," the primary desire of the new soul to merge with its Source. That is, individual desires are measured, called good or bad, by their degree of conformity to this "prima voglia."[36] Truth and goodness are referred to Source in the *Paradiso* as well, where difficult questions of justice and injustice are answered with such statements as this one:

> La prima volontà, ch'è da sè bona,
> da sè, ch' è sommo ben, mai non si mosse.
> Cotanto è giusto quanto a lei consona.
> [*Par.* xix. 86–88]

(The Primal Will, which in itself is good, from itself, the Supreme Good, never was moved; whatever accords with it is in that measure just.)

Whatever most resembles the beloved Source, "prima volontà" calling forth "prima voglia," is therefore the most just. Reason cannot take us to the mysteries of divine justice, because reason cannot encompass or chart our infinite desire to rest in our Source. Those who seek goodness and truth through Lady Philosophy need the receptivity of *infans,* in this texture, not analytical skills—for after all, Philosophy was with God when he created the universe (61. 72, *Con.* III. xv). "The only fixity that there is in the universe is therefore finally hanging on divine good will. Human reason cannot go further."[37]

Finally and most strangely, the Love that "reasons" of philosophy leaves the mind stranded, bewildered without reason. Lady Philosophy may bring the "perverso" back to the origin, yet in the same motion she deprives one of that familiar path of reason: "che lo 'ntelletto sovr'esse disvia" (4). The intellect, unwayed by love of Source, still can find its resting place (*Par.* iv. 127) through philosophical or theological texts—but not literally, not rationally. The intellect must leap, intuiting Source from texts. Thus Beatrice deliberately prophesies in soaring words the pilgrim cannot follow, to demonstrate the limitations of "his school," philosophy (*Purg.* xxxiii). For God has poured into philosophical texts a power beyond the requirements of our nature (61. 29); the texts testify, as though "un spirito da ciel," to a perfection ("valor") transcending humanity (41–44). In other words, the signifiers of philosophy are not sufficient to hold the infinite *vero* and *ben* that have been poured into them. However widely ranging and however persistently returning, *Poet* is of course inadequate to serve *Lover.* The wax of the universe cannot receive God's seal perfectly; his Word remains in infinite excess (*Par.* xix. 43–45). The appropriate response to the Love that reasons of Philosophy, then, is nonverbal, intuitive, religious—Philosophy strengthens our faith (51–53). To have Philosophy thus lead us toward impossibilities, marvels of religious belief, is according to the commentators an "unprecedented" way of calling philosophy the handmaiden of theology;[38] yet this statement is entirely representative of Dante's works. For in the *Commedia* the effort of both narrator and pilgrim is not to reason and word a path back to that original presencing Source, that "luce etterna," but to be presenced by texts or by "autoritadi"—that is, to sense or intuit the light of Source shining through them. The pilgrim gives no physical or metaphysical proofs for hope but alludes instead to "molte

LOVE WORDS

stelle," many presences in texts, like David in the *Psalms* (*Par.*
xxv. 70). And he refers to "filosofici argomenti" and "autorità"
insofar as they are consonant with that "verace autore," God
(*Par.* xxvi. 25–45). The mind in love works to measure the
"bene" that God has bestowed upon these "fronde," these leaves
of texts (*Par.* xxvi. 64–66), but it is not analytical work; it is
rather a thorough feeling acquaintance, an ongoing intuitive
comparison of sources with Source. It is an intuitive response to
unwordable *Lover* in texts, through and despite the worded efforts of *Poet.*

Thus texts become to us not landscapes of reason but luminous presences, and we are drawn to them by their light; we read
their words by the light of our Source, that "gloriosa donna ne la
mente." Thus the *volgare illustre* is vitally irrational, both
nowhere and everywhere, the light of Source shining from the
language we learned from our nurses, moving *with* words but
not *in* words. Thus even words about Beatrice can make others
weep (56. 14); thus the pilgrim spirit often says "Beatrice," after
he sees the lady shining in glory (57); thus even the syllables of
her name, *Be* and *ice*, alpha and omega, master him ("s'indonna") and make him bow down (*Par.* vii. 13–15). The light of
Source, introjected center of the reading self, meets and half
creates the luminous presences of texts: your belief and my
words, says Aquinas, meet in the truth as the center of a circle
(*Par.* xiii. 50–51). When the pilgrim, under John's persistent
questioning, names the "altre corde" (other cords) that draw him
to God, all the teeth with which love bites, he gives not reasons,
not even texts in this ultimate answer:

> 'Tutti quei morsi
> che posson far lo cor volgere a Dio,
> alla mia caritate son concorsi;
> chè l'essere del mondo e l'esser mio,
> la morte ch'el sostenne perch'io viva,
> e quel che spera ogni fedel com'io,
> con la predetta conoscenza viva,
> tratto m'hanno del mar dell'amor torto,
> e del diritto m'han posto alla riva.'
> [xxvi. 54–62]

('All those things whose bite can make the heart turn to God have
wrought together in my charity; for the world's existence and my

own, the death He bore that I might live, and that which every believer hopes for as I do, with the living assurance of which I spoke, have drawn me from the sea of perverse love and have brought me to the shore of the love that is just.')

These are existential beliefs—primal texts of the Unconscious, if you will—that survive at the core *infans* of every self: if we put these beliefs in the language of object-relations, we might call them the existence of self and object (57), the existence of a secure ideal object (60), and a trust that is by nature limitless, infinite (58-59). Our Origin, that internalized good dyad of infant and Maternal Source, is the love that binds texts for us, that gives meaning and coherence to all we read. From these preverbal intuitions we make the original investment of libido that enables us even to perceive the texts. For affect and cognition meet in the preverbal infant, and all motivation and orientation for learning is lighted, set in motion, and continually guided by the maternally presenced core *infans* of the self. "Beatrice is more than the best of eyes . . . ; she is the personality of the beloved, through whom he sees so well, and through whom he is led to ask his questions."[39] And there is nothing *razïonabile* about this lifegiving basic trust, this sensed durability at the unspoken and enigmatic core of the self (*Par.* xxvi. 127-29).

For the *Paradiso* and "Amor che ne la mente" remind us that at our central *infans*, in coenesthetic fantasy, we might wish we could do without texts, without language entirely. We might wish that *Lover* needed no *Poet*, no individuation or detour into words. In the *Paradiso* no signifiers are needed, no memory, no abstract concepts, for angels always see the truth directly in God (*Par.* xxix. 76-81). Thus Beatrice and the other spirits are able to read and even anticipate the pilgrim's thoughts, as infants and young children are sure that their parents can do. Aquinas, the perfect teacher, need only look into the "luce etterna" to know whether Dante has understood him. It is only in condescending love that the spirits manifest themselves in a form perceptible to Dante's senses (*Par.* iv. 40) and agree to use language—Cacciaguda's language is even so "profondo" at first that the narrator cannot record the signifiers until Cacciaguda comes "inver lo segno del nostro intelletto" (towards the mark of our intellect, *Par.* xv. 45). And thus in "Amor che ne la mente," Lady Philosophy receives divine *virtù* without language, as the angels do simply by seeing God (37-38), and the angels in turn gaze at her (23), their vision undimmed by the world of words, *turba* and *tenebrosa*. Like a nursing infant one takes in complete Source without need of words, in uninterrupted communication.[40]

"Amor che ne la mente" is sustained by this wordless, paradisiacal communication between self and Source, this *absent presence*. The poem maternally presenced by Lady Philosophy finds a humbling path to its own origin through disclaiming poems and reason, "dir" and "intelletto." Surely the ineffability topos effects great praise (*Con*. III. iv. 1-4), but the poem is more than praise:

> . . . 'Oh me lassa, ch'io non son possente
> di dir quel ch'odo de la donna mia!'
> E certo e' mi conven lasciare in pria,
> s'io vo' trattar di quel ch'odo di lei,
> ciò che lo mio intelletto non comprende;
>
> [7-11]

('Alas that I am unable to express what I hear of my lady!' And certainly, if I wish to treat of what I hear of her, I must first leave aside what my intellect does not grasp;)

The *verso chiave* here (line 9) is not just a passing ineffability topos, but a center for both *frons* and *sirima:* for the entire first stanza elaborates this conviction that the poem cannot render its Source, that presencing Lady, in words. Here and in subsequent stanzas, the language returns to stress its own inadequacy, for the poem begins and *grows upon* its own consistent deferral to the infinite Presence central to its finite signifiers. While the poem thus energetically conjures its Source, it evokes also the reader's sense of his own wordless Source, a brilliant dyad where being flows in a fixed gaze, unhindered.

> e perch'io non le posso mirar fiso,
> mi conven contentar di dirne poco.
>
> [61-62]

(And since I cannot look steadily at them I must be content to write but little of them.)

Poem and reader are selves in *différance* from this gaze, selves left through primal bereavement with a light that cannot be transcribed. Thus the "nova fantasia" (40. 13) of Beatrice's death leads to the language-free "alta fantasia" (*Par.* xxxiii. 142), the fixed gaze into the face of God.

VI

The *Commedia*, the ultimate love poem, is also sustained by a union between the worded poem and its unspoken Source. Like "Amor che ne la mente" the *Paradiso* reaches toward an unreachable Source, all the more surely infinite as the poem reelaborates and remanipulates the inadequacies of its language. Just as the unattainable fixed gaze supports the canzone, and just as the past Maternal Source supports the continuing self, so the pilgrim's final gaze, a fathomless *profondo* that is essentially *absent* from the poem, supports the poem that goes signifying. Moreover, in the *Paradiso, Poet* and *Lover* meet in restless sequences of metaphors, *figurando,* to re-create within the reader a sense of that first and final Source, as we read at the threshold of the last ten cantos:

> e così, figurando il paradiso,
> convien saltar lo sacrato poema,
> come chi trova suo cammin riciso.
> [*Par.* xxiii. 61–63]

(And so, picturing Paradise, the sacred poem must make a leap like one that finds his path cut off.)

The poem, deprived of a path like the "intelletto" bewildered by reasoning Love, gestures in metaphors toward that infinity beyond the path. Insofar as these metaphors evoke our central *infans,* the pilgrim's "ultima salute" (last salvation) evokes the poem's definitive represencing.

To follow these evocations, we pass over in the *Paradiso* those direct allusions to mothers and infants, and the references to "madre" and specific mythological mothers in periphrasis or metaphor.[41] For these pervade the entire poem as a matter of course, texturing the pilgrim's quest for Source with the *caritas*, the unfraudulent love, of family and *patria*. Instead, we explore the poem's more subtle figurative devices, its metaphoric language of fusion where *Lover* and *Poet* meet to suggest the graced preverbal experience at our central *infans*. For instance, in the first canto, the pilgrim fixes his eyes upon Beatrice's eyes, in turn fixed upon the "etterne rote" (eternal wheels), while the narrator reflects:

> Nel suo aspetto tal dentro mi fei,
> qual si fè Glauco nel gustar dell'erba
> che 'l fè consorte in mar delli altri Dei.
> Trasumanar significar per verba
> non si porìa; però l'essemplo basti
> a cui esperïenza grazia serba.
>
> [i. 67–72]

(At her aspect I was changed within, as was Glaucus when he tasted of the herb that made him one among the other gods in the sea. The passing beyond humanity cannot be set forth in words: let the example suffice, therefore, for him to whom grace reserves the experience.)

This reciprocal pair of metaphors is integral to the effort of that coined word, "trasumanar." For often in the language of the *Paradiso* one incorporates infinite being, by eating or drinking, as Glaucus here tastes the divine herb; and, reciprocally, one is consumed by infinite being, as Glaucus here is moved to plunge into the sea among the other gods. These metaphors are familiar to us: at our central *infans*, we drink in a Maternal Source felt to be infinite, and in turn we sense that we belong to infinite Source, subsumed as part to whole. Being is transmitted ("trasumanar") from mother to infant: *spira / spirito novo*. With ontological need, the pilgrim hungers and thirsts after divine knowledge, for "'l sacro amore" always renews one's thirst "di dolce disïar" (with sweet desire, xv. 64–66). And like his perpetual gazing, his ongoing pleas for this food and drink of wisdom are most often directed toward Beatrice. In this passage, even as Glaucus tastes the herb, the pilgrim takes in Beatrice's sight and is transformed "dentro"—defined, created, transhumanized by her vital Presence, as the self takes Maternal

Source to an intrapsychic center. And in the ensuing cantos the pilgrim finds her sight ever more vital to consume: he shares with the infant the "ever-increasing significance" of that presencing face.[42] With her look, her smile, and her continuing solicitous explications of the universe, she slakes his thirst as with "le dolci stille" (sweet drops, vii. 11–12).

This sweet drinking is neither rational nor simple. A graced paradox holds us all to that everlasting longing of the primal unconscious, where we consume divinity and are in turn consumed as though by the force of our own longing. In the metaphor of that first ascent, "La concreata e perpetüa sete / del deïforme regno cen portava"; that is, "the inborn and perpetual thirst for the godlike kingdom bore us away," as swift as a glance to heaven (ii. 19–21). The God that appears first "outside" oneself ("di fuori," *Purg.* xviii. 43) is taken within, *proodos*, to one's ontological center; in the returning motion, *epistrophe*, the self is pulled "inside-out," its infinite center drawn again "outside" to those divine regions whence the God appeared. Thus *Poet* and *Lover* meet in the invocation of Apollo, with the strangely worded reference to Marsyas: enter my breast and breathe there ("spira"), just as when you drew Marsyas from the sheath of his limbs, "della vagina delle membra sue" (i. 19–21). The satyr Marsyas was flayed for his presumption in challenging Apollo to a singing contest, and of course the narrator beginning the *Paradiso* wonders about presumptuous singing—but more to our purpose, Marsyas is in this wording "inside-out," just like the pilgrim to his Source in response to that engendering breath. The mind leaves itself by way of the Presence it ingests, infinite food (xxiii. 43–45); the pilgrim is raised by his root, Cacciaguida, until he is more than himself (xv. 88–89; xvi. 18). The infant swallows and is swallowed, knowing "himself," in coenesthetic reception, as a total experience of renewed thirst and eternal drinking; the pilgrim also is drawn outward, toward the depths he internalizes.

Through an unswerving gaze we drink and are consumed, at core *infans;* so the pilgrim's gaze, ever more fixed, is his means of assumption into that divine ocean. "Poscia rivolsi li occhi alli occhi belli" (Then to the fair eyes I turned my eyes again, xxii. 154). Eye to eye, one becomes anew, and becomes again, part of a seamless maternal whole. Beatrice's eyes and smile take the pilgrim beyond the reach of his own mind (xiv. 79–81) because in them he can touch the depth ("lo fondo") of grace and paradise (xv. 34–36). He moves toward a "profondo" too deep for mortal justice to penetrate, the sea of God's will that can receive the self unperturbed, as water receives a ray of light (xix. 58–60; iii. 85–87; ii. 34–36). These awesome depths are not for all readers (ii. 1–19) precisely because they *are* indeed at the Source of all selves, the "oceanic feeling" that Romain Rolland knew as a religious impulse. Our ontology is a diffuse, nondifferentiated, synesthetic oneness with maternal presence: to distinguish self from that dyadic Source must be somewhat like finding the outlines of a pearl on a white brow (iii. 13–15).

In the figurative language of light, *Lover* and *Poet* also move together to evoke our dyadic Source. For light, too, can be both consuming and consumed—both a Presence that surrounds one maternally, and an infinite bright point, internalized, for the soul to turn upon. In these metaphors, too, there is no apparent break between Source and self, embracing and introjected light: *spira / spirito novo.* This enigmatic fusion of self with Source is like the sustaining mystery of the Trinity, in Aquinas' periphrasis: the living Light streams from its Source ("suo lucente") so that it is not parted from it, nor from the Love that with them makes Three (xiii. 55–57). At core *infans,* Maternal Source *becomes* the self; and the pilgrim learns that the rays of God's light, unseparated from Him, *become* the new soul, the individual "Subsisto" or "I am" (xxix. 14–15). Thus souls in Paradise are nested or swathed ("fasciato") in light, like Justinian (v. 124–26) and Charles Martel (viii. 52–54) and the pilgrim himself (xxx. 49–51), but this encircling light is also the hub of the soul, divine Presence and ideal object introjected: "The divine point is the very center of the soul; it is God interiorly possessed in a human moment."[43] One's own light, "proprio lume," becomes indistinguishable from the light of grace in this metaphoric texturing. The soul of Peter Damian, enwombed ("m'inventro") in light, is also pierced through by a divine light which sets it spinning upon its center: it is the union ("congiunta") of lights, divine *virtù* and the soul's own vision, that enables his ultimate sight, "la somma essenza" (the Supreme Essence, xxi. 79–87). To journey to the Eternal Light is then the same as to move toward one's own center of being, as to a predestined place, "sito decreto" (i.

124); one is both archer and mark, or, as in "Oltre la spera" (57), both sending and receiving heart.[44] Even the two models of the universe suggest these symbiotic motions. For like the infant whose "surround" is his mother, the pilgrim is embraced by boundless Presence as he travels through spheres of increasing speed and brightness toward the Empyrean; yet also like the infant who introjects his eternal and infinite Source, the pilgrim sees a universe of nine concentric circles enclosing a "punto" (eternal and infinite) of keen light, around which the smaller circles whirl more rapidly in their desire (xxviii). The logical contradiction here is nevertheless an overwhelming ontological truth, a "punto" that conquers, "parendo inchiuso da quel ch'elli 'nchiude" (which seems enclosed by that which it encloses, xxx. 11–12). Here is the enigma of our central being—both embracing and embraced, gazing and gazed-upon, consuming and consumed. Two, three, or many become as one, a limitless whole.

Poet and *Lover* meet also in other features of the verbal texture, even more remarkable than these metaphors. As in Arnaut Daniel's poems, *Poet* is revealed through the very intensity of yearning toward Source, for these verbal devices distinguish the *Commedia* from other poems. For instance, there are neologisms that may suggest being subsumed by some presencing totality (*india, s'indonna, imparadisa, invera, s'insempra,* even *t'annidi*), or that may blur the lines between selves or entities, conflate many to one (*intrea, infiora, inmii, intuassi*). The word "Christ" can rhyme only with itself. We find significant configurations of souls, such as those forming the Eagle of Justice—self-effacing selves to be transparent to God's thoughts,[45] somewhat as the words in "Ne li occhi" work to be transparent to the *donna*. We find periphrases that caress, abjuring the static accidents of names.[46] Even the emphasis upon "babytalk" and the vernacular[47] belongs to the poem's motion toward preverbal and transverbal unity; Source becomes goal. And most significantly, the words again and again bewail their own insufficient significance: the poem knows that it is made of metaphors, knows and mourns its measure of absence from its Source.[48] *Poet* and *Lover* meet in these dramatically impermanent metaphors, placed there to be left behind in the grace of the final vision.

At last, in cantos xxx and xxxiii, *Poet* and *Lover* meet in two epic similes that compare the pilgrim to a suckling infant. In context these work as climactic evocations of Presence, drawing together many of the previous metaphoric threads we have seen. The similes are not unusual: we find comparable language in the *Purgatorio* to suggest literary Source, as when Statius confesses, "dell'Eneïda dico, la qual mamma / fummi e fummi nutrice poetando" (I mean the *Aeneid*, which was in poetry my mother and my nurse, *Purg.* xxi. 97–98). We find it again when Virgil describes Homer in periphrasis as that Greek who nursed at the Muse's breasts longer than his fellow poets (*Purg.* xxii. 101–2). And in several earlier similes in the *Paradiso* the pilgrim has been compared to a nursing animal, or fledgling: Beatrice admonishes him not to be like the lamb that leaves its mother's milk (v. 82–84); the Eagle of Justice circles over him like a stork over the nest where she had fed her young (xix. 91–93); Beatrice, erect and attentive, waits to show him the vision of the Church Triumphant, like a mother bird waiting for the dawn so that she can find food to nourish "suoi dolci nati" (her sweet brood, xxiii. 1–12).[49] But in cantos xxx and xxxiii the similes become crucial, as though with them *Poet* and *Lover* all but satisfy the poem's longing, drawing as close to Source as language allows. The poem as self must become as a suckling infant to enter the Kingdom of Heaven.

In canto xxx light both embraces the pilgrim and usurps his center: for divine love must put out and then relight the candle of his soul to enable his "novella vista," new vision of the river of light. Beatrice guides him to drink:

> Non è fantin che sì subito rua
> col volto verso il latte, se si svegli
> molto tardato dall'usanza sua,
> com fec' io, per far migliori spegli
> ancor delli occhi, chinandomi all'onda
> che si deriva perchè vi s'immegli;
> e sì come di lei bevve la gronda
> della palpebre mie, così mi parve
> di sua lunghezza divenuta tonda.
>
> [82–90]

(No infant, waking long after its hour, throws itself so instantly with its face to the milk, as I, to make still better mirrors of my eyes, bent down to the water that flows forth for our perfecting; and no sooner did the eaves of my eyelids drink of it than it seemed to me out of its length to have become round.)

With his new vision he can take in infinite light (59–60), but still he drinks this flowing river with his eyelids, with his eyes shut. Here seeing and drinking, streaming light and radiant water are one, as they are for the gazing infant who can drink as well without diacritic perception, or with closed eyes. And the pilgrim is swallowed by the infinite sight he drinks, for his new vision is consumed in change. As though in response to his intent, drinking gaze (the rhyme-word "vidi" in 95, 97, 99), his eyes are made better mirrors, perfected (*spegli ... s'immegli*) in mimesis of Source, so that the river, jewels, and flowers become the Rose. Even this new metaphor will soon be dismissed as only a metaphor, a form not universal (xxxi. 1), but the poem, through and by means of the evolving metaphors, moves steadily past this "difetto" (xxx. 80), toward Source.

In Canto xxxiii the pilgrim again drinks in sights, and even in retrospect the sweetness of the draught still drops within the speaker's heart (62–63). His sight is consumed ("consunsi," 84); his drinking gaze is "fissa, immobile e attenta" (fixed, still and intent, 98), as though to turn away would be to become lost, in that familiar term "smarrito" (77). And again his vision is caught up in changes:

> Omai sarà più corta mia favella,
>   pur a quel ch'io ricordo, che d'un fante
>   che bagni ancor la lingua alla mammella.
> Non perchè più ch' un semplice sembiante
>   fosse nel vivo lume ch'io mirava,
>   che tal è sempre qual s'era davante;
> ma per la vista che s'avvalorava
>   in me guardando, una sola parvenza,
>   mutandom' io, a me si travagliava.
>   [106–14]

(Now my speech will come more short even of what I remember than an infant's who yet bathes his tongue at the breast. Not that the living light at which I gazed had more than a single aspect—for it is ever the same as it was before—, but by my sight gaining strength as I looked, the one sole appearance, I myself changing, was, for me, transformed.)

Poet and *Lover* pause, wordless before this concentration of light, again revealing that *Poet*, after all, can attend only to differences, colors, grades of light: words. Yet even as the three circles are differentiated in language, the poem arrives at ultimate *valor* ("s'avvalorava"), and that living light is affirmed as single, "semplice" and "sola," the "ideal object" where all good is gathered (103–4), infinite and eternal "punto." Following Bernard's eyes, the pilgrim's gaze has entered that Eternal Light (52–54), and now in turn the Light penetrates to his center and sets his soul and the poem in motion. He has flown like lightning *to* his own place (i. 92) and now is struck with lightning there, "percossa / da un fulgore" (smitten by a flash, 140–41), in a consummate introjection, a definitive represencing. Now he spins like Peter Damian upon an axis of light: he is represenced forever, "sè in sè regira," and that moment of Presence becomes the eternal present of self and poem.

The "fulgore" that enables the poem is the hyphen between *Poet* and *Lover*. To ask how our image has its place ("vi s'indova") in that circle, then, is to ask the nature of that hyphen, to ask how "nostra effige" (our likeness), finite and intact, the work of *Poet*, can still be painted "del suo colore stesso" (in its own colour) upon the reflected light of eternity, the goal of *Lover* (130–31).

We have been learning all along how difficult it is to belong to that infinite circling in one's own *colore*, for here all is fused ("conflati") to a simple light (xxxiii. 89–90), and the lesser lights have been shut off ("si chiude") one by one (xxx. 1–9). Full Presence obliterates the self as it creates: at the goal of *Lover*, the pilgrim is turned like Semele to ash (xxi. 4–6). For all the words of the poem are erased with that "fulgore," the *vestita* and even the *sentenza* dispersed, like the leaves of the Sibyl (xxxiii. 64–66). Beatrice's beauty and the Creator's glory have indeed conquered the speaker, "poetando" (xxx. 22–33), for here all particulars, substances, accidents, events of history, all *fronde* are lost, and we are left with only the wordless binding of the book, "legato con amore" (bound by love, xxxiii. 86), the light of maternal presence by which we read.[50] Language is *différance*, but now the "nodo" of words has been dissolved in the nondifferentiation of *infans,* and we can only intuit with *Lover* a joy (3) free of words and thought.

Conversely, the Poet-Lover or poem must exist in inexorable distinction from that infinite circling, as a *present absence* held apart from graced experience. For to be "del suo colore stesso," the poem as self must have its comprehensive diversity, "different members" with "various faculties" (ii. 134–35). The pilgrim has all P's erased, and drinks Lethe—but the poem, a being-in-words, must reassume the P's and verbalize the memory of sin. "Diverse voci fanno dolci note" (Diverse voices make sweet music, vi. 124): the worded and reasoned divisions of the poem open it up, so that its *sentenza* may be available to the loving mind.[51] Even in upper Paradise the angels are "ciascun distinto di fulgore e d'arte" (each distinct in brightness and in function, xxxi. 132), and the pilgrim's eyes move up, down, and around the ranks of the Blessed Rose, "mo su, mo giù, e mo ricirculando" (xxxi. 48), a particular and diverse circling limited by words. All this multiplicity is inevitably woven of partial absences: God's glory shines through the universe "in one part more and in another less" (i. 3), and Love's sweetness glows variously, "ferve e tepe" (xxix. 141). The poem, the goal of *Poet, is* detour, negation, deviation, diversity, *nostra effige.* Furthermore, the poem in its primal bereavement knows its own finitude. For *nostra effige* is distinguishable in that circle exactly because it is distinct: limited, circumscribed, subject to the contingencies of time and space. Even if God is a sphere whose center is everywhere and whose circumference is nowhere, still the poem is finite. Like a self, the poem proceeds in awareness of its own termination, held back by "lo fren dell'arte" (the curb of art, *Purg.* xxxiii. 136–41) from its desire to drink forever, and shaped to specifications, like a coat made by a good tailor (*Par.* xxxii. 139–41)—for as the faint allusion here to the weaving Fates reminds us, poems and selves are allowed only a limited measure of cloth for their texturing. Here *Poet,* as care for the limited entity of the poem, may seem in this respect to contradict *Lover.* One might say the poem seems conscious of itself as a specific new presence, distinct and distinctive among other poetic presences: the poem may earn its author reentrance into Florence, and the laurel crown (*Par.* xxv. 1–9), or it may "Chase both

Guidos from the nest," surpassing his contemporaries in fame (*Purg.* xi. 98–99). This poem as self is real, idiosyncratic, vulnerable to time.

Nevertheless, this partial absence is never full absence. Just as the internalized good dyad of mother and infant, inaccessible in reality to the adult self, still allows that self to be, enabling the complex "interstitial web" of object relations that gives strength to the whole structure of self, organizing the self's ability to organize, so that "fulgore" or ultimate Source allows the poem to be, even though it is finally inaccessible to the words of the poem. That "fulgore" binds the book, joins *Poet* and *Lover,* secures meaning, coherence, and intentionality for the poem as equivalent self. Just as the threefold universe was created all at once (*Par.* xxix. 27–33), so that "fulgore" unfolds to the stately, expansive trinitarian rhythm of the threefold poem, "sì come rota ch'igualmente è mossa" (like a wheel that spins with even motion, xxxiii. 144). That "fulgore" is the poem's *absent presence,* illuminating the entire poem with meaning through resemblance to, as well as difference from, its central Light. God's glory shines through all these words, more and less—all words *belong* with that "fulgore" that would consume them, somewhat as the souls manifest in separate heavens all *belong* at their seats in the Empyrean. For this equivalent cosmic Dantean self, *Poet* is enabled by *Lover:* the poem's astounding integrity *allows* its cosmic breadth, the universe within a central point. All the words, even the "orribile favelle e diverse lingue" of hell or the fierce invectives of Paradise, reach down in their difference, *de rive,* to draw the wanderer back to that river of infant wordlessness, "all'onda / che si deriva perchè vi s'immegli" (to the water that flows forth for our perfecting, *Par.* xxx. 86–87). *Lover* subsumes *Poet,* finally. No wandering in these signifiers will conclude in Void, nor in merely the well-shaped poem; all digressions return to that "dritta strada" (straight road; *Par.* xxix. 127–28), and all words lead to that placeless, timeless, wordless "fulgore" that fits our image to our Source.

Finally, the poem as self can presence the reader, draw him with the pilgrim toward ultimate Presence. Thus Beatrice entrusts the pilgrim to Virgil, "quella fonte / che spandi di parlar sì largo fiume" (that fountain which pours forth so rich a stream of speech, *Inf.* i. 79–80); thus Virgil's poems—in Dante's accounting—have converted Statius (*Purg.* xxii). Poems belong with those paradaisical metaphors of fusion: they can be radiant with nourishing and maternal light, food that consumes even as it is consumed. The *Convivio* is the oaten bread with which thousands shall be fed, just as Christ fed the multitude, and the new sun that will give light to those in darkness (I. xiii). And the *Commedia* also is "vital nutrimento" (vital nourishment, *Par.* xvii. 131), with divine light overflowing "questi versi brevi" (these brief lines, *Par.* xviii. 82–87). It exists to presence the reader maternally, both embracing him and feeding him with a gleam ("una favilla sol") of lifegiving Light (*Par.* xxxiii. 70–72). In this maternal sense the poem is effectively Holy Scripture in mimesis of God's book, offered to *Lover infans* within all selves, an oceanic page offered for the drinking:

> Voi altri pochi che drizzaste il collo
>   per tempo al pan delli angeli, del quale
>   vivesi qui ma non sen vien satollo,
> metter potete ben per l'alto sale
>   vostro navigio. . . .
>   [*Par.* ii. 10–15]

(Ye other few that reached out early for the angels' bread by which men here live but never come from it satisfied, you may indeed put forth your vessel on the salt depths. . . .)

5 Petrarch

et perché 'l mio martir non giunga a riva,
mille volte il dì moro et mille nasco,
tanto da la salute mia son lunge.

—[164]

We cannot intuit *Lover infans* in Petrarch's *Canzoniere* so easily
or directly as we can in the lyrics by Dante and Arnaut Daniel.
For through the metaphoric language of fusion, an illumined
dyad sustains Daniel's poems, and a central presencing event
rests at the heart of Dante's poetry; by contrast, in none of Petrarch's various works do *Poet* and *Lover* move harmoniously, in
continual metaphors of fusion, toward some central *arrheton*.
Rather, in these poems *Poet* and *Lover* join in more difficult,
defensive verbal efforts, as though in reaction to an inadequate
or finally unavailable Source. This "as though"—this pervasive
sense of untrustworthy central Source and conflicted central
infans—may serve as our beginning intuition for Petrarch's
poetry. The lyrics of the *Canzoniere* may be understood as works
of self-texturing appropriate to this uncertain ontological
center.

In all of Petrarch's works, final values are never quite final.
Final judgments can be postponed, or retracted. When Reason
receives the Poet-Lover's appeal for justice late in the *Canzoniere*,
she replies that she needs more time to make up her mind (360.
157). Augustine, who often seems the winner in the debates of

Epigraph "And that my suffering may not reach an end, a thousand times a
day I die and a thousand am born, so distant am I from health."

Quotations from the *Canzoniere* or *Rime sparse* are from *Petrarch's Lyric Poems*,
translated and edited by Robert M. Durling (Cambridge: Harvard University
Press, 1976), reprinted by permission of Harvard University Press. In general, I
give line numbers only for the canzoni. Translations are Durling's unless otherwise noted.

the *Secretum,* does not really have the last word. Laura is all but obliterated in the palinode, "Vergine bella" (366), but she is there again at the close of the *Trionfo dell'Eternità,* with those who possess immortal beauty and eternal fame. Perhaps such shifting purposes argue an uneasy ontology for these poems, an inability to fix Source and goal, an inherent restlessness. We recall how the Petrarch of the letters perceived his "wandering life" to have begun at birth:

> But I was conceived in exile and born in exile. I cost my mother such labor and struggle that for a long time the midwives and physicians thought her dead. Thus I began to know danger even before I was born, and I crossed the threshold of life under the loom of death.... I was removed [from Arezzo] in my seventh month and borne all over Tuscany by a certain sturdy youth; as Metabus did Camilla, he wrapped me in a linen cloth suspended from a knotty stick, to protect my tender body from contact. In fording the Arno, his horse fell, and in trying to save his precious burden he nearly lost his own life in the raging stream.
> After the wanderings in Tuscany we went to Pisa. I was removed from there in my seventh year and transported by sea to France. We were shipwrecked by the winter storms not far from Marseilles, and I was nearly carried off again on the threshold of my young life.... Thenceforward, certainly, I have hardly had a chance to stand still and get my breath.[1]

As a young boy, he says, he sensed as "true and almost present" those passages from classical authors about the mutability of life and "time's irrecoverability" (*Fam.* XXIV. 1, p. 201). He was barely in his teens when his mother died, and during those same years his father threw Petrarch's cherished library of classical books into the fire.[2] The Petrarch of the letters would see such incidents as further evidence that "there is no resting-place for me," that he must lie exhausted on the bed of this life (*Fam.* XV. 4, p. 135). He was forever unable or reluctant to find a permanent residence, as though a final sense of belonging, or home, eluded him. For to be by one's very nature deracinated, or homeless, is to lack that definite imagination, that crucial *absent presence*, at one's psychic center: it is not a question of geography, but of how surely one possesses an intrapsychic representation of self-as-Source, toward which one internally is always directed, always "traveling." Without this sure imagination, in Petrarchan texturing, one can hardly even *conceive* of arriving home. Source becomes entirely contingent, a central ground that may always be pulled away. And indeed no ground seems to be truly secure in these letters; even though Gherardo has reached spiritual harbor in a Carthusian monastery, Petrarch nevertheless sends him exhortations to piety, as well as a reading list (*Fam.* X. 3, p. 100). No metaphors of suckling infants belong to this texturing; rather, one exists as though wrapped in a linen cloth and suspended from a knotty stick.

We sense in Petrarch's *Canzoniere* and in his other works a central *infans* moved by the full force of both those original contradictory motions, the dread of Void as well as the longing for Source. It is as though this Poet-Lover lives in the interchange of death and birth: "mille volte il dì moro et mille nasco." For the evocations of Source here are centrally threatened, and any Source that might be intuited from these pages seems to be always already departing. For instance, Laura is typically a shadow, an elusive *ombra*, even in her surest representations. Whereas the *donna* of Donte's *nove rime* approaches and brings life with her gaze, making her presence felt, it is of Laura's essence to vanish, to be summoned only with weeping and imaginative effort. And so *in morte:* Laura as salvific vision, *guida al cielo*, simply does not work as well as Dante's Beatrice. Her eyes do not show the Poet-Lover "la via ch'al ciel conduce" (the way that leads to heaven, 72. 3), despite all intentions. Instead of guiding him step by step to a consummate "fulgore," Laura repeatedly appears and disappears from his bedside: her tender counsel is intermittent, ephemeral—as her memory has always been. And her presence is swept away in the last poems where she becomes merely "tale" (one, 366. 92).

Moreover, except for those tenuous nightly visitations, the Poet-Lover of the *Canzoniere* receives no grace, no responsive, infinite Maternal Source, no presencing or represencing to strengthen his repentance and hope for *salute*. Neither Laura's arms nor God's arms reach down to him in his lifelong wanderings; neither Laura's face nor God's face approaches to bring him definitive rest. One might ask, as Lucia asks Beatrice at the start of the *Inferno*, do you not hear his cries? Such repentant moments as "Padre del Ciel" (62) and "I' vo pensando" (264)

move on unanswered, and the Virgin's exhorted presence sub-
tends the final poem silently. The Poet-Lover's final prayers
move full circle to the first poem in the sequence, where *pietà*
and *perdono* are left to the reader in an unresolvable appeal. This
first poem presents the whole sequence as an endless purgatorial
chain, but without final absolution and remission of sins. There
is no context that assures a sympathetic audience: it is Laura's
role not to listen, of course (223), but there is no sense through
the verbal texture that God and the Virgin Mary are listening,
either. The poems revolve essentially alone, filling the silences
left by their own failing pleas. For in Petrarchan texturing, such
Dantean echoes as "il ver tacito" (the silent truth, 309) do not
really allay the fear that there may be no truth, no trusted listening figure, in the silence. The pilgrim of the *Commedia* can experience nourishing silences, long gazes that lead to the final
eternal gazing—but the *Canzoniere* does not evoke such a "silent
terminal point"[3] to engender and direct the words. The Poet-
Lover must himself fill the silences, while no responsive presences arrive to lead him home. He calls Laura's name into a
Void:

> ... onde con gravi accenti
> è ancor chi chiami, et non è chi responda.
> [318]

(... whence there is one who calls out with heavy accents, but there
is no one to answer.)

The silence that is death shares the maternity of these poems.

In response and reaction to an untrustworthy central Source
and a fully conflicted central *infans, Poet* and *Lover* meet in
difficult textures, where often pain and solitude seem elaborated
almost purposefully, willfully, self-consciously, dramatically. Or,
one might say, defensively. For through several intricate verbal
means that resemble defenses, *Poet* and *Lover* join as though to
guard uncertain Source, or even to reclaim Source from all uncertainty. Like many defensive efforts, these do not work very
well, but the efforts remain to mark Petrarchan texturing. In the
cause of these defenses, whole human presences seem deliberately distanced from these poems, while at the same time parts of

cherished presences seem to be assimilated, possessed in words. Moreover, the Poet-Lover works hard to turn against himself, in distinctive representations of *amant martyr,* so that the rages of incompleted mourning are deflected away from Source and into the verbal texture. Source remains uncertain, but finally, through the verbal negations and deviations of these pervasive defenses, *Poet* takes on weight—becoming perhaps strong enough to subsume, nourish, and compensate *Lover* for the centrally inadequate Source that provoked the defenses in the first place. Strengthened by *Poet,* the Poet-Lover may come to love self, his own being-in-words, almost as he would have loved a securely evoked Source. The expectations and problems of this self-love may lead us to the final self-consciousness of the *Canzoniere,* the Petrarchan "lifelong condition"[4] that we all in some measure share with these poems as equivalent selves.

I

l'aura

It may seem paradoxical that *Poet* and *Lover* would move together in purposeful defense to *distance* important presences from these poems, since intimations of a departing Source can be centrally threatening to the self. But such distancing can allow a crucial, saving measure of defensive control against a Maternal Source felt to be untrustworthy. For if that Source seems by its nature to vanish, the self can defensively take as its own the act of distancing, in order the more surely to circumscribe and hold the imagination of Source, *absent presence,* internalized "ideal object." The self contrives its own "optimal distance" from Source, defensively appropriating its own boundaries. And on the other hand, if Source seems by its nature to be overbearing or overpresencing, such managed distancing can be all the more a saving grace, can allow the self to exist in division. For there are some indications in Petrarchan texts that their evoked always-departing Source may operate, on a deeper level of defense, to screen the opposite evocation: an all-engulfing Source. And in this case, the self through the defense of primal envy would tend to devalue and distance important presences, lest they become entirely overwhelming. Thus ultimately, at some evocative level past the signifiers, that central untrustworthy Source in Petrarchan textures may be too near as well as too far, engulfing as well as abandoning, and these two untrustworthy "imagos" may be always oscillating in mutual reaction to each other. From such a conflicted "core" *infans,* the self would surely move to impose its own distances.

For instance, in an early canzone of the *Canzoniere,* "Una donna più bella" (119), the figure of Glory may suggest a Source both too far away and too near, and some ambivalence may inform the Poet-Lover's reception of her. When she leaves, she winds the garland of laurel around his temples as though to soften her departure: "'Non temer ch' i' mi allontani'" (Do not be afraid that I am going away, 119. 102-5). Formulating this distance from her, the laureled self is discovered; Petrarch is crowned as poet laureate. On the other hand, when several lines earlier, after she presences him with her gaze (88-90), she tells him, "ciascuna di noi due [Virtue and Glory] nacque immortale" (each of us was born immortal, 119. 92), she seems intent to overwhelm him, to provoke his despair.

> "Miseri, a voi che vale?
> Me' v'era che da noi fosse il defetto"
> [93-94]

("Wretches, what does it avail you? It would be better for you that we did not exist.")

Her exclamation here is like the proverb near the close of the *Trionfo del Tempo:* blessed is he who is not born. For he wanes in comparison with her; he can hope at best, through Glory, to live a long time (14-15), but she is overbearingly immortal.

These allusions to literary fame, and to an age without Virtue or Glory, recall certain similar passages in the letters, mixed evocations of abandonment and engulfment by Source, with appropriate defensive distancing. For in the letters also, Petrarch suggests that none of his contemporaries are worthy of Glory, or indeed worth reading, and that for this reason "I exert all my mental powers to flee contemporaries and seek out the men of the past" (*Fam.* VI. 4, p. 68). Bergin offers a more defensive cause for this flight—that Petrarch might have found true rivals among his contemporaries, especially those in Florence. Perhaps the Petrarch of the letters would like to hold his literary sources at a comfortable distance, to devalue those that are not already distanced by time. Such devaluing and distancing could manifest a primal envy of Source, an anxiety of influence. And as for those writers already safely distanced by time, not to mention by language and culture, he could continue to lament their irrevocable departure, taking them—from a distance—to heart. Petrarch, unable to read Greek, could clasp a volume of Homer to his bosom and sigh, "'O great man, how gladly would I hear you speak!'" (*Fam.* XVIII. 2, p. 153). Yet by contrast he could not bring himself to hold so close a copy of Dante's works: "I was strangely indifferent to this one book, which was new and easily procurable. . . . I was afraid that if I should immerse myself in his words, or in those of any other man, I might unwillingly or unconsciously become an imitator. (At that age one is so malleable, so prone to admire everything!)" (*Fam.* XXI. 15, pp. 178–79). Thus even while he carefully explains why he could never hate or envy Dante, the Petrarch of this letter is busy with primal defensive texturing, minimizing Dante's achievements and setting himself at a distance, clearly apart, lest he be immersed, shaped, overborne by a contemporary literary presence.

Perhaps the same defensive patterns inform Petrarch's tendency to avoid close or intimate associations, as well as fixed duties or responsibilities. As Bergin says, "with an art more instinctive than calculated, he managed to keep himself ultimately uncommitted." For example, when he was offered a Papal secretaryship in Avignon, he contrived to disqualify himself.[5] He believed that his own father had been prevented from rising "high in the scholarly world" by the burdens of a job and family (*Sen.* XVI. 1, p. 292), and perhaps in consequence he avoided both; yet he also claims that his ability to reject long hopes—a "natural weakness, or natural soundness"—has saved him "from marriage and from others of life's troubles" (*Fam.* XXIV. 1, p. 201). One leaves, perhaps, before one can be either engulfed or abandoned. And the Petrarch of the letters refuses not only job and family but also a permanent home: he keeps up his travels and changes residence almost incessantly, never becoming definitively "at home," not even in his favorite Vaucluse. He will not belong to a community of close friends, although he several times professes his desire to do so, as when he writes to Guido Sette, "You must know that I never look at pleasant places without recalling my own country home and the friends with whom, God willing, I should most gladly pass there the remnants of my brief life" (*Fam.* XVII. 5, p. 152). He will not choose any city, such as Florence, upon which he might have some claim as "home." His life has often been called a "voluntary exile," and contrasted with Dante's involuntary exile. He cannot explain his "wanderings," which bring him by his own account more trouble than profit, except to say: "If I should be asked why then I do not stand still, I can only respond . . . I don't know why" (*Sen.* IX. 2, p. 260). Perhaps this continual interchange, along with the yearning for the solitary life, helps to preserve the circumference of the self: one keeps home and friends at a safer distance this way, and all evocations of dangerous Source in balance. When Petrarch invites a friend to live with him, he assures him, as he would probably himself like to be assured: "Don't think I am proposing to shackle you, or that you would be confined to a single house" (*Fam.* VIII. 5, p. 71).

The letters may provide a clarifying context, then, for the defensive texturing of the *Canzoniere*, where *Poet* and *Lover* join to distance all intact human presences from the words. After that "primiero assalto" (first assault, 2), Laura is dramatized only as a vanishing presence, so that the Poet-Lover seldom risks encountering her; moreover, few other whole presences—such as, for instance, the consoling ladies of Dante's "Donna pietosa"—are summoned by these poems. Only the distant invocations of apostrophe really belong to these lyrics; even substantial personifications, such as Glory (119) or Reason (360), are exceptional here. Safe from presencing or represencing events, the Poet-Lover can reflect upon his elusive *l'aura*. As Budel says of this distance willingly sought, "in the final analysis, he did not want what he seemed to want."[6] As he wanders "Solo e pensoso" in "i più deserti campi" (Alone and filled with care . . . [in] the most deserted fields, 35), he resembles the Poet-Lover of Arnaut's "En cest sonet," intent to create himself "en desert" (see above, Chap. 3). For at this perpetual distance, he seems to invoke Laura's *absent presence* almost at will, while the landscapes (unlike Dante's) yield their inherent significance to serve as a backdrop for his well-controlled intimations of Source:

> Ove porge ombra un pino alto od un colle
> talor m'arresto, et pur nel primo sasso
> disegno co la mente il suo bel viso.
>
> [129. 27–29]

(Where a tall pine or a hillside extends shade, there I sometimes stop, and in the first stone I see I portray her lovely face with my mind.)

Because she is not there, he can take charge almost entirely of her image, its appearance and disappearance: he "designs" her. And he nourishes himself with this kind of "error," keeps himself symbiotically alive through this *absent presence* he has worked through distancing to create (129. 37–39; 127. 102–6). Perhaps such brief but distinctive metaphors of fusion, *Lover* with *Poet*, are enabled by the defensive distancing.

For he will distance her in time as well as in space. He envisions a future "benedetto giorno" (blessed day, 126. 31) when she would weep at his graveside, and he ranges "ne la memoria" (in memory, 41) to design a spellbinding image:

> Così carco d'oblio
> il divin portamento
> e 'l volto e le parole e 'l dolce riso
>   m'aveano, et sì diviso
> da l'imagine vera,
> ch' i' dicea sospirando:
> "Qui come venn' io o quando?"
> credendo esser in ciel, non là dov' era.
>
> [126. 56–63]

(Her divine bearing and her face and her words and her sweet smile had so laden me with forgetfulness
   and so divided me from the true image, that I was sighing: "How did I come here and when?" thinking I was in Heaven, not there where I was.)

Here again is the language of fusion: Poet-Lover and poem seem almost to disappear into a carefully removed, imaged Presence. He creates his own trance, fixing and directing his memory until it can "mirar lei et obliar me stesso" (look at her and forget myself, 129. 35). Even so, it is a self-conscious trance, where the Poet-Lover in "obsessive" memory[7] still circumscribes and measures his own self-forgetfulness. These textures of fusion are well guarded.

Perhaps the Poet-Lover of the *Canzoniere* even tries to appropriate Laura's death for his own defensive purposes, another act of distancing. His efforts have perhaps caused some readers to believe (probably erroneously) that when Petrarch noted Laura's death in the margin of his Virgil, he was simply tailoring a fiction. After all, when Laura has been removed by death, the Poet-Lover can be even surer of her image. He can summon her presence closer now in the poetry: Laura *in morte,* more than *in vita,* will console, advise, linger a while, and even profess her love. Of course, she is never by any means so direct and immediate a presence as Beatrice. But still, the poems continue to grow in the space cleared by her death: just as the Poet-Lover can *in vita* design her face against a tree or rock, he can mourn both bitterly and sweetly in the landscape that she has abandoned forever:

> et quanto in più selvaggio
> loco mi trovo e 'n più deserto lido,
> tanto più bella il mio pensier l'adombra.
> [129. 46-48]

(and in whatever wildest place and most deserted shore I find myself, so much the more beautiful does my thought shadow her forth.)

In the letters, Petrarch writes to "Socrates" of his reaction to the news that two of his friends have been murdered by brigands: "I feel something fatal, horrible, and yet pleasurable to my mind. Assuredly there is a certain sweetness in mourning . . ." (*Fam.* VIII. 9, p. 76). He was planning to spend the rest of his life with these friends, he says, living together in a single house; but now that they are removed, he will "feed and torture" himself with mourning. And so the Poet-Lover of the *Canzoniere* continues for many years to call Laura's name, for the most part unrewarded—and unencumbered—by her answers. Thus in this defensive texturing *Poet* rises in significance over *Lover,* as words born in solitude and memory come to seem more important than the longing for the present lady.

II

l'auro

Even while *Poet* and *Lover* move to distance whole presences, and especially to hold Laura removed in time and space, they move also to bring worded parts of Laura's presence into the body of the poem. It is as though a sensed untrustworthy Source—too near and too far, engulfing and abandoning— provokes these complementary defensive efforts to draw away from the whole and yet possess the parts. The poems seem to incorporate concrete fragments of Source, worded "part objects" of the unwordable "ideal object," with items taken from Laura and her surroundings. The Poet-Lover works to have her in his own terms, so to speak, to control the poem's genesis by devouring and holding *absent presence* in words that can neither engulf nor abandon the body of the poem. *Poet* and *Lover* join in synecdoche, metonymy, symbol or emblem, and phonic texturing to gather these nourishing fragments.

Any simple, whole, direct representations of Laura as *donna* are soon lost beneath the loving enumerations of her separate beauties, her *belle membra,* her attributes. Most frequent in this collection are her eyes (*begli occhi*), her face (*bel viso*), and her blonde hair (*chiome bionde* or *capei d'oro*); but the poems linger also over her arms (*braccia*), side (*fianco*), feet (*piede*), limbs (*membra*), cheeks (*guancie*), even her hands and fingers, "bella man" and "diti schietti soavi" (199). Cherished parts seem indispensable to these poems: synecdochic presences become habitual substitutes for whole presences, and part-objects are as insistently desired as Source. "Each part of her has the significance of her entire person."[8] In Petrarchan texturing, the distanced whole and the appropriated parts together seem to allow that solid imagination of fusion upon which the self must spin; they provide the equivalent of Dantean "presencing" to define and direct these lyrics. For this Poet-Lover, however long he continues, never can continue long *in vita* or *in morte* without returning to the naming of parts; even the Virgin Mary is praised for her "belli occhi" (366. 22).

The spectrum between synecdoche and metonymy in these poems is a long and full one, so that fragments of Laura accumulate here as in a dream-work to displace the affective charge of her presence among a rich panorama of cathected items, part-presences. She is a glance, a smile, a bearing, sweet whispers, words, angelic singing, an inventory of "mortal bellezza, atti et parole" (mortal beauty, acts, and words, 366. 85). She is a veil, a gown, a white glove; she is *l'auro*, the gold that binds her hair, as well as *l'aura*, the breeze that plays with her hair—even the paronomasia is metonymic. For she is here through whatever she touches, through any reality once contiguous: she becomes her footprints upon the grass, as the "sì bel piede" (so beautiful a foot) becomes "be' vestigi sparsi" (lovely footprints, 125. 53, 60); she can be known only through "quest' erba sì" (this grass, 126. 65). Time is ignored by this contiguity—as when in the *Trionfo dell'Eternità* the speaker exclaims, Happy is the stone that covers her fair face! This touching need not even be quite physical, for she becomes the quality of the air through which her glance has penetrated:

> Ovunque gli occhi volgo
> trovo un dolce sereno
> pensando: "Qui percosse il vago lume."
> [125. 66–68]

(Wherever I turn my eyes, I find a sweet brightness, thinking: "Here fell the bright light of her eyes.")

This Poet-Lover also manages to turn the moment of the original meeting into an enumeration of time and space, as items *near* Laura which he can savor one by one: the hour, the instant, the countryside, the place . . . (61). And of course, metonymy in this texture can move almost imperceptibly toward symbol, when

Laura becomes also the parts of the natural landscape that call her to mind. Mountain by mountain, with water, grass, cloud, rock, the naming of parts continues, though displaced from her body: "in tante parti et sì bella la veggio" (in so many places and so beautiful I see her, 129. 38). The Poet-Lover in "Chiare fresche et dolci acque" (126) summons a gently melancholy sequence, part for part: *acque* (waters) for *membra* (limbs), *gentil ramo* (gentle branch) for *bel fianco* (lovely side), *erba et fior* (grass and flowers) for *gonna* (garment) and *seno* (breast), *aere sacro sereno* (sacred bright air) for those *begli occhi*. It seems as though this list can never be completed, can never constitute a whole. And even when the Poet-Lover designs the final vignette of Laura here, to move himself toward his own trance, the poem still holds her only through parts, through lovely branches, falling flowers, blonde braids like burnished gold and pearls. This kind of effort to make her present brings her there only in treasured synecdoche, metonymy, symbol, *l'auro:* the whole has been scattered into *rime sparse*.

With this texturing of Laura as part-Presence, metaphor is usually not the language of fusion, the inspired evocation of wordless Source—as metaphor can be in the texts of Daniel or Dante. Instead, metaphor and symbol and emblem here often seem merely to extend the uses of synecdoche and metonymy: unsignifiable presences are regularly assumed to become solid objects rendered by concrete, recurring words, *cose in rima*. The reader comes to expect metamorphosis by metonymy; the lady under a green laurel becomes virtually a lady-*lauro*, and the weeping Poet-Lover becomes the stone upon which he sits. In appropriated parts of Ovid, the Poet-Lover becomes a laurel, a swan, a stone, a fountain of tears, a voice, a stag like Acteon (23); emblems of Laura's death, in the corresponding canzone *in morte*, include a deer, a ship, a laurel, a phoenix, a fountain, and a lady like Eurydice (323). For these poems work to transform presences, and ultimately to transform Source, into emblems, into words. All presences, and infinite Presence, are presumed there by contiguity, all but *in* the word, in this closely metonymic texture; it is a kind of verbal metamorphosis. And the Daphne myth suits this defensive texture well: in the tree, the fleeing lady is both forever distanced and yet still entirely available. For in these poems *words* or *parts* of the laurel can be brought close, appropriated by synecdoche: *fronde, rami, legno, scorza, ombra* (leaves, branches, wood, bark, shade). Thus the laurel as metonymic symbol yields in turn its own nourishing parts. Like Apollo, this Poet-Lover can take those "sacra fronde" (holy leaves, 34) to himself, or receive the laurel garland from Glory, and thus he guards himself against untrustworthy Source. He can distance *l'aura* while he yet assimilates *l'auro*, valued part-presences. Perhaps in this way also *l'ombra*, always on the verge of disappearance or dispersion, can be held in words as a reality almost tangible, sweet and sensual, to feed and generate these poems as selves.

> seguirò l'ombra di quel dolce lauro
> [30. 16]

(I shall follow the shadow of that sweet laurel)

> Poi quando il vero sgombra
> quel dolce error ...
> [129. 49-50]

(Then, when the truth dispels that sweet deception ...)

> L'arbor gentil che forte amai molt'anni
> (mentre i bei rami non m'ebber a sdegno)
> fiorir faceva il mio debile ingegno
> a la sua ombra ...
> [60]

(The noble tree that I have strongly loved for many years, while its lovely branches did not disdain me, made my weak wit flower in its shade ...)

The metonymic use of *ombra* can belong in these poems to suggestions of sexual union, as when the end-words of the sestina "Non à tanti animali" (237) seem to be repeated and savored as dark, delectable part-objects: *piaggia, notte, luna, sera, onde, boschi* (rain, night, moon, evening, waves, woods.) For *ombra* is often gathered into the poems with night and evening, in sensual dream-wish: when the Poet-Lover sees the stars "dopo notturna pioggia" (after nocturnal rain), he remembers her eyes "quali io gli vidi a l'ombra d'un bel velo" (such as I saw them in the shadow of a lovely veil, 127. 57, 62).

Through repeating and savoring, *Poet* and *Lover* also join to bring Laura's presence into the poem phonically, so that sounds work as part-presences. In the *Secretum* "Augustine" accuses "Petrarch" of being in love with Laura's *name,* and even apart from the multifold paronomasia, the naming of Laura seems itself satisfying, an activity to be relished: "L'aura che 'l verde lauro et l'aureo crine / soavemente sospirando move" (246). Sometimes in his lists of cherished parts the Poet-Lover seems to include this very naming, "qualche dolce mio detto" (some sweet saying of mine, 70. 17), as when he adds to a catalogue of natural beauties "dir d'amore in stili alti et ornati" (poems of love in high and ornate style) and "dolce cantare oneste donne et belle" (sweet singing of virtuous and beautiful ladies, 312), or as when he blesses, along with all the "parts" of their first meeting, "le voci tante" (the many words) that he has scattered in calling her name (61). Her sweet presence seems almost to be ritualistically incorporated, ingested again and again with liquid consonants and open-throated vowels: *l'aura, lauro, l'ombra, l'ambra, l'aureo, l'aurora, l'oro, l'auro, laureta.* Or the words themselves can become her hair, spread with the *l*'s and *s*'s into delicate, enticing strands:

> L'aura soave al sole spiega et vibra
> l'auro ch' Amor di sua man fila et tesse;
> là da' belli occhi et de le chiome stesse
> lega 'l cor lasso e i lievi spirti cribra.
> [198]

(The soft breeze spreads and waves in the sun the gold that Love spins and weaves with his own hands; there with her lovely eyes and with those very locks he binds my weary heart and winnows my light spirits.)

In the course of this sonnet he takes her presence into his marrow and blood, while his mind reels with the sweetness, "di tanto dolcezza," that has been swallowed with the words—*as* the words, perhaps—into the poem. These are words more than *pexa,* for the very syllables seem delectable: whereas in "Ne li occhi" the words seem to efface themselves before that nameless *donna*, in Petrarch's poems the words themselves become substantial, upstaging the whole human presence. The words themselves attract and overwhelm: "'l dir m'infiamma e pugne...mi struggo al suon de le parole" (speaking inflames me and pricks me on... I melt in the sound of the words, 73. 10–14). The words seem not to let the light of Presence through, but to rest in themselves.

Thus *Poet* and *Lover* join in paronomasia, synecdoche, metonymy, symbol, emblem, and phonic texturing to assimilate nourishing part-presences, worded fragments of Laura's presence, into the Poet-Lover or poem as equivalent self. These part-presences effectively serve as that "image of the lady" which, as Robert Durling points out in his reading of "Giovene donna" (30), seems to become more rigid and more metallic as the Petrarchan lover meditates upon it; these metonymic part-presences, rather than the whole Presence, provide in Petrarchan texture the Aristotelian internalized phantasm of the lady, the impression stamped upon the wax of the lover's soul. The image of the lady hardens into "l'idolo mio scolpito in vivo lauro" (my idol carved in living laurel, 30. 27) because the *parts* so harden, as Durling points out—the branches diamond, the hair gold, the eyes topaz. Furthermore, we might ask exactly *how* the Poet-Lover's "psychological fixation"[9] upon these internalized, imagined parts brings about their hardening, for "hard" images are curiously textured in the *Canzoniere*. Not only is the lady hard, "lei che come un ghiaccio stassi" (she ... who now stands like ice, 125. 11), leaving an unanswered flame within him, but he also is hard as though in response:

> e d'intorno al mio cor pensier gelati
> fatto avean quasi adamantino smalto
> [23. 24–25]

(and around my heart frozen thoughts had made almost an adamantine hardness)

He seems to absorb, ingest, take on her hardness: here are Medusa and victim, of course, or in psycho-ontological terms here is a darker version of that original scene of infant spell-casting (see above, Chap. 1)—unyielding Source becomes frozen self. For Source, however fatally hard, still must be taken in to the vital center of self; we recall the combined responses of mimesis and revenge in Dante's *petrose*. Thus "hard" or "concrete" images come to suggest not only her Medusa gaze, rejecting and petrifying him (197), but also his response in kind, inevitably mimetic of her or joined to her somehow: he is "hard" because he is ice or marble or stone; but his need for her is also unyielding, as when Time binds him in the "più saldi nodi" (tighter knots, 196) of her hair, or when "il giogo et le catene e i ceppi" (the yoke and the chains and the shackles, 89) entrap him, oppress him. For these chains are also treasures, and belong by metonymy to those cherished parts of Source that the poems so eagerly incorporate, those diamond branches, that "oro forbito e perle" (burnished gold and pearls, 126. 48). By this route the Poet-Lover also becomes "hard" in the strength with which he holds these part-presences, and that hardness becomes displaced upon the parts themselves: her name becomes as solid as marble (104). All these associations of "hard" images, and more, are involved with the Poet-Lover's "fixation" as he contemplates the part-images of the lady. She becomes a part-presence both concrete and vital, "hard" both in her treatment of him and in his intense appropriation of her: "questa viva petra" (this living stone, 50. 78). And he is "pietra morta in pietra viva" (a dead stone on the living rock, 129. 51), in the semblance of a man who thinks and weeps and writes; he takes on her fatal hardness in mimetic response, clinging to her for life even as she deprives him of life. It is as though at his central being, at the primary term of the metaphor here, he is "pietra," like her.

Thus in these complex senses, the Poet-Lover's "contemplation," his motion toward Source, works to harden the part-images of the beloved. Moreover, *Poet* and *Lover* move defensively in these words toward yet another kind of "hardening." For one might describe the vocabulary of the *Canzoniere,* made of small groups of frequently recurring words, as "hard"—refined, restricted, well fixed. The Poet-Lover's metonymic tenacity affects not only the worded fragments of Laura's presence but also the words for his own suffering: *pensieri, sospiri, dolor, occhi molli, danni, giogo, vita acerba* (thoughts, sighs, grief, soft eyes, pain, yoke, bitter life). He seems to hold to limited sets of words, with little variation: this is hardly a *vario stile* in vocabulary. In a way the repetitive vocabulary seems almost to encrust these poems with the conventional, the familiar—so that an unusual image would seem intrusive. Bergin notes that the imagery of these poems is "personal," not remaining distinct or "objective" or sharply visual, like Dante's imagery; rather, "with Petrarch the image is absorbed and devoured, and it is precisely this emotional solidarity that the poet seeks."[10] Through images made ever more familiar, both Laura and Poet-Lover become constant, possessed in "solidarity." And when in some poems the metonymic vocabulary becomes both substance and audience, as in "Chiare, fresche et dolci acque" (126), the "solidarity" between Poet-Lover and image becomes all the more intense. Poet-Lover becomes a being-in-words defensively, with a vengeance. For in these poems *Poet* and *Lover* do not move in *infans* receptivity, open to the wordless influence of Laura or other whole human presences. In Dante's poems the path to Source, ultimate "fulgore," is clear despite all *orribile lingue,* so that the language is cosmically diverse, but there is little such "negative capability" in Petrarch's poems. It is as though in Petrarchan texture Source had become treacherous, perhaps both too far and too near, so that individual words are not free to roam and generate worded differences; rather, words seem almost to be circumscribed, taken as part-presences, repeatedly devoured. Through this kind of rigidity, worded part-presences are firmly held, as though in place of a central *absent presence,* and again *Poet* comes to seem more important than *Lover.*

Even the religious language of the *Canzoniere* does not usually work as the metaphoric language of fusion, but is instead textured with this fixed vocabulary. For usually in the repentance sequences the words themselves remain constant while the references shift from secular to Christian,[11] so that even as the Poet-Lover professes change he is holding stubbornly to the language, the words resisting almost all diversity: the unusual "croce" or "miserere" (62) in such instances becomes the exception that proves the rule. And more generally, the very repetition of certain clusters of religious terms establishes them as part of the "hardened," carefully possessed vocabulary: *salute, benedetto, beata, miracolo, meraviglia, paradiso, divina* (salvation, holy, blessed, miracle, wonder, paradise, divine). And through further allusions, Christian ceremony and ritual are appropriated, and the "commune dolor" (universal woe) brought to the service of "miei quai" (my misfortunes), in religious terms that are savored as insistently as any others (3). These terms can fill out items of synecdoche, as when her voice is "chiara, soave, angelica, divina" (clear, soft, angelic, divine, 167). They can consecrate metonymic presences:

> Qual miracolo è quel, quando tra l'erba
> quasi un fior siede.
> [160]

(What a miracle it is, when on the grass she sits like a flower!)

> Benedetto sia 'l giorno e 'l mese et l'anno
> [61]

(Blessed be the day and the month and the year...)

But even when these poems approach the language of fusion, as when the Poet-Lover exclaims, "Costei per fermo nacque in paradiso!" (She was surely born in Paradise! 126. 55), the "blessing" of the Christian words does not seem to enable the words to reach past themselves. The religious terms are, instead, included with the hair, the pearls, the grass, the flowers, the voice—with the treasured metonymic parts, so worded and so named, signifiers as Signified, *Poet* over *Lover*.

III

> guerra è 'l mio stato
> [164]

(war is my state)

Thus in Petrarchan texturing, whole presences are distanced while part-presences are hoarded in words. *Poet* and *Lover* move together in these complementary defenses, and in their difficulties the individuating *Poet* emerges; the poem, as a being-in-words, rises to distinction. But there is still further defensive texturing in these poems—intricate *amant martyr* representations through which the distinctive Petrarchan "voice" emerges even more clearly. Here *Poet* and *Lover* move in continuing, subtle displacements to deflect negative impulses from the problematic Source of the poems; by contrast, in Dante's works with their secure presencing events, primal rages seem to be diverted simply, as with a single clean stroke, to the walled compartments of the *petrose* and the *Inferno*.

Thus in the *Canzoniere* aggression appears displaced or transmuted into that wearying and interminable sorrow, *dolore, pena,* that will mark the Petrarchan lover through several generations of love poetry. In his use of Ovid, this Poet-Lover does not include Daphne's sexual fear, and he does not follow the story of Acteon through to his dismemberment:[12] in these poems, one turns from rage and passion, in painful flight. Of course, he is reluctant to rail at the beloved;[13] what is more, he slights the representations of Laura as "cruel," and instead turns his attentions to his own afflicted image, *amant martyr.* For in this verbal texture, the presences and personifications that always wound the speaker seem perhaps less important than the pain of the blows:

> Voglia mi sprona, Amor mi guida et scorge,
> Piacer mi tira, Usanza mi trasporta;
>
> [211]

(Desire spurs me, Love guides and escorts me, Pleasure draws me, Habit carries me away;)

Here and elsewhere, as in the canzone "I' vo pensando" (264), the active, angry verbs become the speaker's continuing pain, passively endured. Potential rage or invective is turned away from Laura as Source, and becomes woven into the vocabulary of his martyrdom: *martiri, sospiri, piaghe, mal, duol, pena, dolore, affanno, danno, tristi, duri, miseri, amare, paura, sconsolato, dispietata.* That is, war becomes this Poet-Lover's state of being, and he can thereby avoid actively waging war.

Thus as *amant martyr,* this Poet-Lover turns against himself centrally, from the beginning of the sequence, to emphasize his swift and lasting departure in time from Laura's presence. Unlike Dante's speaker, he does not linger in the universal moment of presencing; he moves immediately *de via,* away from that briefly invoked "luogo e tempo" (time and place, 2) to reflection upon the moment, and within a very few poems this moment must be called upon from the past. In this way he avoids making Laura's cruelty the target of his invective. For it is Time that here becomes cruel and implacable, that carries the ever-vanishing Source of these poems all the more surely away. And indeed, Time in its merciless turning, *volgendo,* could eventually scatter that first moment entirely:

> Quand' io mi volgo indietro a mirar gli anni
> ch' ànno fuggendo i miei penseri sparsi,
> et spento 'l foco ove agghiacciando io arsi,
> [298]

(When I turn back to gaze at the years that fleeing have scattered all my thoughts, and put out the fire where I freezing burned . . .)

Time, as the agent of the Poet-Lover's martyrdom, renders him helpless, himself absorbing the possible anger toward the elusive beloved, and thus guarding that problematic Source from aggression. For not only does he typically receive the weight of the transitive verbs: even more frequently, the intransitive verbs governed by the speaker seem to have absorbed the wearing of time: "piango et ragiono" (I weep and speak, 1), "vegghio, penso, ardo, piango" (I am awake, I think, I burn, I weep, 164), "vo mesurando" (I go measuring, 35), "I' vo pensando" (I go thinking, 264. 1), "Là 've cantando andai di te molt'anni / or, come vedi, vo di te piangendo" (Where I went singing of you many years, now, as you see, I go weeping for you, 282).[14] In these present tenses and present gerunds, the entropic force of time acts upon him: these are verbs of habitual endurance, always bearing the implicit threat of full dissolution and absence. With these verbs, time takes the speaker ever further from that first moment, and the painful moments of increasing distance are stretched out as though upon a rack of time. He addresses Laura in one of the earlier poems:

> ... i' vi discovrirò de' miei martiri
> qua' sono stati gli anni, e i giorni, et l'ore;
> [12]

(I shall disclose to you what have been the years and the days and the hours of my sufferings;)

For moments are the elements of his martyrdom—in the recurring present tenses, a war of attrition continues to be his present state.

There are some momentary truces in this war, of course. Several defenses appear to cancel each other: even while time threatens to dissolve the memory of Laura's presence, the defensive distancing allows the Poet-Lover to re-create, elaborate, even improve that memory in moments of *pace*. There is such "breve conforto" (brief solace, 14) in the solitude canzoni, and also when Laura returns *in morte*. In these cases his endurance seems almost to have earned a renewal, a recovery of presencing, for she appears unmarked by time, "qual io la vidi in su l'età fiorita" ("just as I saw her in her flowering, 336), and the visions bring him "pace" (126. 55), "soccorso" (help, 283), "tregua" (a truce, 285). But these truces are also subject to time, and indeed time will remove these peaceful illusions:

> ... se l'error durasse, altro non cheggio.
> [129. 39]

(... if the deception should last, I ask for no more.)

> i' come uom ch' erra et poi più dritto estima
> dico a la mente mia: "Tu se' 'ngannata. . . ."
> [336]

(I, like one who errs and then esteems more justly, say to my mind: "You are deceived. . . .")

Eventually these poems always turn time back against themselves: the cherished memories, like the original moment, yield to the sweep of time. Dante's *Commedia* moves steadily toward definitive represencing, but Petrarch's *Canzoniere* is carried away from all represencing scenes. Even though Petrarch in his daily routine fought time like Rabelais' Gargantua, reading while he shaved or ate, and writing in the middle of the night (*Fam.* XXI. 12, pp. 174–75), he still could acknowledge to Guido Sette, "there is no standing still for man here below; there is nothing but continual flow and down-slipping and at the end the collapse of all" (*Fam.* XIX. 16, p. 161). "La vita fugge et non s'arresta un'ora" (Life flees and does not stop an hour, 272). There is really no contest in time's war against the self. Time wears away the Poet-Lover, continues to dissolve presencing and represencing scenes: the laurels become oaks and elms (363), and the *morte* poems reiterate their own fatigue: "Omai son stanco" (Now I am weary, 364). The vaunted moral or religious progress must at best coexist with time's war against all central meaning for this self-in-words. The verbs here appear to have absorbed the rages of primal separation, so that Time in ongoing present tenses keeps drawing the poems toward their own Void, their own unpresenced final appeals.

Moreover, in the *amant martyr* texturing of these poems, it is not only Time that is turned against the self. The very moment of Presence, such as it is, is turned against the self also, in the elaborated pain of the experience and the memory. In this way also, the Poet-Lover exists in a state of war from the first few sonnets, with the military language of the enamorment as "'l colpo mortal" (the fatal blow) or "primiero assalto" (the first assault, 2) or the time "quando i' fui preso" (when I was taken, 3). Thus far we have only an echo of some of the textures, perhaps, of Dante or Cavalcanti; but Petrarch's Poet-Lover continues insistently to turn the violence of these metaphors upon himself, appropriating the language of *colpo, piaghe, giogo, ancide, pena,* and taking these words of the pain, as it were, to the heart of the poems. He becomes inseparable from this pain. In this way he manages usually, though certainly not always, to deflect his rage from Laura; it is the moment, the day, the experience that is cruel, "crudo" (298), and not her. But there may be also a *causa sui* wish defensively textured in this continuing self-affliction. Especially if Source is felt to be untrustworthy—engulfing or abandoning (or both)—the self moves in defense to take charge of, to "write," its own conflicted presencing scene. Thus the self intensifies and receives its own rage toward a Source "too near" or "too far," and perhaps thereby comes to earn a remembered sweetness; the self can design its own nourishing scene of Presence, its own conflated suffering and reward. Indeed, in the *Canzoniere* that first moment is not really *dolce;* its sweetness is largely conjured by memory, as though partly in response to the emphatic pain.

Perhaps other defenses are involved here, too. But in any case, surely the complex, defensive representations of the enamorment serve to establish and focus the oxymoronic texture of the *Canzoniere*.[15] For that first "blow" sets up a radical ambivalence that lasts throughout the sequence, so that no luminous meeting in the light of the lamp, no pure drinking of *spiriti* with the eyes, is ever quite possible in this texture. Evocations of that first moment are virtually always conflicted, scrupulously including pain; the memory can burden him as well as give him rest. Time renews "le prime piaghe sì dolci profonde" (the first deep sweet wounds, 196); the speaker will bless his wounds (61); anniversaries recall a "per me sempre dolce Giorno et crudo" (Day to me always sweet and cruel, 298), a "dolce amaro / colpo" (sweet bitter blow, 296). And this central ambivalence underlies the rich ambivalences of the sequence, where *Poet* and *Lover* move together in the oxymorons, antitheses, and paradoxes—the pain with the joy, the bitter with the sweet—that have come to mark the poetry as "Petrarchan." The love that ensnares him is "l'onesta pregion" (the worthy prison, 296), both a promise and a threat: "Amor, con quanto sforzo oggi mi vince!" (Love, with what power today you vanquish me! 85). For in this oxymoronic texturing, the state of war continues. Laura's eyes can emanate a sweet and nourishing light that keeps him alive (71. 76–82), but they can also dazzle or burn him, or wound him (195), or turn his heart to marble (197). Laura makes him feel "dolcezze amare et empie" (sweetness . . . bitter and cruel, 210), and one can "take in" her presence only through paradox:

> Così sol d'una chiara fonte viva
> move 'l dolce et l'amaro ond' io mi pasco.
> [164]

(Thus from one clear living fountain alone spring the sweet and the bitter on which I feed;)

He would die content of "tal piaga" (such a wound) and live in "tal nodo" (such a bond, 296); she brings life and death at once, and death itself is made sustaining, "bel morir" (beautiful death, 278).

Besides these familiar phrases, there are other textures of ambivalence in these poems, also growing from their centrally ambivalent moment. For even "dolce ne la memoria," the interludes of *pace* are so slight that they are virtually oxymoronic, disappearing almost at once back into the prevailing *guerra*. Paradoxically, even these sustaining memories need expression in negative language:

> Da indi in qua mi piace
> quest'erba sì ch'altrove non ò pace.
>
> [126. 64-65]

(From then on this grass has pleased me so that elsewhere I have no peace.)

> pur mentr' io veggio lei, nulla mi noce.
>
> [284]

(As long as I see her, nothing pains me.)

> né trovo in questa vita altro soccorso;
>
> [283]

(Nor do I find any other help in this life.)

After all, "dolce giogo" (sweet yoke) is a characteristic oxymoron for his memory itself; his heart is nourished by sighs (1). And of course, the central ambivalence will at times seem to govern the very construction of the sonnets, binding sonnet divisions that would separately express "dolce" or "amaro"; often the Petrarchan *volta* between octave and sestet seems to be thus formulated. And there are other variations: in one *morte* sonnet, for example, the first eleven lines savor Vaucluse in its natural beauty, while the last tercet knows the grief of Laura's death (303). More broadly, the ambivalence informs the alternating hope and despair in the *morte* poems: now he is dazzled by Laura's return as a vision, radiant yet familiar (282; 284); and now he despairs of writing when he realizes that her *belle membra* are all "poca polvere . . . che nulla sente" (a bit of dust that feels nothing, 292). And of course, the periodic and final poems of repentance add an overriding ambivalence. Now he blesses that first moment (61), and now he rejects it, a "dispietato giogo" (pitiless yoke) no longer sweet (62). Reinforced by the *Secretum,* this has been the ambivalence most striking to readers of Petrarch's works. Recently, Aldo Bernardo speaks of the "irreconcilability of Petrarch's haunting polarities," his vacillation between Laura as "myth" and Laura as "living Christian witness."[16] It is as though the Poet-Lover wishes to write a new Source for himself, when he senses that the presencing event he has helped to design is inadequate, after all, and finite.

Thus *Poet* rises to prominence in these *amant martyr* representations, in which both Time and the "premiero assalto" are turned against the Poet-Lover. For these poems are *defined* as *rime sparse* partly by their war with Time. The speaker is adamant about including the weight, the pain, the dissolution that Time brings. "Cure me, and I shall be stronger, but my bed will be no smoother and softer" (*Fam.* XV. 4, p. 135). After all, the motions of *Poet* are served through this defensive texturing, for this Poet-Lover "chi pianse sempre" (who weeps eternally) finds immortality among the blessed precisely through his unending pain, his ongoing passive defeat before Time.[17] By suffering endlessly, he gains endless distinction. Moreover, the oxymoronic texture, established perhaps by that first ambivalent moment, works even further to individuate the Petrarchan "voice." For the tropes of antithesis, oxymoron, and paradox are perhaps those most clearly visible to Petrarch's long line of imitators.[18] We can see the introduction of this texture even in the first sonnet: the Poet-Lover names his own style as the "vario stile in ch'io piango et ragiono / fra le vane speranze e 'l van dolore" (varied style in which I weep and speak between vain hopes and vain sorrow). There are many ways of interpreting the stylistic variety of the *Canzoniere,* of course. But on the most basic level, "vario" is defined by these very lines, as ranging between hope and despair.[19] In this sense the self is "varied," or endlessly vacillating, between the polarities of the oxymorons and antitheses, with no further range or progress possible: "né per mille rivolte ancor son mosso" (nor for a thousand turnings about have I yet moved, 118). And the "van" of the first sonnet surely gestures toward that ultimate defensive ambivalence, rejecting that original moment entirely. For even the interludes of repentance, along with those intermittent protestations of moral progress and those late evocations of Dantean *luce*,[20] can be read in the contexts of this vacillation. The path here is almost always "rivolte," not Dante's steady journeying. This self is less centrally secure than the Gherardo who proceeds straight to the top of Mont Ventoux; but for that very reason, the wandering route of "error," more fully informed by *Poet,* makes this self more distinctive. Thus John Freccero can speak of "real literary strength from fictionalized moral flaws."[21] And thus Petrarch can almost proudly apply to himself a sentence from one of Plautus' plays: "'I beat everybody in torturability of soul'" (*Fam.* IX. 4, p. 83).

There are other strengths for *Poet* in this antithetical texturing. For through the established habits of oxymorons, antitheses, paradoxes, and contradictions, these beings-in-words become self-generating, in a sense inexhaustible. Through these devices the language comes to feed on its own negations: there must be a pain counterpoint to every pleasure, and each antithetical pair seems to breed further pairs. The sequences of paradoxes (132; 134) gather energy as they continue, as though they could go on forever; they are brought only arbitrarily and temporarily to a graceful close, "In questo stato son, Donna, per vui" (In this state am I, Lady, on account of you, 134). In this texturing the eternity lost at that ambivalent presencing is reclaimed, in a sense, in the very interminability of the tropes. This Poet-Lover, being-in-words, can resonate between *speranza* and *dolore* essentially forever; these poems are sustained, born a thousand times a day, by their very lack of rest or repose, their incessant deaths. Thus certainly the last sequence of "conversion" poems, or any other announced closure, would seem inherently unsuitable here. But it is fitting that *pace* would be the last word for these warring antitheses.

IV

Benedette le voci tante ch'io
chiamando il nome de mia donna ò sparte,
[61]

(Blessed be the many words I have scattered calling the name of my lady.)

As *Poet* and *Lover* move through these complex defensive textures, the words themselves rise to importance, and the Poet-Lover is clearly distinguished as a being-in-words. *Poet* emerges as a strong individuating motion in the negations and deviations of these defensive verbal devices—the savored parts of metonymy and synecdoche; the intensified, melancholy distancing of whole presences; the unending oxymorons, antitheses, and verbs of endurance. This *Poet* motion, in its unusual pervasiveness and strength, seems in several ways to answer that endemic longing, *Lover infans:* that is, the poems come in large measure to serve as their own Source, to work as "substitute" Source. These poems seem to offer their own worded beings to themselves in the place of unwordable Source, designing themselves in a negative mimesis to possess the qualities *lacked* by the elusive, untrustworthy Source intuited at their center.

Some of these qualities we have seen achieved through the defensive texturing itself, which works with *Poet* to make these poems inexhaustible and self-generating, secure, closely held, unique, full of treasured ideal parts. But the poems also imitate ideal Source through some further texturings where *Poet* and *Lover* cooperate: individually, the poems become unified wholes that are sweetly, musically, coenesthetically nourishing. They may also become timeless, permanent "ideal objects" that are places of infinite repose. In these ways the "ben colto lauro" (well-tended laurel, 30, 36) replaces Laura; the self feeds its own longing; the poems become themselves that wholly present *donna* or Source that they do not receive into their texture. In Kohut's terms, perhaps, secondary narcissism absorbs the charge of primary narcissism, and the poems, with a "constant and conscious egocentricity,"[22] usurp for themselves the place of Source. Thus Freccero is right about the poems' "self-contained dynamism" and "auto-reflexive" thematic,[23] in this sense: these are not *nove rime*, where Source shines through effaced words; rather, these words, in all their opacity and dense music, seem designed to be poetic selves-as-Source.

Petrarch in the letters seems to know that a literary text could work like a maternal presence, arousing and fulfilling expectations at the coenesthetic level of deep sensibility, until the text becomes an integrated and satisfying whole, allowing one to "coenesthetically fantasize" primal identification with Source. For he speaks of his study of Cicero in early childhood:

> At that age I could really understand nothing, but a certain sweetness and sonority so captured me that any other book I read or heard read seemed to me to give off a graceless, discordant sound. I must admit that this was not a very juvenile judgment, if one may call judgment what was not based on reason. But certainly it is remarkable that while I didn't understand anything, I already felt exactly what I feel today, when after all I do understand something, little though it be. That love for Cicero increased day by day, and my father, amazed, encouraged my immature propensity through paternal affection. And I, dodging no labor that might aid my purpose, breaking the rind began to savor the taste of the fruit, and couldn't be restrained from my study. I was ready to forego all other pleasures to seek out everywhere the books of Cicero. [Fam. XVI. 1, pp. 292–93]

Whatever this "certain sweetness and sonority" that marks Cicero as a literary presence, it seems to be more profound than mere "understanding," and more lasting—it seems perhaps to reside even at that "level of deep sensibility" posited by Spitz.[24] Perhaps Petrarch, having thus been rapt with the sweetness of another's wit, sought himself in the *Canzoniere* to devise poems that could likewise be capturing presences; perhaps he refers partly to this captivating sweetness when he insists that he wants any reader, while reading, to be "entirely mine" (*Fam.* XIII. 5, p. 115).[25] But whatever the reason, the poems have a lulling, maternal *sound*. Even while the poems defensively distance whole presences and rigidly possess worded parts, they *sound* sweetly nourishing. To this end, the coherence and affective energy of each individual *Canzoniere* poem inheres in an elaborate, tightly woven "interstitial web" in which logical, causal, and syntactic patterns merge and are overlaid with rhythmic and phonic equivalences. Thus Durling notes that "Giovene donna" (30), with its "sense of balance, cyclical recurrence, and progressive intensification and enlargement," outdoes its predecessor, Dante's "Al poco giorno."[26] Similarly, Bergin points out that

Petrarch, both in syntax and in the stanzaic patterns that seem to flow so easily from syntax, achieved a unity and integrity markedly greater than that of his predecessors who wrote in the medieval pattern of coordinate clauses. For over and above his rhetorical and prosodic virtuosity, Petrarch typically devises a clear statement, straightforward in syntax and diction, "united and musically set forth."[27]

These poems can be aural presences, with a "certain sweetness and sonority" enhanced by the syntactic unity and balance—presences that address *Lover infans* on that primal level explained by Spitz, of "rhythm, tempo, duration, pitch, tone, resonance, clang." And on this aural or phonic level most of the poems are quintessentially sweet, a consoling and nourishing music. One might apply to these poems as constructions of sound the same adjectives that cluster around the *donna* of Dante's *nove rime: soave, piano, umile, dolce.* Or their sound might remind one of Laura in her *morte* visitations, as she speaks "col dolce mormorar pietoso et basso" (with . . . sweet, low, pitying murmur, 286). Granted, in several poems after Laura's death, the Poet-Lover undergoes harsher texturing, *roche rime* (332, 32), for as he explains,

> non posso, et non ò più sì dolce lima,
> rime aspre et fosche far soavi et chiare.
>
> [293]

(I cannot—and I no longer have so sweet a file—make harsh, dark rhymes into sweet, bright ones.)

But the uses of the rougher consonant groups seem to be, on the whole, short-lived; in sound, this highly selective vocabulary resembles Dante's *pexa* words. As in the sweet, incorporative naming of Laura, the resulting aural presence of the poem seems indeed maternal—*soave, chiare, dolce.*

> Chiare fresche et dolci acque . . .
> [126]

> Quel rosigniuol che sì soave piagne . . .
> [311]

Soleano i miei penser soavemente . . .

[295]

Quando io v'odo parlar sì dolcemente . . .

[143]

We come as readers to rest in "confident expectation" of this lulling voice, the voice of poem as substitute Source, and the *music* of the individual poem can serve in a way to override or reward the painful negations and deviations of the defensive texturing, somewhat as the sweetness of the memory rewards the Poet-Lover for suffering its "blows."

> Ma ben veggio or sì come al popol tutto
> favola fui gran tempo, onde sovente
> di me medesmo meco mi vergogno;
>
> et del mio vaneggiar vergogna è 'l frutto,
> e 'l pentersi, e 'l conoscer chiaramente
> che quanto piace al mondo è breve sogno.
>
> [1]

(But now I see well how for a long time I was the talk of the crowd, for which often I am ashamed of myself within; and of my raving, shame is the fruit, and repentance, and the clear knowledge that whatever pleases in the world is a brief dream.)

In this "sweet, low, pitying murmur" of the introductory sonnet, we are told that everything that follows will record only a brief dream, worthy of nothing but shame and repentance. And yet we are enticed to read on even by sound alone—for example, by the dolorous o's and mournful m's of this beautifully weeping voice. For weeping is sweet in the *Canzoniere*, so that sighs, as this first sonnet also tells us, can themselves be nourishing, and the sighs of these poems are indeed easy to "drink in" with the ear. In the margin of his Virgil, Petrarch writes that he records Laura's death with a certain "bitter sweetness,"[28] and when he writes of the death of two good friends, he confesses, "Assuredly there is a certain sweetness in mourning; on this theme I am unhappy enough to feed and torture myself and find pleasure for days at a time" (*Fam.* VIII. 9, p. 76). This is not a simple masochism, here or in the lyrics of the *Canzoniere: Poet* and *Lover* move in defensive textures that convert rage to pain, and then nevertheless, as though in answer to conflicted *Lover infans,* the pain is made sweet, musical. The poems are rocked with their own intonations, fed with their own sweetness, as they revolve alone in time.

These poems themselves become the significant maternal presences, ultimate systems of equivalences rewarding all "confident expectations," and perhaps therefore the poems are less than successful in assembling Laura as a whole presence. For as we have seen, the evocations of Laura *in vita* tend to be lists of her treasured parts, and often the poems *in morte* continue this cataloguing in the *ubi sunt* tradition (282; 292; 299). For the Poet-Lover is not trying, finally, to evoke Laura as Source, unwordable Presence; the presence of Laura is not ultimately the point here, though it may indeed seem to be. The poem is mimetic of ideal Source while it holds Laura distant. For this is a texture of complex verbal defenses, not Dante's texture of primal receptivity. Dante's pilgrim can hold up the very syllables of Beatrice's name, BE and ICE, as diaphanous to the light of Source (see *Par.* vii. 13–15), whereas Petrarch's Poet-Lover seeds his own octave and sestet with the syllables of Laura's name, weaving LAU, RE, and TA into his own carefully formed syntactic unit: "Quando ... poi ... Così ... se non che ... " (5). The tribute to the lady or her name is lost to, or indeed becomes, the word-play itself, the opaque music of syntax and sound.[29] It is his own presence he is assembling from these fragments of her name, just as throughout the lyrics it is his own presence he assembles from all the synecdochic and metonymic parts of Laura. The poem is the distinctive and recognizable presence; Laura remains a shadow, *l'ombra* or *l'aura,* cast by the worded fragments of her.

One wonders whether perhaps this Poet-Lover treats his literary sources in the same way, assimilating them in fragments in order to reconstitute them as himself. He does specify that only a deeply hidden resemblance to the parent literary work should be observable in the child, the successor (*Fam.* XXIII. 19. pp. 198–99); and his oral, incorporative metaphors for this process of making new works from old tend to stress a total assimilation by the new text as self:

...I have read Virgil, Horace, Livy, Cicero, not once but a thousand times, not hastily but in repose, and I have pondered them with all the powers of my mind. I ate in the morning what I would digest in the evening; I swallowed as a boy what I would ruminate upon as a man. These writings I have so thoroughly absorbed and fixed, not only in my memory but in my very marrow, these have become so much a part of myself, that even though I should never read them again they would cling in my spirit.... It has cost me great labor to distinguish my sources. [*Fam.* XXII. 2, pp. 182–83]

Those who read poetry, "sweet to the taste," should feed on it and absorb it, not just "taste the Pierian honey with their tongue's tip" (*Fam.* XIII. 7, p. 120). Sometimes the features of Petrarch's sources seem almost deliberately recognizable, as with the entire quoted lines from predecessors in the love lyric (70), or perhaps more subtly with such Dantean fragments in the *morte* poems as "l'alma, che tanta luce non sostene" (my soul, who cannot bear so much light, 284), or "la mia debile vista" (my weak sight, 339), or "l'occhio interno" (my internal eye, 345), or even "vera beatrice" (366. 52). But usually this Poet-Lover knows how to devour and digest literary presences thoroughly. Thomas Greene demonstrates that Petrarch aims to produce texts that must be deeply sub-read, and Adelia Noferi discusses Petrarch's style as a blending of the styles of Cicero, Augustine, and Seneca.[30]

There is another sense in which these poems take on the qualities of ideal Source—in the continual application of the *lauro* emblem to the poems themselves. In this way, the poems as selves reclaim the eternity so doubtful in that elusive central Source. For as *lauro,* the poems themselves become the desired lady, taking one step further a familiar use of emblems in these poems: "Each of the major emblems for Laura thus at some time or other also stands for the lover, and vice versa."[31]

This mimetic effort is not like the straightforward construction of ideal Source in the poems' music; rather, involved here are several defenses—negations and deviations. For as *lauro,* the poems become the whole presence of the lady forever distanced, and they become thereby an emblem of the Poet-Lover's own unassuageable and ongoing pain. Moreover, by calling them-

selves *lauro* the poems imply that they are evergreen, permanent, even petrified—and they are all the more permanent for
including the "hardness" of the lady, the rejection and the distancing. Those branches are "sempre verdi" (eternally green, 5)
partly because the lady-*lauro* never yields, indeed is immobilized
in her refusal. Eternal desire, as the Gnostics knew, is at least
eternal. In this way the poems as *lauro* become their own treasured part-presences, their own laurel leaves or crown; they
"crown [themselves] with the symbol of [their] defeat."[32] This
sonnet addressed to Apollo even makes for itself a conclusive
laurel crown, in those shading arms:

> sì vedrem poi per meraviglia inseme
> seder la donna nostra sopra l'erba
> et far de la sue braccia a se stessa ombra.
>
> [34]

(Thus we shall then together see a marvel—our lady sitting on the
grass and with her arms making a shade for herself.)

Finally, the poems as *lauro* try to weave into themselves a
receptive future audience, moving further to assure their own
eternity. These efforts, like other defenses here, are not felt as
secure; but at least, in this understanding of *lauro* both self and
Source are intended to live together forever. Petrarch wrote in
an early Latin lament on his mother's death, "Vivimus pariter,
pariter memorabimur ambo."[33] And in the emblem of *lauro,* the
Poet-Lover and Laura are verbally fused: thus in this one
opaque word *Poet* and *Lover* try to accomplish a fusion that they
rarely join to evoke beyond the words. Moreover, the invocation
of a sympathetic public helps to confirm these poems as places of
infinite repose, to bestow *lauro* upon these poems as *lauro.* For
an audience can work as Source (see above, pp. 56–61), whether
it be the masses with their "windy applause" that Petrarch
scorned when Dante earned it, or only a circle of initiate readers
and lovers, such as those invoked for the *Canzoniere.* From the
first "Voi," those textured listening presences allow a chance of
pity and pardon, and they encourage the Poet-Lover's hope: "i'
spero / farmi immortal" (I hope to become immortal, 71. 95–96).
Laura, God, and the Virgin Mary are possible audiences, too,

but they hardly care for the poems as *lauro;* it is with their future readers that the poems make their largest effort, to texture their own "stade du miroir" and reclaim themselves from the void.

V

ma ricogliendo le sue sparte fronde
dietro le vo pur così passo passo,
[333]

(but . . . gathering up her scattered leaves, I still follow after her step by step.)

Thus in the music of single poems, and in the application of the term *lauro*, these poems are made as beings-in-words that resemble ideal Source—to answer *Lover infans*, their own central longing. Nevertheless, as a group the poems remain *rime sparse, rerum vulgarium fragmenta*, as though there is not a strong enough sense of Maternal Source in these texts to integrate them beyond the level of the individual poem. For it is positive maternal affect that organizes the self's ability to organize, and that allows to texts their coherence, affective energy, and intentionality. These poems as a book are *fragmenta* in response to their uncertain ontological center.

For example, the poems are episodic, and on the whole they are arranged with no felt integration moment to moment; they are joined to each other by only the slightest of narrative threads. No immediately evident design, chronological or otherwise, governs the poems. Bergin has said of the *Trionfi* and of all Petrarch's longer works that they are composed of fragments, very loosely united, and that this "basic flaw derives from a constitutional incapacity of Petrarch to handle the grand design" for "the synthesizing resolution eluded Petrarch."[34] Those who have found patterns in the *Canzoniere* have had to work hard to do so, as though any real integration in the sequence were well hidden. For instance, Ernest Wilkins has carefully traced the various orderings of the poems, exploring rationales for each of them. Bernardo has recently sought to connect the search for form with the development of Laura's image, especially in the *Triumphs;* he stresses the frequent reorderings of the last thirty poems. Thomas Roche has suggested that the Christian liturgical calendar may offer a map for the sequence.[35] By contrast, Freccero sees the episodic nature of the sequence as a self-contained strength: the poems "spatialize time" and are "free of the threat of closure."[36] But even with such an implied rhetorical infinity, *Poet* still threatens *Lover,* for the poems are also "free," in their fragmentation, of those secure organizing affects that could enable integration and closure. As a whole, the sequence hardly forms a densely integrated presence, even though the rich defensive texturing is insistently distinctive, always identifiable as Petrarch. Durling speaks of Petrarch's "intensely self-critical awareness that all integration of selves and texts is relative, temporary, threatened."[37] But the best description of the fragmentary nature of the sequence is Petrarch's own, or his adoption of Dante's metaphor: the leaves of this book are scattered, *rime sparse,* because they have not been well bound with Love. The Poet-Lover must keep toiling, step by step, in the endless task of collecting again all the scattered leaves of *lauro,* self and Source.

Moreover, some of the defensive texturing seems finally to fail, to threaten the intentionality of the sequence, to cut rather too deeply into the *Canzoniere* as self. For instance, time as antagonist seems not only to distinguish this Poet-Lover but also gradually to remove the purpose of his existence. As the sequence endures through twenty-one years "ardendo" (burning) and another ten years "piangendo" (weeping, 364), he tells us ever more often that he is weary, "stanco di viver (weary of life, 363), and we sense a relaxing of his will to continue in those potentially inexhaustible antitheses, *Poet* without *Lover.* At several points the weight of time, and the grief at Laura's death, seem to usurp for him even his "sense of an ending," to bring this weeping and writing figure to an abrupt close.[38] Also with the experience of Laura's death, the Poet-Lover seems to lose his defensive confidence that he can possess worded parts of Laura's presence. He seems to move beyond his earlier inexpressibility tropes and now fully to acknowledge, at moments, the distance between his worded part-presences and a Presence beyond words. Whatever I spoke or wrote about her, he once says, "fu breve stilla d'infiniti abissi" (was a little drop from infinite depths; 339).[39] As she tells him in her last visionary appearance, she is now a "Spirito ignudo" (naked spirit), inaccessible to mortal words and far above the level of his sweet music, "queste dolci tue fallaci ciance" (these sweet deceptive chatterings of yours, 359. 60, 41).

Even more troubling for the coherence of the sequence are those intermittent repentance poems and the final "conversion" poems, where *Poet* and *Lover* turn against the self centrally, at the presencing moment. Here defensive ambivalence surely jeopardizes the very reason for the existence of poems and Poet-Lover, their entire foundation of affective energy. The poems contend that they should be otherwise created, that they should be "più belle imprese" (more beautiful undertakings, 62). In this thorough self-doubt, Laura becomes an invalid Source, a mistake, and poems that grow from her *absent presence* are likewise invalid:

> ... i' chiamo il fine per lo gran desire
> di riveder cui non veder fu 'l meglio.
> [312]

(... I call out for the end in my great desire to see her again whom it would have been better not to have seen at all.)

All the poems of Laura have been a wandering, an error, better never to have been. When in *De Librorum Copia* Joy boasts, "I possess countless books," Reason replies, "And countless errors...."[40] In the last poems even *lauro* disappears:

> terra è quella ond' io ebbi et freddi et caldi,
> -spenti son i miei lauri, or querce et olmi.
> [363]

(She is dust from whom I took chills and heat; my laurels are faded, are oaks and elms.)

With *lauro* no longer evergreen, Laura ceases to be named: "tale è terra" (366. 92). The Virgin Mary is brought forward as legitimate Source, new ground of the poems' being:

Vergine, i' sacro et purgo
al tuo nome et pensieri e 'ngegno et stile,
la lingua e 'l cor, le lagrime e i sospiri.

[366. 126–28]

(Virgin, I consecrate and cleanse in your name my thought and wit
and style, my tongue and heart, my tears and my sighs.)

But this consecration works only for future poems, not for past
ones, and now the sequence is over. The whole sequence seems
to have been merely a prelude to its palinode: these retractions,
if one takes them at all seriously (and many readers have been
understandably reluctant to do so), draw all purpose and intentionality from the poems and leave them grounded on full absence. In this sense we have perhaps not literary strength, but
literary weakness, from fictionalized moral flaws. As the first
sonnet announces, the poems to follow are to be understood as
valueless: raving, "vaneggiar," and cause for repentance, and
"giovenile errore." They have taken their being from one who is
dust. Who would ask integration or coherence, then, from such
fully devalued poems as these?

Perhaps this ultimate turning-against-the-self works as a last,
desperate defense—a "splitting" away of almost all the poems as
"bad" in order to preserve the ensuing silence after the sequence
as "good." That is, the poems seem to annihilate themselves, to
renounce their long-held purposes, in order to purify the blank
spaces beyond themselves, to conjure the Void as God or true
Source. To put it another way, one must renounce all, must be
"revolted by physical pleasures and nauseated by unremitting
joys," in order to reach "the still, secure harbor of life" (*Fam.*
XXI. 13, pp. 175–76). And among these possible joys the Poet-
Lover surely includes the formation of the self in words, "queste
dolci tue fallaci ciance." For in these defensive textures some
would recognize the "Augustinian" Petrarch holding sway over
the "Ciceronian." Bergin finds in the *Africa* a "melancholy
acknowledgment that nothing in this world is of lasting importance," and in the *De remediis* a "continuous disparagement of
life's joys" that seems "to come very close to a negation of the
value of life itself and to press the pessimistic attack somewhat
beyond the Christian frontiers."[41] If poems and self are fully

renounced, then it is all the more likely that God may lie behind the poems, "il ver tacito . . . / ch'ogni stil vince" (that silent truth which surpasses every style, 309), cradling their lamentations.

But if there is this "splitting" defense at work, it too is ultimately a failure. These poems cannot quite bear to throw themselves away. Thus they reclaim themselves from the silence, gathering their scattered leaves and presenting them to the reader: "Voi ch'ascoltate in rime sparse il suono / di quei sospiri" (You who hear in scattered rhymes the sound of those sighs). For these poems, despite all doubts, fall back upon themselves as Source. In this texturing, Eternity is not other than, but merely *più bella* than Laura,[42] and correspondingly the Poet-Lover's Eternity is not other than the painful, defensive response to her in these words. To belong in Eternity, this Poet-Lover must be one "chi pianse sempre."

6 *Shakespeare's Sonnets*

I

... this rich praise, that you alone are you—
[84]

In the sonnets the language of fusion recurs in paradox, hyperbole, and incantation. There are several versions of a "matrix sentence" at the root of such language: for the paradoxes, "I am you" or "you are another you"; for the hyperboles, "you are all to me"; for the incantations, "you are you." These simple sentences may help to reveal that in this language of fusion *Poet* and *Lover* join to evoke wordless Source, an infinite I-and-thou in perpetual renewal like the dual unity at the "core" of self.

The sonnets, of course, have their conventional echoes of the paradox of shared identity, "I am you": the heart, the soul, the picture, or the loved one is said to reside in the breast of the lover (22, 109, 24, 48). But further, in this texture such formulaic contradictions as "my next self" (133) or "that other mine" (134) tend to grow into difficult juxtapositions of pronouns—crowded structures where the symbiosis between "I" and "thou" seems to reverberate as one extracts the several possible meanings:

'Tis thee, myself, that for myself I praise
[62]

223

> . . . thou teachest how to make one twain
>
> [39]¹

As we try to read "one twain" or "thee, myself," the paradox "I am you" appears cryptic, without even the resolving force of the verb "to be": this language brings us up short, as though before some irreducible and urgent truth. We recall the similarly gnomic language of that "mystic" poem *The Phoenix and the Turtle*, which echoes the sonnets exactly at this dyadic mystery, "I am you," two are one. For example:

> Let me confess that we two must be twain,
> Although our undivided loves are one. . . .
> In our two loves there is but one respect,
> Though in our lives a separable spite,
>
> [36]

> So they love as love in twain
> Had the essence but in one,
> Two distincts, division none:
> Number there in love was slain.
>
> [*The Phoenix and the Turtle*, 25–28]

Almost stubbornly brief, as though hardly condescending to words at all, these paradoxes are the language of fusion—love past reason, religious love, primal identification. Many readers have sensed the intensity of the paradox "I am you" within the sonnets; J. B. Leishman, for example, hears almost a parody of St. Paul's "I live; yet not I, but my friend liveth in me."² And Montaigne knew the same ontological paradox, speaking of his friendship with Etienne de la Boëtie—it was as though the line that separated them had been effaced.

In the related paradox of the procreation sonnets, "you are another you," we find again a difficult arrangement of pronouns:

> Thou of thyself thy sweet self dost deceive
>
> [4]

> That's for thyself to breed another thee
>
> [6]

O that you were yourself, but love you are
No longer yours than you yourself here live
[13]

Here the "I" and "thou" belong to the same repeated word, so that the language gestures toward the enigma of shared being between parent and child. A single word like "yourself" thus comes to imply a continual interchange of being, a perpetual renewal that all selves intuit in the sensed infinity between an "I" and a "thou." In response to *Lover infans*, miracles of rejuvenation and distillation belong in the texture of the sonnets to this symbiotic dyad, this "mutual flame" (The *Phoenix and the Turtle*, 24). The "you" and "other you" of the procreation sonnets become an I-and-thou in their ability to preserve between them the flow of being:

This were to be new made when thou are old,
And see thy blood warm when thou feel'st it cold.
[2]

To give away yourself keeps yourself still
[16]

As fast as thou shalt wane so fast thou grow'st—
In one of thine. . . .
[11]

It is within this paradoxical dyad, "I am you" or "you are another you," that being can never be lost or expended in a waste, but rather ebbs and flows in the interpenetration of "loss" and "store." In this sense age becomes youth, death becomes life, and the paradoxes absorb the give-and-take of chiasmus, a figure retained even in the "dark lady" sonnets to secure I-and-thou: "Therefore I lie with her, and she with me" (138).

But the dual unity of the procreation sonnets, "you" and "other you," gradually gives way to the main evocation of Source that sustains the sequence, the eternal I-and-thou of Poet-Lover and youth. We can see this direction early in the sonnets, as the Poet-Lover or "I" seeks to insinuate himself into that eternal flow between "you" and "other you" in his addresses to the youth: "Make thee another self for love of me" (10). For he seeks to belong to that same abundance of being that he invokes—as later in his role of "decrepit father" to the youth he asserts, "I make my love engrafted to this store" (37), the "store" of the beloved's worth and truth. And as the repeated metaphor of "engrafting" reminds us, it is the Poet-Lover as *worded* being who reaches toward the sustaining paradox of "you" and "other you," who seeks to make the lines of his "pupil pen" one with those "lines of life" he is encouraging (16), so that the dyadic mystery of parent and child is overtaken, transformed to the insistent I-and-thou of poem and Source: "I engraft you new" (15).

> But were some child of yours alive that time,
> You should live twice in it and in my rhyme.
>
> [17]

The worded "I" or Poet-Lover here joins the lines of immortality[3] because he becomes a symbiotic dual unity with the "thou" of the sequence, like parent and child or child and parent. For in this language of fusion, the self as being-in-words must be an "I" linked to a "thou," or "consecrate to thee" (74), in order to be eternal. It is this I-and-thou, this symbiotic evocation of Source, that allows this being-in-words a self-renewal, "Spending again what is already spent" (76), from an infinite well of affective energy. Both lines of procreation and lines of verse can "distill" this fluid interchange of being, self to self (5, 54),[4] for both can carry the felt miracle of primal identification, I-and-thou. As Murray Krieger implies, the windows to eternal life are another pair of eyes.

Another matrix sentence for the language of fusion here might be stated: "To me, you are all the world." For one needs a sentence that would generate those regular hyperboles through which the youth becomes All—all lovers, all fortune, all nature. And this hyperbolic language works to extend the dyadic I-and-thou, to reveal it as infinite and oceanic, through an all-inclusive "thou." Perhaps we can see here the workings of that "intimate hyperbole" that Boyde suggests for the *nove rime*, where the *donna*, like Beatrice later, becomes a "beacon of orientation" to the speaker. For the sense of the hyperbolic terms is intimate—to the "I," the "thou" is All, all worth and all truth, and there is no exaggeration. (Perhaps in this context, the universal never becomes the impersonal, and even sonnets without their quota of personal pronouns are not really detached from the I-and-thou.[5]) Thus in these hyperboles the first and second person pronouns are extended to "all" and "every." The Poet-Lover tells the youth that those lovers praised in books with "ántique pen" have been "all you prefiguring" (106), for example, so that the juxtaposition of pronouns implies a continuum of being between "all" and "you." And the pronouns can become again characteristically dense when "all" is woven into the dyad of I-and-thou: when the Poet-Lover finds in the youth "all those friends" who have died, he builds through a chain of dyadic paradoxes to the conclusion, "And thou, all they, hast all the all of me" (31). We see these hyperboles linger even in accusation and betrayal, when the youth is more literally the repository of all present lovers:

> Take all my loves, my love, yea take them all . . .
> All mine was thine, before thou hadst this more.
>
> [40]

Since the "thou" is All to the "I," it seems almost necessary that the youth would have been read as both homosexual and heterosexual lover, as well as friend. For the I-and-thou at the basis of the sequence becomes the more truly infinite when the youth can be both Adonis and Helen, known through "every blessèd shape" and "all external grace" (53). For this Poet-Lover, this passion, one must have a "master mistress" (20), a composite of all that is loving and lovable, all lovers.[6] The long history of varied interpretations of the youth surely helps to demonstrate his inclusive nature, "thou" as All. At the very least, as Rosalie Colie says, the hyperbolic praises are emphasized by the fact that the sonnets are addressed to a man.[7] And some would see further a suggestion of Hermaphrodite as a powerful bisexual symbol of wholeness, completeness, self-containment, or "peculiar unity."[8] Such a self-sufficient creature might well be "Unmovèd," a Source that could save or betray. C. S. Lewis calls love

227

in the sonnets "the quintessence of all loves ... we cease to ask what kind," and Leishman reads "some effluence of *il primo amore*" in this love.[9]

The "thou" of the sequence is All in more expansive senses, too. In further reaches of hyperbole, the Poet-Lover will direct lists of Fortune's favors toward the "all" of the friend, in conclusive lines:

> And having thee, of all men's pride I boast
>
> [91]

> Or any of these all, or all, or more,
> Entitled in thy parts do crownèd sit.
>
> [37]

The youth is equivalent to all beauty, wealth, and high birth, and he compensates for their loss: this I-and-thou thus includes all "state" (29), stands by itself "hugely politic" (124). And just as this "thou" is all fortune, so he is all nature: Nature stores him in his abundance as a map of all beauties (67, 68), and he must have a child to regenerate this store (14). Thus summer and day are defined by the presence of "thee," and winter by his absence (43, 97, 98, 56)—the "I" of the sonnets finds in this "thou" all seasons, all times, all terms of nature and fortune. Presence or absence becomes an all-or-none issue, as in one incorporation metaphor the Poet-Lover either starves or surfeits, "Or gluttoning on all, or all away" (75).

Thus in the intimate hyperboles of fusion, the "thou" of the sonnets becomes All, becomes a prototype, becomes the One in whom the many reside. He is the "pattern" of the lily and the rose (98), the fulfillment of prophecies and former praises (59, 106), the substance toward whom others are shadows, or the real figure whom others counterfeit (37, 53).

> For nothing this wide universe I call,
> Save thou, my rose; in it thou art my all.
>
> [109]

This Poet-Lover might well ask, "Why write I still all one ...?" (76), for by his very breadth of allusion he writes all into one, sweeping all values from fortune, nature, and even religious doctrine into the "thou." Leishman calls this method "inverted Platonism,"[10] and in a Freudian sense he seems right, for in "condensation" the many are layered upon the ideal object, Idea of the Good, "thou" evoked as Source for the poems. For we have here not a "position" on Platonism, but a movement toward I-and-thou: *Poet* and *Lover,* in these hyperboles of fusion, join in disregard of worded differences, with no "irritable reaching" after religious doctrine. In the soft focus of multiple allusion, all is taken into "thou."

Thus the "thou" of the sonnets becomes both All and One, and we reach the last matrix sentence beneath the language of fusion here: "you are you." Generated by this sentence are a small group of "incantatory" words that often seem designed to evoke *all* qualities of the "thou" with a *single* term; the words used in this way include worth, truth, beauty, fair, love, rose, sweet, kind, best, the second personal pronoun, and certain demonstratives. The sense here is almost talismanic, like the tautology "you are you"; one summons all magically inclusive qualities of the "thou" by these single syllables, as though these small words are all that one can say or need say to invoke the "thou." These words in context often seem luminous with their failed effort to reach Source, *absent presence,* the quintessential "thou" toward whom the "I" of the sequence exists in dyadic relationship, and they are all the more luminous in their brevity and compactness, like the single syllables of BE and ICE transparent to the light. Often the sonnets seem in certain ways built around these single syllables—built to stress them in the rhythm of the line, or to focus them through the octave-sestet structure, or to repeat them lovingly.

Here are some examples of these "incantatory" words stressed by the rhythmic structure of the line (my italics):

How with this rage shall *beauty* hold a plea
[65]

Take all my comfort of thy *worth* and *truth*
[37]

I will be *true* despite thy scythe and thee
[123]

By that sweet ornament which *truth* doth give
[54]

Let me not to the marriage of *true* minds
[116]

The rhythmic stresses can be subtle, involving placement before
the caesura, placement in later accented positions of the line,
and variations from expected rhythmic patterns. And often, too,
these "incantatory" words seem to occur near some "turn" of
sonnet structure,[11] near the end of the second quatrain or at the
end of some catalogue—the pronoun "thee," especially, can
serve to "turn" a sonnet:

Why should poor beauty indirectly seek
Roses of shadow, since his rose is *true?*
[67. 7–8]

Be thou the tenth muse, ten times more in *worth*
[38. 9]

All these I better in one general *best*
[91. 8]

O know, sweet love, I always write of *you*
[76. 9]

But *thy* eternal summer shall not fade
[18. 9]

When *thou thyself* dost give invention light?
[38. 8]

But from *thine* eyes my knowledge I derive
[14. 9]

Haply I think on *thee* . . .
[29. 10]

. . . the conceit of this inconstant stay
Sets *you* most rich in youth before my sight.
[15. 9–10]

Again, these simple words can be chosen for some figures of repetition:

> Look what is *best,* that *best* I wish in thee
> [37]

> But *best* is *best,* if never intermixed?
> [101]

> O let me *true* in love but *truly* write
> [21]

> Thou *truly* fair wert *truly* sympathized
> In *true* plain words by thy *true*-telling friend
> [82]

You are you—these vital incantations allow the sonnets an *absent presence* that is secure, personal, yet universally inclusive. It may be their simplicity, or their repetition, or their very lack of precise detail that enables these words to evoke "thou" as Source. Since they are somewhat abstract or opaque, such words as *worth* and *fair* and *best*—already charged by the "signifying universe" with a sense of Source—can better summon that intuitive *Lover infans* alive in readers. And the antonomasiac pronouns, words that *almost* tell names, can remind one of the self-effacing style of the *nove rime,* whose *donna* is a whole lifegiving presence, undivided into particular referents or part-presences. With the frequent word "true," this whole presence takes on constancy, becomes in appeal a secure "thou" to enable and renew the self.[12] At the same time, these monosyllables can belong to the plain-speaking or "homely" language of the sonnets which seems for many readers to reveal genuine emotion.[13] The simple words then become a kind of liturgy in the sequence, a sparely worded obeisance to the essential, wordless I-and-thou that sustains this Poet-Lover.

Often it is through this vocabulary of incantation that the echoes of Christian doctrine are brought into the sonnets. One critic who seeks to "justify the vocabulary of devotion in a strictly mundane poetry of love" remarks, "what particularly engages the imagination is the notion of confinement to singularity as a warrant against depletion."[14] In a similar "notion" of object-relations theory, a stable or constant "thou" is a warrant for continually renewed being in symbiosis, I-and-thou. The monotony of Source is life itself, and "you are you" becomes not sterile repetition but assurance that being will always flow between "I" and "thou":

> Why write I still all one, ever the same,
> And keep invention in a noted weed,
> That every word doth almost tell my name,
> Showing their birth, and where they did proceed?
> O know, sweet love, I always write of you,
> And you and love are still my argument.
> So all my best is dressing old words new,
> Spending again what is already spent:
> For as the sun is daily new and old,
> So is my love still telling what is told.
>
> [76]

Here are eloquent plain words of fusion: with *you, love, best,* that dyadic interchange is insistently evoked, and loss always becomes store. And we notice the same language in the "Christian" sonnets, where the eternity that belongs at this dyadic "core" of self is elaborated in Christian allusions:

> ... yet, like prayers divine,
> I must each day say o'er the very same;
> Counting no old thing old, thou mine, I thine,
> Ev'n as when first I hallowed thy fair name.
>
> [108]

Incantation is repetition, because the need for that primal identification with Source never ends—or the end is always that flowing chiasmic paradox, "thou mine, I thine." The point of the incantatory words is to evoke a constant *you,* a nourishing still point around which the poems can form themselves:

> Kind is my love today, tomorrow kind,
> Still constant in a wondrous excellence;
> Therefore my verse to constancy confined,
> One thing expressing, leaves out difference.
> Fair, kind, and true, is all my argument,

> Fair, kind, and true, varying to other words;
> And in this change is my invention spent—
>
> [105]

The echo of the Trinity belongs in this texture with the vocabulary of repetition, and all "confinement" serves the quintessential dual unity, I-and-thou, a sensed eternity, "A god in love, to whom I am confined" (110). In this poem the repetition in the phrase, "most most loving breast" can belong also to the incantations—"all one, ever the same"—for to be welcomed again to the friend's breast is the sameness of renewal. In Shakespeare's texture the marriage of true minds is always the marriage of two minds, and the Christian phrases are brought to serve a symbiotic unity. All supplication, all "oblation," work toward that paradoxical dyad that centers poems and selves— "mutual render, only me for thee" (125). The "I" will sacrifice himself in appeal for full communion with the "thou."

Thus through the language of incantation, "you are you," the poems summon I-and-thou with simple words—and they use some other even less articulate devices toward that wordless union. The demonstrative pronoun "this," meaning poem (Poet-Lover, "I"), can seem stubbornly unexplained, a degree more opaque than the pronoun "thee" that shares its life:

> When thou reviewest this, thou dost review
> The very part was consecrate to thee . . .
> The worth of that is that which it contains,
> And that is this, and this with thee remains.
>
> [74]

> So long lives this, and this gives life to thee.
>
> [18]

In such structures, *Poet* and *Lover* seem bent to reduce words to gestures, in what Krieger calls the regressiveness of words, the "pointing and grunting."[15] For in the language of fusion, language seems designed to fail: "Hearing you praised, I say, ''tis so,' ''tis true'" (85). Perhaps the references to love or the beloved abiding in thoughts, or eyes, or breath, complete this motion beyond the words (see 81, 83, 85), or at least they sugg⸱ ⸱an

233

active silence, as in Dante's works, ready to redeem the limitations of words.

> You live in this, and dwell in lovers' eyes.
>
> [55]

For the matrix sentences that underly the language of fusion in the sonnets all imply an eventual impasse of language before the union of I-and-thou, a sense that no more can be said: because it was he, because it was I. Shakespeare's "magical poetic" moves in paradox, hyperbole, incantation, and at last, silence.

II

> No love, my love, that thou mayst true love call
>
> [40]

At least two kinds of defensive texturing are prominent in the sonnets: those poems about moral fault, inconstancy, or sexual betrayal seem to grow from one kind of defensive effort, and the poems concerned with fortune, reputation, or time (see III, below) seem to grow from another.[16] In the first group, *Poet* and *Lover* join in some difficult verbal strategies to secure the "thou," *absent presence,* as *good*—or, if the effort thus to preserve an "ideal object" fails, the direction is in any case toward a definite, unchanging I-and-thou, however flawed or compromised. Sometimes the defensive textures of the youth sonnets and the dark lady sonnets resemble each other, but often they can be distinguished. For many sonnets to the youth are engaged in defensive naming and renaming, as though to shift the labels of "bad" and "good" until, by whatever means, the youth is securely named *good:* the Poet-Lover calls himself "bad" in order to call the youth "good," for example, or the youth is truly "good" though he may seem "bad," or "bad" always looks "good" on the youth. Again, other sonnets to the youth may use sarcasm, irony, innuendo, or even direct anger to insinuate or state that the youth is *bad*—always for the purpose of moral exhortation, in order that he and the Poet-Lover may be reclaimed, and the I-and-thou renewed, as *good*. The sonnets to the dark lady follow a somewhat different defensive pattern. Some effort is made to label her "good," but it is more desperate, as though the Poet-Lover is asking to be deceived, to have her try to seem good to him, although she is bad. Or, admitting that she is bad, the defensive effort in some intricate wordplay is to preserve in words a "thou" to the Poet-Lover's "I," at any price of moral compromise. Of course, this defense fails in part, for this flawed I-and-thou is hardly ideal, hardly lifegiving. Nonetheless, the poems cling to this dual unity: even in the darkest of the poems to the lady, as well as in most of the sonnets to the youth, the wordplay can move toward some verbal echo of I-and-thou. It is often through these verbal strategies of defense that *Poet* can emerge so strongly in Shakespeare's sonnets, in myriad-minded allusions, in semantico-logical tricks, in puns or sarcasm—*de via* from Source, in individuating play with words.

This Poet-Lover will seem almost congenially to "identify with the aggressor"; that is, he will deflect aggression away from the beloved by quite deliberately taking anger or hatred upon himself, labeling himself as "bad" (see 49, 88, 89, 149). In this texture, the turning-against-the-self seems almost eager, vivacious, as though this Poet-Lover had labels to spare in this game of defensive naming; and the goal, to preserve I-and-thou, is often straightforwardly admitted. Sonnets 33 through 36 seem to deflect the label of "bad" from the youth, often through applying it to the Poet-Lover, and one might read the affirmation of I-and-thou in the couplet of 36 as the goal of this effort. In sonnet 33, it is not the beloved who has become bad, but the "basest clouds" or "region cloud" that have covered his "celestial face," and through the double meaning of "stain" ("to sustain a moral blot" or "to outshine"), the last line may be read as seeming to blame while truly praising: "Suns of the world may stain when heav'n's sun staineth." True good shines through apparent bad. In sonnet 34 the language of "disgrace" and "shame" and repentance momentarily touch the youth on the way through the poem, but in the couplet the ransoming tears turn the youth's bad to good. The Poet-Lover, "him that bears the strong offence's cross," takes on the weight of the beloved's guilt especially in the couplet, even while in the displacement of the ransoming tears, "which thy love sheeds," the beloved himself is allowed to be the Christ figure who cancels his own ill, and thus is renamed as good. And of course in sonnet 35 the speaker turns blot, disgrace, and shame quite cleverly upon himself:

> All men make faults, and even I in this,
> Authórizing thy trespass with compare,
> Myself corrupting salving thy amiss,
> Excusing thy sins more than thy sins are;

As Stephen Booth puts it, "The quatrain develops a competition in guilt between the speaker and the beloved"; it is as though to preserve the youth from being named bad, the speaker must take the words of blame upon himself, making himself "áccessary" so that the thief can be all the more "sweet." In the next line, "For to thy sensual fault I bring in sense," both meanings of "sense" ("reason" and "corporeal faculties") might help to exonerate the youth, the second meaning by implicating the speaker. Finally, sonnet 36 completes this defensive naming—the speaker takes all "blots" upon himself in order that, absolved from the threat of the name "bad," two may be repeatedly made one: "our undivided loves are one . . . one respect . . . love's sole effect." Even the first line, which seems to admit separation, can be read as a fusion of two into one: to say "we two must be twain" is at least briefly to play upon the meaning of "twain" as "couple" or "married pair."[17] And in the motion toward the couplet we see all the more clearly the accomplishment of this group of sonnets; the defensive naming has preserved the "thou" as good, has allowed his name to keep its "honour," so that finally the "I" merges with a purified and ideal "thou," and the threats of *bad* are forogtten:[18] "Thou being mine, mine is thy good report."

In many of the sonnets involving the youth's supposed "faults," the definition of "good" has been confusing to many readers, especially when one considers also the procreation sonnets. Marriage, or abstinence, or constancy in friendship or in heterosexual or homosexual relationships—all may by turns seem to be offered as "good." Perhaps just as that *prima voglia* measures moral value in Dante's *Paradiso* (see above, Chap. 4), so in Shakespeare's sonnets "good" and "bad" are measured by that dual unity, I-and-thou. That is, "good" comes to be defined as whatever preserves or secures I-and-thou, and "bad" as whatever threatens or shatters it. Thus in the procreation sonnets, sexual "use" becomes good because it promotes that paradoxical dyadic bond between parent and child: "That's for thyself to breed another thee." But in the later sonnets, sexuality can become "bad" insofar as it threatens the I-and-thou of Poet-Lover and youth. Whether the issue is friendship or homosexual passion, the youth's intimate relationships with others are seen as a deception, a stain, an infection because they endanger the dual unity of Poet-Lover and youth. In the same way, perhaps, a certain aloofness would be bad or heartless when directed toward the Poet-Lover ("Unmovèd, cold") but good when directed toward the speaker's rivals ("to temptation slow").[19] There is much opportunity for complication of "bad" and "good" because the threats to the dyad I-and-thou are myriad, both sexual and nonsexual; that dual unity, in its symbiotic perfection, can be vulnerable to most of the contingencies of reality. And in the hyperbole of *amor hereos,* morality in this sense becomes a life-or-death issue—if the rival poet thrives, the speaker will be "cast away" (80); the Poet-Lover will die without the youth's love (92). The dyad of self and Source holds a mortal risk, against which Coriolanus struggles in his *causa sui* defensiveness.[20]

Thus to keep the youth "good" is to keep the "thou" constant to the "I," to preserve the dyadic "core" of poem and self. Sonnets 92 through 96 are another group occupied with this defensive texturing: in their effort of renaming, they often seek to cover the suspected bad with the visible good, so that all intimations of the youth's inconstancy are met by stating and restating that he appears to be good. In this group, the emphasis on seeming good keeps abreast of the accusations and the moral warnings, and the poems as a group move toward the same concluding couplet as in sonnet 36. In sonnet 92 the problematic subject is announced: "Thou mayst be false, and yet I know it not." Yet in the next sonnets, as though appropriate to the speaker's effort to live like a "deceivèd husband," the possible false seems to be matched with the seeming fair, line for line and phrase for phrase: "so love's face / May still seem love to me, though altered new" (93). In sonnet 93 three of the fourteen lines essentially repeat themselves to stress that the youth appears good, constant, trustworthy:

> For there can live no hatred in thine eye . . .
> That in thy face sweet love should ever dwell . . .
> Thy looks should nothing thence but sweetness tell.

And of course sonnet 94 has provoked multiple interpretations because it keeps turning its blame to praise; it "Cannot dispraise but in a kind of praise" (95). In the continual effort to keep the "thou" positive, the language itself is "beauty's veil" (95), defensively used and re-used, however transparently:

> Naming thy name blesses an ill report
> [95]

> Thou mak'st faults graces that to thee resort
> [96]

Again and again the lines themselves, in words and names, make faults into graces—errors become truth, basest jewels seem well, sexual "sport" is termed gentle (96). The couplets of 94 and 95 seem to warn the youth to live up to this apparent good; the couplet of 96 repeats the warning and adds to it, as though in accomplishment, the dyad of I and thou, arranged in chiasmus—"thou . . . mine, mine . . . thy":

> But do not so; I love thee in such sort,
> As thou being mine, mine is thy good report.

It may even be that this couplet deliberately repeats the similar achievement at the end of sonnets 33 through 36. Through the persistent defense of naming and renaming, I-and-thou has been preserved intact.

In some of the other defensive verbal textures, the youth is indirectly or directly called *bad* as though in order to reform or reclaim him—in "beneficial ill," to acknowledge bad and thereby turn it to good. In the sonnets' given ordering, the youth in the course of the sequence is subject to innuendo, irony, sarcasm, and even direct charges, but as the "youth" group of poems draws to a close, in sonnets 109 through 112 and 117 through 120, the dual unity of Poet-Lover and youth is strengthened and restored, and bad transformed to good. Finally, the couplet of sonnet 120, like the couplet of 36 and 96, is another perfect chiasmic expression of the paradox, I am you. It is as though to label the youth *bad* had acted as a "moral" cure, insofar as "moral" is defined as working toward that perpetual destination, I-and-thou.

For the young man does not lack accusations and rebukes, even though he does not receive so many as the dark lady. He can be rebuked through irony, as in sonnets 57 and 58 where the Poet-Lover is careful to specify the angry thoughts he supposedly does not feel:

> Nor dare I chide the world without end hour
> Whilst I, my sovereign, watch the clock for you.
> Nor think the bitterness of absence sour
>
> [57]

Sonnet 58, also in the language of "slave," again blames though irony, making the charges it says it is not making; the speaker will suffer "without accusing you of injury," and will not "blame your pleasure." The cover of irony is designedly thin, and in one half-line here the anger becomes more open: "though waiting so be hell." In the opening of sonnet 87 the irony is a little more opaque; there an aggressive meaning can be teased out of an apparent compliment:

> Farewell, thou art too dear for my possessing,
> And like enough thou know'st thy estimate
>
> [87]

This same charge is made more openly in the couplet of sonnet 84:

> You to your beauteous blessings add a curse,
> Being fond on praise, which makes your praises worse.

And often, rather direct accusations will appear in what Colie might call a *sal* couplet, after a sonnet preoccupied with the tensions between seeming good and being good. Sonnet 70 seems at first to be renaming the youth as good—"slander's mark was ever yet the fair." Yet the couplet gives words to the suspicion: "If some suspéct of ill masked not thy show." And other couplets are more unconditional, almost like invective:

> But why thy odor matcheth not thy show,
> The soil is this, that thou dost common grow.
>
> [69]

> For thee watch I, whilst thou dost wake elsewhére,
> From me far off, with others all too near.
>
> [61]

In one sonnet, there is even a barely disguised gesture of retribution:

> But for his theft, in pride of all his growth
> A vengeful canker ate him up to death.
>
> [99]

All in all, the anger or even rage in these sonnets is unusually clear, so that any turning-against-the-self seems almost freely chosen, a defensive ploy strangely self-aware. This is far from Petrarch's endless pain; nor is it, as G. B. Shaw has so clearly asserted, the posture of a sycophant: "A sycophant, when his patron cuts him out in a love affair, does not tell his patron exactly what he thinks of him."[21]

In sonnets 109 through 112 and 117 through 120, the Poet-Lover is acknowledging his own "bad," his own straying or threat to I-and-thou, in order that he may return, converted to "good," to the youth: "thy breast . . . my home of love" (109). But perhaps implicitly he is also reclaiming the youth from bad to good, or at least that theme finally emerges in sonnet 120, a poem of mutual repentance and reparation: "That you were once unkind befriends me now." For in these poems one can perhaps see the Poet-Lover moving gradually out of his defensive naming to a more direct application of accusatory terms, "bad" uncovered by "good." He begins with the protest, "O never say that I was false of heart," and places his "bad" in conditional terms: "if I have ranged" (109). But the language becomes more confessional: "I have looked on truth / Askance and strangely" (110). His terms are more direct: "blenches," "worse essays" (110), "my harmful deeds" (111), "wretched errors" (119), "my transgression" (120). Of course, all this admitted "bad" is defined by the I-and-thou, as this Poet-Lover knows:

> For what care I who calls me well or ill,
> So you o'er-green my bad, my good allow?
> You are my all the world . . .
>
> [112]

For the unflinching self-accusations are supposed to cure the "bad," to be "Potions of eisel 'gainst my strong infection" (111), just as the transgressions themselves have been "bitter sauces" (118) to restore the palate. For the effort is to renew the I-and-thou as "more strong, far greater" by naming and therefore recognizing bad, to turn it to good: "O benefit of ill" (119). And surely these sonnets often reach the language of fusion, especially in their couplets—as though perhaps they had earned such language through their direct, confessional naming. The beloved as All is frequently invoked, and there are Christian and Platonic echoes: "my heav'n," "sum of good." And finally in the couplet of sonnet 120, when *both* have been named "bad" with the references to "your trespass," the poems reach a conclusive expression of that paradoxical I-and-thou, again in chiasmus like the couplet of sonnets 36 and 96:

> But that your trespass now becomes a fee:
> Mine ransoms yours, and yours must ransom me.

The "But" seems to signal a surprise like heavenly grace,[22] a gift, perhaps a definitive resolution of bad to good. One might read the strength of this couplet, its secure evocation of fusion, as an ontological basis for that assertion in the next poem: "I am that I am" (121).

To keep "thou" constant to "I," and thus to secure the dyad I-and-thou, becomes a more conflicted effort in the poems to the lady, but the effort is still so intense that even the label of "good" is sacrificed to it. Perhaps, after all, inconstant women are a more deeply felt ontological threat than inconstant men. Certainly in these poems the lady is a perpetual danger to I-and-thou, so that through her actions neither she nor the youth can provide a secure "thou" for the lyric "I." In this context of inconstancy, sexual union becomes a "waste" precisely because it is outside the I-and-thou, outside the flow of being in the lifegiving dyad that spends again what is already spent. One recalls Othello's explanation of the depth to which cuckolding affects him:

> But there, where I have garner'd up my heart,
> Where either I must live or bear no life,
> The fountain from the which my current runs
> Or else dries up: to be discarded thence!
> Or keep it as a cistern for foul toads
> To knot and gender in!
>
> [IV. ii. 57–62]

In this language, sexual constancy seems to promise primal fusion, to assure a Source vital to self. And correspondingly, Desdemona's supposed infidelity is felt as a primal danger—she has even lost the handkerchief, a guarantee of love, once used by Othello's mother. Thus, in a moral scheme centered by Source, by I-and-thou, the figures of inconstant women generate the language of moral evil, in plays and in poems: rank weeds, infection, disease, a cistern for foul toads, Hamlet's "unweeded garden," or "things rank and gross in nature." She must die, or she'll betray more men. For sexual union, however vulnerable to the "hell" of inconstancy and impersonal lust, can still *seem* to offer the "heaven" of eternal fusion, the merging of selves, I-and-thou. The desire is infinite, the act a slave to limit: in the phallic overtones of the language of the sonnets, words associated with "straight" can suggest constancy or endurance, while words like "bent" imply the vulnerable, flawed, or untrue.

Thus in the defensive texturing of the dark lady sonnets, there is some limited effort to name her "fair" just as there was to name the youth "good"—in order to keep "thou" constant to "I." Some of this renaming seems straightforward enough, although it may hide a negative second meaning:

> Thy black is fairest in my judgment's place
>
> [131]

> Then will I swear beauty herself is black
> [132]

The first line here can carry the echo "in place of my judgment" and leads to the charge that her deeds are black; the second line follows a suggestion that she has a black heart.[23] But other poems here are a desperate plea for deception, so that he can take the "worst" as the "best" (137). The defensive naming here is an insistence that bad *seem* good. He begs her not to "glance thine eye aside" when he is watching, and he devises ingenious excuses for her roving glances: "Let me excuse thee" (139). He asks her to *say*, at least, that she is constant to him:

> If I might teach thee wit, better it were,
> Though not to love, yet, love, to tell me so
> [140]

Thus in these sonnets the defensive naming of "good" is obviously a failure, and the effort toward a constant "I" and "thou" is virtually abandoned.

Instead, the defensive verbal texture seems to work toward stating lovers as pairs, despite all complications of lies, inconstancy, or forswearing: these sonnets appear to insist upon some verbal equivalent of that dual unity, I-and-thou, even though constancy, security, and truth have been lost. In these defensive texturings, perhaps, *Poet* seems the most visible of all: sometimes in "festivals of verbal ingenuity"[24] the allusions to rivalry and sexual betrayal, to triads or to multitudes, are verbally worked and worried until they yield some simpler statement of a pair, of I and thou. This kind of verbal ingenuity has been used before, in sonnets 40 through 42, to counter the threats of a triangular relationship:

> Then if for my love thou my love receivest,
> I cannot blame thee for my love thou usest
> [40]

In the wordplay here, the term "my love" can mean the speaker's affection, the youth's love for the speaker, the youth himself, and the mistress, and the combination of possible meanings for the lines is dazzling.[25] But most important, with these words all reference to "her" has been eclipsed, and there remain only I, thou, and my love. Here is another verbal solution to the triangle:

> But here's the joy, my friend and I are one;
> Sweet flatt'ry, then she loves but me alone.
>
> [42]

In these words, both I-thou dyads are reclaimed: the first line solves the loss of the youth—"That she hath thee is of my wailing chief"—and the second restores the pairing of speaker and mistress. Of course, moral compromise is necessary to this verbal play; he loves offenders so that the offenders will be loving to him: "Loving offenders, thus I will excuse ye."

Similarly, in the sonnets to the lady, the terms of I-and-thou can strangely persist in the face of sexual betrayal. In sonnet 144, reminiscent of sonnet 42 in situation and phrasing, the youth and the mistress operate as a team in relation to the speaker, "both from me both to each friend," and the motivation for their coupling is to seduce him, in this language: "To win me soon to hell." Further, the speaker in these words retains pronominal possession of each, even to the couplet: "Two loves I have . . . my female evil . . . my better angel . . . my saint . . . my angel . . . Till my bad angel fire my good one out." As in sonnet 42, the words seem to persist in implying that both youth and mistress are "thou" to the speaker's "I." At other moments, too, the triad of lovers can seem to be governed or enclosed by the pronouns of "I" and "thou":

> Be it lawful I love thee as thou lov'st those
> Whom thine eyes woo as mine impórtune thee
>
> [142]

> So run'st thou after that which flies from thee,
> Whilst I, thy babe, chase thee afar behind
>
> [143]

These lines seem to resemble the language of sonnet 40, with the inclusive term "my love" eclipsing the rival party, for here the rivals to "I" and "thou" are rendered only as "those" and "that which." And often the defensive insistence upon "I" and "thou" can occur in the couplet. Those sonnets with multiple puns on "will" are effectively invitation poems, whose couplets ask, as Sidney's Astrophel beseeches Stella, "take me to thee":

> Think all but one, and me in that one will.
> [135]

> And then thou lov'st me for my name is Will.
> [136]

In a way, this is a morally compromised version of the language of fusion: let me be one among all your lovers, he asks, instead of saying, "you are all the world to me." And other couplets can also resolve the complications of more than two lovers, of flawed truth or constancy. In sonnet 133, a metaphor of "imprisoning" with dense and entangled pronouns, the couplet reads,

> And yet thou wilt, for I being pent in thee
> Perforce am thine, and all that is in me.

And of course sonnet 138 reaches its own chiasmic version of dual unity, its own perjured "mutual flame":

> Therefore I lie with her, and she with me,
> And in our faults by lies we flattered be.

Perhaps here the pronoun "her" instead of "thou" is itself a sign of compromise or distancing. Sonnet 147 even insists upon the coupling of "I" and "thou," however black, in a circular motion from its last line to its first: the past tense of the couplet, "I have sworn thee fair," recalls the lingering present tense of the first line, "My love is as a fever."

For in this darker texture, relationships are not renounced, however perjured they become; all couplings hold fast in the verbal texture, despite sexual betrayals. This language insists upon the pairing of lovers, the resolution to an I-and-thou however "bad," with aggressive ingenuity, somewhat as Venus insists upon Adonis, or, in the Ovidian myth that is one source for Shakespeare's poem, as Salmacis insists upon Hermaphrodite.

> And when a woman woos, what woman's son
> Will sourly leave her till he have prevailed?
>
> [41]

The confusion of the pronoun here, "he" or "she,"[26] seems exactly the point: it may be that some wish for primal completion or wholeness, self and Source, can lie beneath man's fear of sexually aggressive dark ladies. Perhaps the price for the self-sufficiency of the Hermaphrodite figure is the rage ("perjured, murd'rous, bloody, full of blame") of one's insistence upon the "heaven" of fusion, man and woman inextricably bound together; in this sense, Salmacis resembles the dark lady or Shakespeare's Venus. Ultimately this is an ontological "heaven" upon which one must insist for survival, and the potential aggression of the Poet-Lover who will "prevail" is mirrored in the unyielding seductiveness of the dark lady. One recalls the speaker of Dante's "Così nel mio parlar": perhaps, as Margaret Mahler believes, man born of woman must live with a fierce, repressed desire to reclaim his wholeness, self and Source, I and thou.

III

> How with this rage shall beauty hold a plea,
> Whose action is no stronger than a flower?
>
> [65]

Even apart from sexual betrayal, there are many contingencies that can intrude upon or weaken that timeless dual unity, I-and-thou: thus we find sonnets that confront the multiple threats of fortune and time, through another sort of defensive texturing (see above, n. 16). The verbal strategies involved here are suggested by the couplet of sonnet 146:

> So shalt thou feed on death, that feeds on men,
> And death once dead, there's no more dying then.

That is, these sonnets seem almost to devour all possible worded dangers to I-and-thou that are posed by time and fortune, and to make from these dangers their own coherence and affective energy as verbally textured selves. In this way Time, "Eater of youth" (*Rape of Lucrece,* 1. 127), nourisher turned consumer, becomes again a source of strength, even of the poems' own immortality. In these textured defenses, *Poet* and *Lover* join in the "soft focus"[27] of words that seem to include all possible threatening features of Time and "the times." Moreover, these poems generate affective energy by personifying elements of fortune and time as "bad," and elaborating these elements with various energetic verbs. And in negative constructions, the poems defy these enemies to I-and-thou, and thus further define themselves. In such negations and deviations as these, *Poet* moves to distinguish these sonnets from all others: the poems have fed on death, that feeds on men. Finally, these verbal strategies work toward the ultimate purpose of all such defensive textures; they clear the way for some evocation of Source among these threats. For often in these sonnets the language of fusion will rest in the couplet, as though by the "raging" of a multitude of threatening circumstances the sonnet earns a fragile, persistent affirmation of I-and-thou.

What seems to be a verbal "devouring" of the threats to time and fortune might be stated also as a "not-me" defense: the poems *seem* to be naming and rejecting all that I-and-thou is *not,* by choosing words that suggest a broad sweep of references.[28] But of course "not-me" is also "me," and these inclusive words persist in the poems. And the poems reach their amazing coherence, their "soft focus" that allows the reader to contemplate many meanings simultaneously,[29] partly because the defensive motion of "not-me" blurs the focus, taking threats to be general and universal. For in a sense, all reality is threatening to that perfect, primally repressed identification of I-and-thou, and thus all threats can be conflated in "soft focus."

> If my dear love were but the child of state,
> It might for fortune's bastard be unfathered,
> As subject to time's love, or to time's hate,
> Weeds among weeds, or flow'rs with flowers gathered.
> [124]

This language moves to exclude; and since the following phrases are set *apart* from "my dear love"—purified away, as in Arnaut's texture—they draw to themselves all impure reality, all

vicissitudes of meaning. Arthur Mizener mentions several contextual meanings of state: fortune, status, wealth, beauty, pomp,
the body politic, policy. He uses the plays to demonstrate that
"weeds" can connote moral or spiritual evil as well as natural
decay, the disease of rotting flesh. And he points out that either
the love or the hate of "th'inviting time" can be suspect. But all
these meanings are held together in suspension partly because
they are all banished from "my dear love"—all "not-me," all
equally threatening. In the context of, say, a history play, there
might be reasons to give weight to several of these meanings
over others. But this language offers a more compact version of
Dante's cosmic diversity, where all gradations of light have dis-
appeared; the only light rests in "my dear love," and the succeed-
ing darker threats are almost interchangeable.

The images can work in similar ways even when the "not-me"
defensive texture is not so obvious:

> Nativity, once in the main of light,
> Crawls to maturity, wherewith being crowned,
> Crookèd eclipses 'gainst his glory fight,
> And time that gave doth now his gift confound.
>
> [60]

That first line, with its unmatched evocation of fusion, itself
helps to distance the next lines, for they are only a sequence of
flaws interrupting a perfect original state. One recalls Dante's
pilgrim drinking the river of light with closed eyelids, like a
nursing infant. And one recalls also the texture of fusion in
these sonnets, where *Lover infans* is in motion toward a "home of
love" or a "most most loving breast"—this seems a "main of
light" true to Romain Rolland. By contrast, surely the referents
of "Crookèd eclipses," for example, would tend to blur: this
quintessential "Nativity" can be crushed alike by omens of ill
fortune, or the progress of time, or the bending of old age. (Or,
one might say, "Nativity" after the first moment comes to take on
its original meaning of "destiny," or astrological fate.) All threats
to such a "Nativity" tend to merge, as in the passage from Job
that Booth finds echoed here, for that ontological vulnerability
concentrates them all in opposition: "Man that is born of a
woman hath but a short time to live."[30] Men as plants "at height
decrease" (15); only Love that is a babe continues to grow (115).

Thus the sonnets can build their own coherence by defending I-and-thou against all conceivable threats, and absorbing the threats into the layered allusions of their own words. This texture in its "constructive vagueness" can become whole, seamless. And the language may seem to be "wantoning on the verge of anarchy,"[31] because here *Poet*, moving *de via* from the language of fusion in several directions at once, can thereby establish an individual voice for these poems as equivalent selves.

Also through this "not-me" defense, the force and severity of these threats is used to generate the affective energy of the poems. The softly focused abstractions often appear as those "shadowy personifications" Booth keeps remarking, figures of polarized evil like those in a morality play. And often in the same lines, further heightening the emotional charge, we find verbs suggesting fierce destruction. By contrast, in Petrarch's poems the active verbs are muted because they come to register the speaker's pain, passively endured; they become a means for an *amant martyr* defense (see above, Chap. 5). But in Shakespeare's sonnets, the speaker is not usually the object of these verbs—the personified destructive presences such as Time are allowed their universality, their full strength:

> Time doth transfix the flourish set on youth,
> And delves the parallels in beauty's brow
> > [60]

> For never-resting time leads summer on
> To hideous winter and confounds him there
> > [5]

> When I have seen the hungry ocean gain
> Advantage on the kingdom of the shore
> > [64]

When the elements of fortune and time become active, evil presences, the "I" of poem and Poet-Lover can at the same time borrow their strength and defy it. He can define himself through phrases with "against" and "despite," and through negatives. For example, sonnet 49 begins each of its quatrains with "Against," and sonnet 63 takes up its first two quatrains with an "Against" clause that is echoed in line 10, "Against con-

founding age's cruel knife." And negatives that distinguish the
"I" are common:

> Not marble nor the gilded monuments
> Of princes shall outlive this pow'rful rhyme
>
> [55]

> Have I not seen dwellers on form and favor
> Lose all and more by paying too much rent
> For compound sweet forgoing simple savor,
> Pitiful thrivers, in their gazing spent?
> No, let me be obsequious in thy heart...
>
> [125]

In this texture, the affective energy of the poem as self grows
from the vehemence with which the enemy is isolated, personified, and defied. The self is affirmed in negation: "No, I am
that I am" (121). For in these negations, and in these dangerous
presences that would "take my love away" (64), *Poet* is revealed:
those passages woven of negative constructions, personified
dangerous figures, and strong verbs or verbals are perhaps the
most memorable of all in the sonnets:

> ... Love is not love
> Which alters when it alteration finds,
> Or bends with the remover to remove.
> O no, it is an ever-fixèd mark....
> Love's not time's fool, though rosy lips and cheeks
> Within his bending sickle's compass come
>
> [116]

> It suffers not in smiling pomp, nor falls
> Under the blow of thrallèd discontent,
> Whereto th'inviting time our fashion calls
>
> [124]

> Nor Mars his sword nor war's quick fire shall burn
> The living record of your memory
>
> [55]

> Against my love shall be as I am now,
> With time's injurious hand crushed and o'erworn
>
> [63]

Among all these defensive textures, the evocation of that protected *absent presence* can appear simple, even vulnerable; the
language of fusion maintains a gentle persistence. Booth notes
in sonnet 124 that the slight pronoun "it," referring to "my dear
love," carries the "key to the poem's power" because it keeps
reappearing as "sure, constant, forthright, simple, and blank."[32]
It is an ever-fixèd mark, like the focal word "you" in the sonnets.
And yet this I-and-thou has no power in the manner of those
destructive presences, fortune and time; rather, it is almost by
definition outnumbered by them, vulnerable to them:

> Ruin hath taught me thus to ruminate,
> That time will come and take my love away
> [64]

> This thou perceiv'st, which makes thy love more strong,
> To love that well which thou must leave ere long.
> [73]

Thus the verbs that belong with the affirmations of I-and-thou,
in the language of fusion, are no match for those more savage
verbs in the defensive texture. To assert that the youth will "pace
forth" in "this pow'rful rhyme" is almost exceptional; more usual
is the claim that the poem will "outlive" marble and monuments
(55). For these affirmations, like the insistence on incantatory
words or pronouns, can seem almost verbless:

> How with this rage shall beauty hold a plea,
> Whose action is no stronger than a flower?
> [65]

At a first reading, these lines strike a clear dissonance: a flower is
not an action. And even when one reads in the allusions to military or legal actions, the suggestion of simply enduring, holding
out, or withstanding is still perhaps the most prominent one—
love bears it out.[33] The couplets of these sonnets often depend
on simple verbs of continued existence: live, dwell, stand, shine
(17, 19, 55, 60, 63, 65).
Thus these sonnets will often seem to drive "home" to the
couplet, to that vulnerable but persistent I-and-thou that they

have achieved, in a sense, through their defensive texturing. Several readers have pointed out the sense of "forward thrust" or drive of the lines, or their sense of decreasing complication as they move through the third quatrain to the couplet.[34] One might be able to demonstrate rhythmically that the sonnets move through contraction in need to relaxation in fulfillment, or that they trace a coenesthetic pattern of hunger-feeding-satiety (see above, Chap. 2) to their "core" or goal, I-and-thou. But at the least, the quatrains in some way allow the couplet, or prepare for the couplet, whether they do so with an implied "therefore" (18, 54, 55, 81) or with a sense of "despite" or "nevertheless" (15, 17, 19, 60, 63, 65). For in the couplet, the multiple threats of the quatrains must often be borne, or resolved, or evaded. If some readers have found certain couplets to be "failures," it may be because these readers sense that the couplet is vital to the poem as self: they expect the couplets to hold logically fortified assertions, or defiant, transitive verbs. But instead, these couplets invoke a simple mystery, illogical and fragile—in them I and thou can meet in continual renewal and interchange of being. These terms seem to conjure the infinite "inner space" at the core of every self, appropriate to eyes, light, breath, and those verbs of endurance:

> O none, unless this miracle have might
> That in black ink my love may still shine bright.
> [65]

> So, till the judgment that yourself arise,
> You live in this, and dwell in lovers' eyes.
> [55]

> You still shall live—such virtue hath my pen—
> Where breath most breathes, ev'n in the mouths of men.
> [81]

Such lines evoke that inherent sense of Source which the sonnets insist upon as "within" themselves. Whether between Poet-Lover and youth, or poem and reader, or one lover and another, these lines preserve I-and-thou, inexhaustible before words:

> So is my love still telling what is told.
> [76]

Conclusion

Renaissance love lyrics written by men have prompted these efforts to read the literary text as equivalent to the self, and Renaissance love lyrics written by men have served as the testing ground for these theories. But since this psycho-ontological hermeneutics can encompass—without ignoring—differences of sex, historical period, and genre, this model of text as self might be more fully elaborated into a general theory of literary interpretation. Such a theory might indeed be relevant to most literary texts born of selves, or all those that bear the marks of their birth—for since the model is defined by our humanity, we cannot outgrow it individually or historically. Or in the terms of the second chapter, the poetics allows the worded differences of *Poet,* but it allows also that universal longing, *Lover,* indispensable to our human nature. To texture these drives that I have called *Poet* and *Lover* is the work that is the self, the text, the Poet-Lover.

If we read text as equivalent to self, we can understand and encompass in our interpretations the variety of sexual nuances in these lyrics—the questions, for example, of whether the author is male or female, and whether the beloved is male, female, or hermaphroditic. For these differences belong to *Poet,* but not to *Lover.* Granted, we have discussed Source as a maternal presencing that enables the self; and granted, the metaphors of fusion in most of these lyrics belong to a female beloved, the figure of a lady. But the metaphoric language of fusion in Shakespeare's sonnets belongs just as easily to the figure of a young man, and there is no reason that it should not. For in the text, as in the self, it is through the motions of *Poet* that the beloved becomes gendered; *Lover,* in self and poem, is an ontological motion that essentially has nothing to do with gender. That wordless fusion that engenders poems and selves is itself *not* gendered, and in this fundamental sense the ultimate fusion longed for is always the same, out of worded ideological differences. Source, that non-specific mother, has no more gender than it has specificity; Souce is an infant sense of boundlessness that cannot truly be rendered by a figure, male or female. Moreover, with *Lover,* there is no discrimination among issues, positions, statements, finalities, worded "things" to be sought for in love. These matters do make all the difference with *Poet,* the drive for individuation, so that through *Poet* we have all the worded colorations, the definitions of the "nature of love," the accomplished realities of specific adult sexual relationships in poems and in selves. But the texturing *Poet* cannot exist alone. Source organizes the self's ability to organize: *Lover infans* is irreducible within the self. Thus by allowing both *Poet* and *Lover,* this model could be adapted to the poems of Sappho, or Michelangelo, or Donne, or the female troubadours—to any worded particulars about sexual relationships in the literary text. Of course, neither this nor any other model can explore all the nuances that it is the business of *Poet* to suggest.

If we read text as equivalent to self, we can also include in our interpretations the cultural and historical contexts of the text, the problematics of literary tradition. Of course, we work within limitations of time and space, and I have not been able to use in the preceding chapters as much historical perspective as I would have liked. But the model would certainly allow this approach: history belongs to the separation of selves, and such matters are therefore entirely relevant to *Poet,* albeit not to *Lover.* The model simply insists we not forget *Lover,* in our interpretations of any historical period. Take the current debates in literary criticism as an example. Today some theorists would seem to stress exclusively the *Poet* motion in texts; they would expose the "centers" of texts as non-meaning instead of meaning, absence instead of presence; they would evaluate central meaning in our culture as a deception upon which we have built language; they would urge us to embrace the infinite deferral of meaning, the joy of intertextuality in structures that have only "operative centers" devoid of meaning, such as Lévi-Strauss's myths. But Gerald Bruns, who concludes that the "modern poetic act . . . is a refusal to mean," nevertheless reveals, in his discussions of Mallarmé and Blanchot, a persistent *Lover* moving with *Poet* in the metaphoric language of fusion. For example, Bruns says that Mallarmé seeks in poetic utterance to consign the world of things and people to oblivion, for only in this condition of absence can one contemplate *le Néant,* the "pure idea" utterly without content or meaning. He quotes Mallarmé: " 'My work was created only by elimination. . . . Destruction was my Beatrice.' "[1] Yet he further explains that this "pure idea" or beauty is described by Mallarmé as "something all music, essence, and softness: the flower which is absent from all bouquets," a cradling aesthetic presence that is infinitely reassuring—a sense of Source, it finally seems, not strictly the "meaning" of the words, but nevertheless something enabling the words, indispensable to the words, bringing them into being. To Mallarmé, it seems, the text moves with *Lover infans* toward this something, this essence, this Source, even as content and meaning are dismissed.

Similarly, Bruns explains that to Blanchot the poet in negative discourse demonstrates to the reader the primordial void to which speech and language belong and *thereby maintains,* out of language, the *plenum,* the immediate presence of the world in plenitude, certitude, and silence. He quotes Blanchot: " 'The language of literature is the search for the moment which precedes it.' "[2] Again, text is enabled by Source, the sense of this preverbal moment, and the text returns one, in the metaphors of this poetics, to a fusion with a world that has been purified, by the text, of texts, contents, meaning, fragments, doubts. Thus for Blanchot and Mallarmé *Lover* persists, yearning past the words. We might ask whether even the most negative, impersonal, and anti-intentional of these theories is quite able to do without its metaphors of fusion. Perhaps today one often finds in literary texts the motion of *Lover* toward Source, a "meaning" that is distorted, displaced, or even denied, but still not eradicated. Here, of course, "meaning" would not be a definitive, valid, wordable interpretation of the text, but rather a sense of unwordable Source that presences the text, motivates the text, allows it a justification for being, a sense of self, its own presence or aura, its tie to a wordless *plenum* felt to be infinite. Just as a self cannot exist without some enabling intrapsychic vestige of maternal presence, so the literary text, equivalent self, cannot exist without its center, an intuited Source that sustains the text in its absence and contingency. We do not give up our inexpressibility tropes: "Beauty means inexpressibility. . . . Literature tries to create with words this state of wordlessness."[3] This motion of *Lover* is alive in all selves in all historical periods; *Lover* moves in texts along with the *Poet* motion that must work within particular historical periods and contexts.

Finally, if we read text as equivalent to self, we can include in our interpretations the differences of genre and subgenre. For these again are matters for *Poet,* not for *Lover.* In this model, to question the literary text is to question the human condition, and the model might well be elaborated toward the interpretation of epic, romance, or satire, for example. But of course, to build such a monolithic model would frustrate the *Poet* motion within us all. Surely all readers, as Poet-Lovers to the text of this book, will find their own differences from the model here suggested. I do not intend to homogenize texts—or theories of the text—but to suggest a common center of human being from which all selves and texts then freely deviate. Texts have centers, but texts must also find their own directions away from those centers.

Notes

Notes to Chapter 1

1. James Hillman, *Re-Visioning Psychology* (New York: Harper & Row, 1975), p. 154.

2. Ernest Becker, *Escape from Evil* (New York: Macmillan, 1965), chap. 3 et passim.

3. Margaret S. Mahler, Fred Pine, and Anni Bergman, *The Psychological Birth of the Human Infant: Symbiosis and Individuation* (New York: Basic Books, 1975), p. 197.

4. Paul Ricoeur, "Art and Freudian Systematics," trans. Willis Domingo, in *The Conflict of Interpretations: Essays in Hermeneutics*, ed. Don Ihde (Evanston, Ill.: Northwestern University Press, 1974), p. 206.

5. Sigmund Freud, "Civilization and Its Discontents" (1930), in *The Standard Edition of the Complete Psychological Works of Sigmund Freud*, ed. James Strachey (London: Hogarth Press), XXI, 113. Subsequent references are to this edition.

6. Norman O. Brown, *Love's Body* (New York: Random House, 1966), p. 264.

7. Anton Ehrenzweig, *The Hidden Order of Art* (Berkeley: University of California Press, 1967), pp. 186ff.

8. Owen Barfield, *Poetic Diction* (London: Faber & Faber, 1928), p. 64; see also chaps. 3 and 4.

9. Paul Ricoeur, "A Philosophical Interpretation of Freud," trans. Domingo, in *Conflict of Interpretations*, pp. 169–70.

10. Walter Benjamin, "Theses on the Philosophy of History," in *Illuminations*, trans. Harry Zohn, (New York: Harcourt Brace, 1968), pp. 259–60.

11. D. W. Winnicott suggests an "isolated core" of the personality, even *in health*, which "knows it must never be communicated with" or altered by external reality; it would follow that our inability to word the secret core of self could mask our reluctance or even our terror. See

"Communicating and Not Communicating, Leading to a Study of Certain Opposites," in *The Maturational Processes and the Facilitating Environment* (New York: International Universities Press, 1965), p. 187; cited in Mahler et al., p. 223.

12. Jacques Derrida, "The Supplement of Copula," *Georgia Review* (1976), p. 535.

13. Freud thought it probable that this hymn "Vor Sonnenaufgang" (from *Also Sprach Zarathustra,* III) was an expression of Nietzsche's longing for his father, who had died when Nietzsche was still a child (XII, 54).

14. E. H. Gombrich, "The Mask and the Face," in *Art, Perception, and Reality* (Baltimore: Johns Hopkins University Press, 1972), pp. 34ff.

15. He refers to the "equipment" for establishing the original libidinal object, and thus enabling the self to be. See René A. Spitz, *The First Year of Life* (New York: International Universities Press, 1965), p. 95. The same author demonstrated in a famous earlier study that infants deprived of sufficient mothering, even when all their physical needs are met, simply cannot develop at all and will in fact die if the deprivation continues. See "Hospitalism: An Inquiry into the Genesis of Psychiatric Conditions in Early Childhood," *The Psychoanalytic Study of the Child* (New York: International Universities Press, 1945), I, 53–74.

16. Evoking this unnamable enigma with any name is at best a perplexing task. Terms from Freudian theory, such as "symbiotic orbit," "ideal object," "preoedipal mother," "archaic omnipotent self-object," "non-specific mother," or even "mass of two," can seem rather bloodless, part of a relentless search for objectivity. Some terms have been preempted by other writers, such as "Presence" (Derrida, the Geneva school of criticism), or "Other" (Lacan, Hegel), or "Imago" (Melanie Klein); others seem too plain or literal ("Mother," "Womb," "Whole"), or even too ugly ("Omphalos"). From all these considerations I have selected the term "Maternal Source," or alternatively "Source," "Presence," or "maternal presence," assuming that any possible confusion with Derrida's usage will disappear in context.

17. Mahler et al., p. 5.

18. Spitz, *First Year,* pp. 44, 99. Spitz's "preobjectal stage" seems to be equivalent to Mahler's "symbiotic orbit."

19. Freud, "On Narcissism," XIV, 100.

20. Mahler et al., p. 59.

21. Hillman, p. 50.

22. Mahler et al., p. 227.

23. Otto F. Kernberg, *Object-Relations Theory and Clinical Psychoanalysis* (New York: Aronson, 1976), p. 60.

24. Helen E. Durkin, *The Group in Depth* (New York: International Universities Press, 1964), p. 76. See also Mahler et al., pp. 15, 199, 223.

25. Jean Laplanche, *Life and Death in Psychoanalysis,* trans. Jeffrey Mehlman (Baltimore: John Hopkins University Press, 1976), pp. 22, 33.

26. Spitz, *First Year,* pp. 141, 107.

27. Maurice Merleau-Ponty, "The Child's Relation with Others," trans. William Cobb, in *The Primacy of Perception,* ed. James Edie (Evanston, Ill.: Northwestern University Press, 1964), pp. 119, 125, 153.

28. Philip E. Slater, *Microcosm: Structural, Psychological and Religious Evolution in Groups* (New York: John Wiley, 1966), pp. 63, 69-70, 106-7. Brown, p. 35.

29. Spitz, *First Year,* pp. 51-52, 65, 74, 94, and more generally chaps. 3 through 5. He explains in chapter 8 that with the emergence of the "second organizer," at the establishment of the "8th month anxiety," the maternal face becomes unique.

30. Becker, pp. 36, 134, 122.

31. Kernberg, pp. 58, 59.

32. Claude Lévi-Strauss, *Tristes tropiques* (Paris: Plon, 1955), pp. 48-49.

33. Durkin, pp. 75, 77, 79. She adds that the controlling and dangerous preoedipal mother, and not the father who often inherits her role, is ultimately that "paramount and dangerous personality" of whom Freud speaks (1921), and toward whom one must surrender one's will and adopt a passive, masochistic attitude (p. 79).

34. Laplanche, p. 24. Spitz, *First Year,* p. 129. Melanie Klein, *Envy and Gratitude: A Study of Unconscious Sources* (New York: Basic Books, 1957), p. 11. See also Melanie Klein, *Contributions to Psycho-analysis, 1921-1945* (London: Hogarth Press, 1950).

35. Freud, XII, 20-21.

36. Merleau-Ponty, p. 124. Spitz, *First Year,* pp. 97, 127-28.

37. Merleau-Ponty, p. 109. Barfield, p. 89.

38. For example, Kernberg has several reservations about Klein's theories, but he seems to agree with much of her structuring of the "depressive position" (pp. 39-41, 67-68).

39. Hillman, p. 110. See Richard E. Palmer, *Hermeneutics* (Evanston, Ill.: Northwestern University Press, 1969), pp. 195-96.

40. Heinz Kohut, "Thoughts on Narcissism and Narcissistic Rage," *The Psychoanalytic Study of the Child* (New York: Quadrangle, 1973), XXVII, 378.

41. G. W. F. Hegel, *The Phenomenology of Mind,* trans. J. B. Baillie (New York: Macmillan, 1931), p. 159.

42. Mahler et al., pp. 206, 230. Slater, p. 182.

43. Spitz, *First Year*, pp. 104-5; my italics.

44. Mahler et al., p. 68. Spitz, p. 105. Kernberg, p. 51.

45. Mahler et al., pp. 103-4. Kernberg, p. 73. Wheelwright, pp. 61-62.

46. Mahler et al., p. 109; my italics. Spitz, *First Year*, p. 170.

47. Mahler et al., p. 111, quotes an unpublished work, 1972.

48. Slater, p. 219.

49. Laplanche, pp. 123-24.

50. Soren Kierkegaard, *Purity of Heart*, trans. Douglas V. Steeres, (New York: Harper, 1938), p. 85; cited by Mahler, p. 73.

51. Hillman, p. 48.

52. Ernst Kris, *Psychoanalytic Explorations in Art* (New York: International Universities Press, 1952), p. 60. Ehrenzweig, p. 102.

53. Susan Sontag, *Against Interpretation* (New York: Dell, 1961), p. 33; Suzanne Langer, *Feeling and Form* (New York: Scribner's, 1953), p. 22; William K. Wimsatt, *Day of the Leopards* (New Haven: Yale University Press, 1976), p. 212.

54. Ricoeur, "A Philosophical Interpretation of Freud," p. 168.

55. The concept of "signifying universe" is borrowed from Thomas Greene, *The Light in Troy: Imitation and Deconstruction in Renaissance Poetry* (New Haven: Yale University Press, to be published in 1982).

56. Kenneth Burke, *Language as Symbolic Action* (Berkeley: University of California Press, 1966), p. 379.

57. Fredric Jameson, *The Prison-House of Language* (Princeton: Princeton University Press, 1972), p. 208.

58. Paraphrased by Murray Krieger, *Theory of Criticism* (Baltimore: Johns Hopkins University Press, 1976), p. 231.

59. Paul de Man, *Blindness and Insight* (New York: Oxford University Press, 1971), pp. 17-18.

60. Hanna Segal, "A Psycho-analytical Approach to Aesthetics," in *New Directions in Psycho-Analysis,* eds. Melanie Klein, P. Heimann, and R. E. Money-Kyrle (London: Tavistock, 1955), pp. 384-405.

61. Krieger, p. 237.

62. Barfield, p. 88. Cary Nelson, *The Incarnate Word* (Urbana: University of Illinois Press, 1973), pp. 4-5.

63. Morse Peckham, *Man's Rage for Chaos* (New York: Schocken, 1967), p. 202.

64. Jonathan Culler, *Structuralist Poetics* (Ithaca: Cornell University Press, 1975), p. 163.

65. Edward Said, "Notes on the Characterization of a Literary Text," in *Velocities of Change,* ed. Richard Macksey (Baltimore: Johns Hopkins University Press, 1974), p. 39.

66. These are the first two of the four types of humanist imitation described by Greene in his book. See n. 55.

67. Geoffrey Hartman, *The Fate of Reading* (Chicago: University of Chicago Press, 1975), p. 123.

68. Hartman, p. 19.

69. Frederick Crews, "Anaesthetic Criticism," in *Psychoanalysis and Literary Process* (Englewood, N.J.: Winthrop, 1966), p. 23.

70. Discussed by Jameson, p. 131.

71. Georges Poulet, "Criticism and the Experience of Interiority," in *The Structuralist Controversy,* eds. Richard Macksey and Eugenio Donato (Baltimore: Johns Hopkins University Press, 1970), pp. 60-62.

72. Stanley Fish, *Self-Consuming Artifacts* (Berkeley: University of California Press, 1972), p. 3.

73. Kris, p. 46.

74. Roland Barthes, "To Write: An Intransitive Verb?" in *The Structuralist Controversy,* p. 141.

75. Crews, p. 19.

76. Merleau-Ponty, p. 134. Culler, p. 95.

Notes to Chapter 2

1. Margaret S. Mahler, Fred Pine, and Anni Bergman, *The Psychological Birth of the Human Infant* (New York: Basic Books, 1975), p. 227. See above Chap. 1.

2. "a part of the heart, one of man's eternal aspects." H. I. Marrou, "Au dossier de l'amour courtois," *Revue du Moyen Age Latin,* 3 (1947), 89; cited by Roger Boase, *The Origin and Meaning of Courtly Love: A Critical Study of European Scholarship* (Manchester: Manchester University Press, 1977), p. 52.

3. See above Chap. 1, n. 11.

4. Werner Jaeger, *Paideia: The Ideals of Greek Culture,* III (New York: Oxford University Press, 1944), 208, citing Ep. 7.341c. He also quotes *Timaeus* 28c: "It is hard to find the creator and father of the universe, and when he is found, it is impossible to describe his nature publicly." See also Marcia L. Colish, *The Mirror of Language: A Study in the Medieval Theory of Knowledge* (New Haven: Yale University Press, 1968), chap. 1, "St. Augustine: The Expression of the Word," esp. pp. 48, 80.

5. See Linda M. Paterson, *Troubadours and Eloquence* (Oxford: Clarendon Press, 1975), p. 82, in reference to Peire's "Be m'es plazen," and p. 168, concerning Raimbaut's "Assatz m'es belh."

6. James J. Wilhelm, *The Cruelest Month* (New Haven: Yale University Press, 1965), pp. 140, 226.

7. See René A. Spitz, *The First Year of Life* (New York: International Universities Press, 1965), p. 103, for use of the term "somatopsyche."

8. Raimbaut, "Ben sai c'a sels seria fer," 44-48, translated in L. T. Topsfield, *Troubadours and Love* (Cambridge: Cambridge University Press, 1975), p. 143; Bernart, "Le gens tems de pascor," 37-38, in *Anthology of the Provençal Troubadours*, ed. R. T. Hill and T. G. Bergin (New Haven: Yale University Press, 1964), p. 38.

9. Otto F. Kernberg, *Object-Relations Theory and Clinical Psychoanalysis* (New York: Aronson, 1976), p. 68.

10. Moshé Lazar, *Amour courtois et fin' amors dans la littérature du XIIᵉ siècle* (Paris: C. Klincksieck, 1964), p. 278, cited and translated by Elizabeth Salter, "Courts and Courtly Love," in *The Mediaeval World*, ed. D. Daiches and A. Thorlby (London: Aldus, 1973), p. 416.

11. Jaeger, II, 287, quotes *Theaetetus* 176b, and calls this statement the "noblest expression of Plato's paideia."

12. Baldassare Castiglione, *The Book of the Courtier*, trans. Charles Singleton (New York: Doubleday, 1959), pp. 350, 269.

13. Ibn Hazm, *The Ring of the Dove*, trans. J. Arberry (London: Luzac, 1953), pp. 23, 118.

14. Bernard, *Sermones in Cantica Canticorum*, ed. LeClerq, Talbot, Richais (Rome: Editiones Cisterciences, 1957), LXXXIII, i, 3; cited by Joan Ferrante, *Woman as Image in Medieval Literature* (New York: Columbia University Press, 1975), p. 28.

15. Topsfield, pp. 45, 157, 190-91.

16. Heinz Kohut, "Thoughts on Narcissism and Narcissistic Rage," *The Psychoanalytic Study of the Child* (New York: Quadrangle Books, 1973), XXVII, 364, 385.

17. Jonathan Saville, *The Medieval Erotic Alba: Structure as Meaning* (New York: Columbia University Press, 1972), p. 267.

18. Andreas Capellanus, *The Art of Courtly Love*, trans. John Jay Parry (New York: Norton, 1969), p. 122.

19. Uc Brunec, "Pus lo dous tems," and Guiraut Riquier, "Als subtilz aprimatz," cited and translated by Maurice Valency, *In Praise of Love* (New York: Macmillan, 1961), pp. 187, 192.

20. See Steven Runciman, *The Medieval Manichee* (Cambridge: Cambridge University Press, 1974), p. 176; Denis de Rougement, *Passion and Society* (London: Faber & Faber, 1940), p. 66; and René Nelli, *L'érotique des troubadours*, Bibliothèque Méridionale, 2d ser., 38 (Toulouse: E. Privat, 1963), p. 73. See also Boase, pp. 39, 78-79.

21. *A Glossary of Psychoanalytic Terms and Concepts*, ed. B. E. Moore and B. D. Fine (New York: American Psychoanalytic Association, 1967), p. 14.

22. "*Ishk* designates a depressive state which is combined with deep

anxiety . . . caused in some unknown manner by love," and the word is from "*ishka*, meaning a creeper which twines round a tree and gradually causes its death," according to Gregory Zilboorg, in *A History of Medical Psychology* (New York: Norton, 1941), p. 124. See also Boase, pp. 66–67, 95, 124, 132.

23. Raimbaut, "Non chant per auzel," 32; Peire, "Al dessebrar del païs (II)," 39–40. See Topsfield, pp. 150, 168.

24. Raimbaut, "Non chant per auzel," 27–28; Peire, "L'airs clars," 46–48. See Topsfield, pp. 149–50, 171–73.

25. Valency, pp. 150–53.

26. "Mout jauzens me prenc en amar," 25–30, in *Anthology of the Provençal Troubadours*, p. 8.

27. Topsfield, p. 105.

28. Peire, "Amors, La fuelhs e·l flors," 64–66; Raimbaut, "Escotatz ma no say que s'es," 33–34. See Topsfield, pp. 152–54, 164–66.

29. Jaeger's volume II is entitled, "In Search of the Divine Centre." See for example his remarks on the *Meno* (p. 169) and the interpretation of Eros as "the yearning to make Good one's own forever," so that "its object, eternal goodness and beauty, must be the very heart of the Self" (p. 195). See also Colish, pp. 76–80, and Frederick Goldin, *The Mirror of Narcissus in the Courtly Love Lyric* (Ithaca: Cornell University Press, 1967), esp. chap. 5, "The *De Trinitate* of St. Augustine and the Lyric Mirror."

30. Goldin, p. 103.

31. Philip Slater, *Microcosm: Structural, Psychological and Religious Evolution in Groups* (New York: John Wiley, 1966), pp. 144–45.

32. Goldin, p. 159.

33. Peter Dronke discusses Geoffrey de Vinsauf in "Medieval Rhetoric," in *The Medieval World*, ed. Daiches and Thorlby. Geoffrey anticipates Coleridge and the Romantics with his faith that the imagination can "fuse" (Coleridge's word) matter and manner. Geoffrey describes poetic imagery (*collatio occulta*) as a "plant best planted in the garden of one's matter [*materia*]" (p. 330).

34. Leo Spitzer, "Speech and Language in Inferno XIII," in *Dante*, ed. John Freccero (Englewood Cliffs, N.J.: Prentice-Hall, 1965), p. 95. Also Brian Vickers, in *Classical Rhetoric in English Poetry* (New York: Macmillan, 1970), argues that language is all but infinitely flexible, and one rhetorical figure can record many states of mind (p. 113).

35. Paterson, esp. pp. 58–74.

36. Mahler, p. 57.

37. See the discussion in Nathaniel B. Smith, *Figures of Repetition in the Old Provençal Lyric*, NCSRLL, 176 (Chapel Hill: University of North Carolina Press, 1976), pp. 29–35. Perhaps one of the reasons that

Molinier never completes his plan to teach the "proper sort of love" (p. 33) is that its symmetries are implicit in the artistic fruit of love, figures and flowers of the "Gay Saber."

38. David I. Masson, "Vowel and Consonant Patterns in Poetry" (1953), in *Essays on the Language of Literature,* ed. Seymour Chatman and Samuel R. Levin (Boston: Houghton Mifflin, 1967), p. 4.

39. Spitz, *First Year,* pp. 98, 135-36.

40. Marshall Edelson, *Language and Interpretation in Psychoanalysis* (New Haven: Yale University Press, 1975), p. 175.

41. Roman Jakobson, "Linguistics and Poetics" (1960), in *Essays,* ed. Chatman and Levin, pp. 296-322.

42. Nancy Streuver, *The Language of History in the Renaissance*, pp. 71, 74.

43. Judith Mitchell, *Psychoanalysis and Feminism* (New York: Random House, 1975), pp. 111-12, 119.

44. John Halverson, in "Amour and Eros in the Middle Ages," *Psychoanalytic Review,* 57 (1970-71), considers the "historical dimension" and concludes that political and economic changes in Western Europe were the "matrix of the literature of love" (p. 254). Richard A. Koenigsberg, in "Culture and Unconscious Fantasy: Observations on Courtly Love," *Psychoanalytic Review,* 54 (1967) accepts courtly love as a "social institution" and praises it for resolving Oedipal conflicts more admirably than the Greek and Christian social institutions that revealed men's hostility toward women (pp. 48-49). See also Herbert Moller, who points out in "The Social Causation of the Courtly Love Complex," *Comparative Studies in Society and History,* I (1958-59), 137-63, that medieval sex ratios show a shortage of females in the upper strata of society; and Melvin W. Askew, "Courtly Love: Neurosis as an Institution," *Psychoanalytic Review,* 52 (1965), 19-29.

45. Goldin, p. 87. William D. Paden, Jr., et al., "The Troubadour's Lady: Her Marital Status and Social Rank," *Studies in Philology,* 72 (1975), 48-49.

46. This passage from "Assatz sai d'amor," 17-24, is cited and translated by Topsfield, p. 147.

47. Raimbaut, "Ar resplan la flors enversa," stanza IV, cited and translated by Topsfield, pp. 154-57. See Cavalcanti's "L'anima mia vilment'è sbigottita," and "Donna mi prega." See also Chap. 4, below.

48. See "Quiconque voudra suivre Amour ainsi que moy," in *Les oeuvres de Pierre de Ronsard, texte de 1587,* ed. Isidore Silver, II (Chicago: University of Chicago Press, 1966), 124-25.

49. Kernberg, p. 71.

50. León Hebreo (Judah Abravanel), *The Philosophy of Love,* trans. Friedeberg-Seeley and Barnes (London: Soncino Press, 1937), p. 19. Freud, *Standard Edition,* XIX, 169.

51. Giraut de Bornelh, "Si·m sentis fizels amics," stanza III, cited and translated by Paterson, pp. 125, 127.

52. Jaeger, II, 135.

53. Raimbaut, "Dona, si m'auzes rancurar," 38-40, cited and translated by Topsfield, p. 143.

54. Kernberg, p. 68; see above, at n. 9.

55. Valency, p. 157.

56. Andreas Capellanus, p. 122. Mitchell, p. 128.

57. John Charles Nelson, *Renaissance Theory of Love* (New York: Columbia University Press, 1955), p. 35.

58. Arnaut Daniel, "Doutz brais e critz," 25-32, in *Canzoni,* ed. Gianluigi Toja (Florence: G. C. Sansoni, 1960); my translation.

59. This term for the *lausengiers* is used by Ferrante p. 72; see also Frederick Goldin, "The Array of Perspectives in the Early Courtly Love Lyric," in *In Pursuit of Perfection,* ed. J. M. Ferrante and George D. Economou (Port Washington, N.Y.: Kennikat Press, 1975), pp. 51-100.

60. Wilhelm, p. 225.

61. Raimbaut articulates a rhetorical commonplace here. For instance, Paterson explains Giraut de Bornelh's version of *trobar clus* by reference to Geoffrey de Vinsauf and Isidore (pp. 90-101). Giraut in this effort seeks a mean between obscurity and naked, public exposure of meaning; like Raimbaut in the tenso, he does not want to sing "a totz . . . comunalmen."

62. See Jerrold Seigel, *Rhetoric and Philosophy in Renaissance Humanism* (Princeton: Princeton University Press, 1968), chap. 1.

63. Mahler, et al., p. 206.

64. E. Neumann, *The Origins and History of Consciousness* (New York: Pantheon, 1954), p. 121; cited by Slater, p. 244. Spitz, *First Year,* chap. 11.

65. See Edelson, pp. 31 and 98, and Richard Ohmann, "Prolegomena to the Analysis of Prose Style," in *Essays,* ed. Chatman and Levin, p. 409.

66. Wilhelm, p. 221.

67. Lines 36-42, cited and translated by Frederick Goldin, in *Lyrics of the Troubadours and Trouvères* (New York: Anchor, 1973), pp. 178-81.

68. Vickers, p. 79. Robert Rogers, "On the Metapsychology of Poetic Language: Modal Ambiguity," *International Journal of Psycho-Analysis,* 54 (1973), 71-72.

69. Jakobson, p. 321.

70. Richard Lanham, *The Motives of Eloquence: Literary Rhetoric in the Renaissance* (New Haven: Yale University Press, 1976), p. 29.

71. Streuver, p. 12.

72. Paul Zumthor, in "Style and Expressive Register in Medieval Poetry," in *Literary Style: A Symposium,* ed. Seymour Chatman (London:

Oxford University Press, 1971), draws this picture of the *registre* on p. 272, calling it a configuration of "the 'space' proper to this kind of discourse."

73. Eugene Vance, "Love's Concordance: The Poetics of Desire and the Joy of the Text," *Diacritics*, 5.1 (Spring 1975), 46, 52, 51.

74. Stephen Booth, *An Essay on Shakespeare's Sonnets* (New Haven: Yale University Press, 1969), pp. 170-71.

75. Freud, *Civilization and Its Discontents*, trans. and ed. James Strachey (New York: Norton, 1962), p. 30.

76. Zumthor, p. 267.

77. Peter Haidu, "Making It (New) in the Middle Ages: Towards a Problematics of Alterity," *Diacritics*, 4.2 (Summer 1974), 8. (This article reviews Zumthor's *Essai de poétique médiévale* [Paris: Editions du Seuil, 1972]).

78. Scholars seem to agree on this assessment of the *trouvères:* Paterson, for example, alludes to their "apparent uniformity" (p. 7), and Haidu calls medieval French literature "a cold, uncommunicative Other" whose "text-specific intentionality . . . escapes us" (p. 3).

79. Haidu, p. 3.

80. This passage is cited and translated by Edward I. Condren, "The Troubadour and His Labor of Love," *Medieval Studies*, 34 (1972), 189.

81. Smith (p. 43) discusses the complex etymology of *trobar*, perhaps from **tropare*, "to write poetry," or even from *turbare*, "to drive and catch fish by troubling the water": from either word *trobar* could come to mean *invenire*, "to find" in a poetic sense. Both etymologies seem to carry the sense of deviating or making trouble, rather than harmonizing and fusing.

82. Smith, p. 61. Paterson, pp. 211-12.

83. Vance, pp. 50, 51.

84. Mitchell, p. 291.

85. Leo Spitzer, *L'amour lointain de Jaufré Rudel et le sens de la poésie des troubadours*, UNCSRLL, 5 (Chapel Hill: University of North Carolina Press, 1944), p. 21. Topsfield, p. 169.

86. *Canzoni*, ed. Toja. This is my translation of "En cest sonet," 36-39, after consulting the translations of Toja, Goldin, Paterson, Topsfield, and Valency, who reach no agreement on the subject of the verb "ten" and the referent of "·n." See below, Chap. 3.

87. Condren, p. 195.

88. Mahler uses Bouvet's term "optimal distance," p. 230. See also her description of children after the "rapprochement phase," pp. 94-101.

89. Stephen G. Nichols, Jr., "Toward an Aesthetic of the Provençal Lyric II," in *Italian Literature: Roots and Branches*, ed. G. Rimanelli and

K. J. Atchity (New Haven and London: Yale University Press, 1976), p. 32.

Notes to Chapter 3

1. Compare Raimbaut d'Aurenga, "Mas mi ten vert a jauzen joys," line 7 of "Ar resplan," cited in *Anthology of Troubadour Lyric Poetry*, ed. and trans. Alan R. Press (Austin: University of Texas Press, 1971), p. 106, and Peire d'Alvernhe, "un nou ioi qe·m fruich' e·m floris" (a new joy that ripens and blossoms for me), line 4 of "Deoista·ls breus iorns," cited and translated in Linda M. Paterson, *Troubadours and Eloquence* (Oxford: Clarendon Press, 1975), p. 87.

2. Melanie Klein believes that internalization proceeds in oral metaphor, as incorporation of "good imago" or "bad imago." More recently, Otto F. Kernberg would specify that introjection is derived not necessarily from incorporative fantasies but from primary autonomous apparatuses of perception and memory, and that not simply an "object" or "imago" is internalized but, rather, dyadic constellations, composed of self-representation, object-representation, and affective coloring. See *Object-Relations Theory* (New York: Aronson, 1976), pp. 34–39, 56–59.

3. See also René A. Spitz, *The First Year of Life* (New York: International Universities Press, 1965), pp. 43–46, on the coenesthetic and diacritic organizations, and pp. 53–85 and 102–7 on the beginning of perception.

4. L. T. Topsfield discusses the sestina in *Troubadours and Love* (Cambridge: Cambridge University Press, 1975), pp. 213–17, Paterson on pp. 193–201. Here are their translations of the lines in question. Paterson: "For my self thus grafts and inserts its scions into her as the bark into the rod" (31–32); "for from this my soul's joy in Paradise shall be doubled" (35). Topsfield: "For my whole being fastens on her and clings to her with its nails like the bark on the branch" (31–32); "so that my soul will have double joy in Paradise" (35).

5. Charles Jernigan, "The Song of Nail and Uncle: Arnaut Daniel's Sestina 'Lo ferm voler q'el cor m'intra,'" *Studies in Philology*, 71 (April 1974), 127–51. His translation of the same lines: "My body is just as rooted and enfingernailed in her as the bark on the rod [branch]" (31–32); "and my *arma* will have double joy of her in paradise" (35). References are to pp. 149, 147, 140–44, 151.

6. See Kernberg, chap. 7, "Barriers to Falling and Remaining in Love," especially pp. 186–97, on narcissistic tendencies to devalue and spoil sexuality, thus making it "disconcerting."

7. Toja, pp. 304–10.

8. See below for a translation of this entire poem.

9. Toja, p. 307; my translation.

10. See Kernberg, p. 36, citing Jacobson and Sandler and using the phrase "purified pleasure ego." See also pp. 63-64, and Sullivan's theories summarized on pp. 121-22.

11. In Raimbaut's "Cars, douz e feinz," line 55, "Cars con argens, esmer e cresc," is cited and translated by Paterson, pp. 147-50, "Precious as silver, I become purified and grow in value." Her reading of this difficult poem is on pp. 151-56. Even the phrase *fin' amor* may be connected with this metaphor: see the phrase by Peire d'Alvernhe, "de fina afinatz," or "purified by pure friendship," cited by Paterson, from "Sobre·l vieill trobar," line 50 (p. 73).

12. Paterson, p. 156. Topsfield, p. 140.

13. "Lanquan li jorn," lines 41-42, comment by Topsfield, p. 215. This particular illumination metaphor is Topsfield's, not Rudel's, but it does suggest rightly that in Rudel's poems, remembered presences sustain the Poet-Lover.

14. Freud, *Standard Edition*, XII, 35-79.

15. James J. Wilhelm, "Arnaut Daniel's Legacy to Dante and to Pound," in *Italian Literature: Roots and Branches*, ed. G. Rimanelli and K. J. Atchity (New Haven and London: Yale University Press, 1976), pp. 67-83. Topsfield also calls Arnaut "metaphysical" and compares him with Peire d'Alvernhe, Marcabru, Rudel, and Guillem de Montanhagol, pp. 183, 186.

16. A. Del Monte, *Studi sulla poesia ermetica medievale* (Naples: Giannini, 1953), p. 94; my translation.

17. Paterson, p. 82.

18. Paterson, p. 156.

19. A. Berry, *Florilège des troubadours* (Paris: Firmin-Didot, 1930), p. 187.

20. See Toja, "Versificatione e Technica Metrica," in *Canzoni*, pp. 35-64; Paterson, pp. 140-41, 172, 187, and 205; Topsfield, passim.

21. Topsfield, pp. 197-98.

22. Paterson, pp. 58-76, p. 189; Topsfield, p. 184.

23. Consult Nathaniel B. Smith, *Figures of Repetition in the Old Provençal Lyric*, NCSRLL, 176 (Chapel Hill: University of North Carolina Press, 1976).

24. Toja calls the monosyllabic line "very rare" and the bisyllabic line "rare also" (p. 37).

25. See for example Canello's·description of the sound effects of Arnaut's sestina: "the ear is left as though it were lost in a discordant void, which little by little is filled" (Toja, pp. 54-55).

26. "His innovations are evident in the number, kind, and disposition of rhymes" (Toja, p. 41). Arnaut uses 100 separate rhymes in a total of 962 lines of verse.

27. Even in an early song with no original *caras rimas,* "Chansson do·ill mot" (2), Arnaut planes syntax and word endings to fit the difficult *coblas capfinidas* form, so that *iois* and song can reach a peak, "capduoilla," together.

28. See Paterson, pp. 179, 191, and 155, for paraphrases of L. Pollman and S. Battaglia, and a comment on Raimbaut d'Aurenga.

29. Toja, pp. 43-44. They are *-òutas, -ampa, -òbra,* and *-endi.*

30. In the *Leys d'Amors, rima estrampa* is in fact what Arnaut is using in this song, composed of *rimas dissolutas,* or rhymes without correspondence within the stanza. *Rims espars,* on the other hand, is a completely unrhymed line. See Paterson, p. 204, and Toja, p. 41.

31. Toja's notes here refer to Spanish history, and some scholars have even fixed Arnaut's birth year by this alluded crowning at Etampe. The last lines, "Eu l'agra vist, mas estiei per tal obra, / c'al coronar fui del bon rei d'Estampa" (I would have seen that, but I stayed for such work that I was at the crowning of the good king of Estampa), do echo lines 7 and 8, and it would be a good joke if he simply meant he was staying for the crowning of the king of rhyme (cf. estampida), to write the poem.

32. Vida, l.6, in Toja, p. 166. Petrarch, *Trionfi,* IV, 40-42. See also Toja, "Arnaut e la critica," pp. 65 ff.; Paterson, p. 203; Topsfield, p. 197, "brief words pared to the limit." Thomas G. Bergin, in "Dante's Provençal Gallery," *Speculum* 40 (1965), calls him "very often willfully obscure" (p. 20).

33. 16. 3-5. Compare Geoffrey de Vinsauf, "Let the craftsman's skill effect a fusion of many concepts in one, so that many may be seen in a single glance of the mind. By such concision you may gird up a lengthy theme; in this bark you may cross a sea," lines 700-703 in *Poetria Nova,* trans. M. F. Nims (Toronto, 1967), p. 41.

34. Toja and Lavaud believe "asauta" means "attacks"; Paterson translates, "delights"; Canello, "inspires."

35. Paterson discusses Marcabru's *braus* style, pp. 52-54, and Peire's *braus* style, pp. 74-76. See also pp. 87, 204.

36. Sir Maurice Bowra, "Dante and Arnaut Daniel," *Speculum,* 27 (1952), 468-69.

37. "Cars, douz, e feinz," line 27, quoted by Paterson, p. 148.

38. Topsfield, p. 205.

39. The last "it," or "la," might signify Love, throat, or lady, according to various translators. See Paterson's comments on *trobar braus,* pp. 74-75, 141.

40. Perhaps "D'autra guiz' e d'autra razon" (6), the single poem with no tornada, and with no *caras rimas* according to Toja's list on p. 44, is a poem self-described as suffering false accusations, the threat of total absence.

41. Toja, p. 337.

42. Topsfield, pp. 76-77, 92.

43. See Paterson, pp. 19-28. The citation and translation are on pp. 21-22.

44. Topsfield, pp. 95, 169-70.

45. Paterson, pp. 77, 79.

46. Paterson quotes B. Marti, "E qui belhs motz lass' e lia," p. 15. See also p. 81.

47. Paterson, contrasting Arnaut with Raimbaut d'Aurenga and earlier troubadours, concludes that Arnaut uses such words as *clus,* and images of closing and concealing, "not to describe a style, but to suggest a mood of mystery, of restrained and concentrated thoughts and feelings" (p. 193). Karl Vossler believes that Dante and Arnaut shared a certain *Seelenzustand* or "standing place for the soul" (Paterson, p. 186).

48. See Toja, pp. 15-19, for the documentation of conjectures about Aragona, Ebro, Guillem de Bouvila.

49. The four original *caras rimas* are *-aura, -èri, -èrna, -óli*. From Paterson's "Appendix II: Versification," one might conclude that a seven-syllable line is relatively short, especially when contrasted with the stately measure of "Si·m fos Amors" (17) or "Sols sui qui sai" (15).

50. From "Quan lo rius," lines 24-25; translated by Press, p. 31.

51. Toja, p. 281.

52. We find "pecs," "precs," "secs," and "penill" in the servente "Pois Raimons" (1). Other words with sexual connotations here may include "mon," "m'encreis," "cucs," "cor," and "encubit." The lines are difficult to translate, like those of "Lo ferm voler" (18), perhaps because of the double meanings. A full discussion of possible meanings would be lengthy.

53. Paterson, p. 202. Arnaut has been assigned a variety of labels: Jeanroy and Bowra call his style *trobar ric;* Battaglia and Del Monte, *trobar clus;* Mölk, *trobar prim.* See Paterson, pp. 190-91.

Notes to Chapter 4

1. Citations and translations of Dante's lyrics are from *Dante's Lyric Poetry,* eds. Kenelm Foster and Patrick Boyde (New York: Oxford University Press, 1967). 2 vols. I adopt their numbering. In the following discussion of the lyrics and the *Commedia,* I leave untranslated words that are cognates, that are paraphrased or otherwise made clear in context, and that are used as specialized terms.

2. René A. Spitz, *The First Year of Life* (New York: International

University Press, 1965), p. 95. And to Mahler, of course, the growth through and from this direct presence, in the separation-individuation process, constitutes the psychological birth of the self.

3. Otto F. Kernberg, *Object-Relations Theory and Clinical Psychoanalysis* (New York: Aronson, 1976), pp. 114, 63. The "spirito novo" of *Purg.* xxv seems to integrate or organize the lower faculties in order to bring about the "alma sola," the single soul. This ability to integrate or organize still seems in current object-relations theory to be a "magic" that enables the new self to develop, and it seems to be a function of the maternal presence: a good self-object constellation, internalized, becomes an organizing nucleus of the self, and a bad self-object representation has a disorganizing effect. See Spitz, p. 105.

4. *Gentilezza* is defined in "Le dolci rime" (69) as the seed of happiness placed by God in the soul innately disposed to receive His engendering breath. See Foster and Boyde, I, 107, translation of 69. 119–20, and II, 223, commentary. See also *Convivio (Con.)* IV. xx. The particular "disposition" of this soul before God's breath seems a matter of fortune or luck—except, of course, in "Ne li occhi," where the lady can bestow *potentia* and thereby *gentilezza*.

5. Kenelm Foster, "Dante's Idea of Love," in *From Time to Eternity*, ed. Thomas Bergin (New Haven: Yale University Press, 1967), p. 75.

6. See especially "Amore e 'l cor gentil" (34), "Tanto gentile" (43), "Vede perfettamente" (44), "Io mi senti'" (42), "Sì lungiamente" (46), and "Oltre la spera" (57). The canzone "Donne ch'avete" (33), in a similar style, will be discussed later in this chapter.

7. Gianfranco Contini, "Introduction to Dante's *Rime*," trans. Yvonne Freccero, in *Dante*, ed. John Freccero (Englewood Cliffs, N.J.: Prentice-Hall, 1965), p. 35. See also Erich Auerbach, "Dante's Early Poetry," in *Dante: Poet of the Secular World*, trans. Ralph Manheim (Chicago: University of Chicago Press, 1961), pp. 24–68.

8. See the definition of the anagogical sense, *Con.* II. i. 52–65. See Auerbach, p. 44.

9. Patrick Boyde, *Dante's Style in His Lyric Poetry* (Cambridge: Cambridge University Press, 1971), chap. 3, "Tropes," pp. 119, 123, 135, 138: cited p. 124.

10. The terminology used by Dante, of course, included *frons, pedes, sirima, voltae*. See Foster and Boyde, I, xliv-li. I am using the later terminology that became conventional for sonnets: quatrain, octave, tercet, sestet.

11. See Spitz, pp. 50–52, 65–75; cited p. 72.

12. See for example Foster and Boyde, II, 155, the commentary on 57. 2 and 8, where *sospiro* and *spirito* seem to be used interchangeably.

13. Freud, *Standard Edition*, XII, 78.

14. See *De Vulgari Eloquentia (DVE)*, ii. vii. See also *Con.* IV. vi on the legendary verb "auieo," and the concept of vowels as the bonds of words: the word "auctor," Dante says here, descends from this legendary verb.

15. Contini, pp. 30-31.

16. *Purg.* xxvi. 94-114. Foster and Boyde gloss "leggiadre" as "soave" in their commentary on "Poscia ch'Amor" (70), II, 229.

17. Foster and Boyde respond to the surprising phrases in lines 19-20 and 42 by calling them "theologically absurd" and "theologically incoherent." They try to explain them by adding: "He is a young poet working rather insecurely on the borderlines between orthodox Christianity and the 'religion' of courtly love" (II, 100).

18. Of course, these techniques belong to the *dissimulatio* that Dante discusses approvingly, as in *Con.* II. xi. 6 and III. x. 7. And Boyde, in *Dante's Style*, suggests that "dissimulation in a broader and much more subtle form is wholly characteristic of Dante's poems," including the stated inability to praise the lady, the praise through her effects, and the contrivance of a fictitious rhetorical situation (p. 287).

19. Foster and Boyde, II, 129-30.

20. Joan Ferrante, "The Relation of Speech to Sin in the *Inferno*," *Dante Studies*, 87 (1969), 33-46, provides a good collection of examples demonstrating that Hell is a "great mouth."

21. Boyde, *Dante's Lyric Poetry*, pp. 230ff. See Foster and Boyde, II, 275, for a listing of consonants and consonant groups professedly *dolci* and *aspri*. In the first stanza of "Così," for example, the consonants within the rhyme considered harsh are *-pr, -tr,* and *-rm*.

22. See Thomas M. Greene, "Dramas of Selfhood in the *Comedy*, in *From Time to Eternity*: "Capaneo embodies that tragic rigidity of the personality common to all the damned, condemned as they are to repeat endlessly the gestures of their crippled loves" (p. 107). See also Irma Brandeis, *The Ladder of Vision* (New York: Doubleday, 1961), p. 174.

23. This is Contini's phrase, cited in Foster and Boyde, II, 266. See also their line-by-line commentary, pp. 273ff.

24. Glauco Cambon, in *Dante's Craft* (Minneapolis: The University of Minnesota Press, 1969), says of Nimrod: "Incommunicability is here enacted by language as the utterly fallen, indeed demoniac condition" (p. 33). See also Ferrante, "The Relation of Speech to Sin."

25. See Kernberg's analysis of splitting as a defensive mechanism, throughout his book. "The conflict is not 'unconscious' in the strict sense connected with repression, and, as long as the *rigid barrier* between contradictory ego states is maintained, the patient is free from anxiety" (p. 46; my italics).

26. These lines seem to recall the *tornada* of Arnaut's "Lancan son passat li giure" (4), cited above, Chap. 3.

27. With Kernberg and other object-relations theorists, there seems to be considerable uncertainty as to what "happens" to the aggressively invested representations as the self becomes integrated: are they split off, repressed, or somehow modified or neutralized? The question seems to be how, and indeed whether, an intrapsychic equivalent of hell might be brought about. For example, Kernberg believes that repression is the more effective defense, but repression "requires strong countercathexes because, unlike splitting, it is characterized by the blocking of discharge" (p. 46). See pp. 39–46, 67–72. Perhaps we need not ask precisely whether the stern Beatrice here represses or "splits off" sin; at least, she integrates the pilgrim.

28. Sinclair's commentary to his translation, *Purgatorio* pp. 415–16.

29. This is the argument by Mark Musa, trans. and ed., *Dante's Vita Nuova* (Bloomington: Indiana University Press, 1973), essay and notes, pp. 89–210.

30. "In periods of crisis . . . the individual can temporarily fall back upon his internal world. . . . One aspect of regression in the service of the ego is a reactivation in fantasy of past good internalized object-relations which provide 'basic trust' to the self. Basic trust, of course, ultimately derives from the first internalization" of a good dyad, mother and infant (Kernberg, p. 73). Klein, Spitz, Mahler, and others hold similar views.

31. John Freccero, introduction to Dante's *Paradiso,* trans. John Ciardi (New York: Signet, 1970), x.

32. Compare, in the poems with which this canzone is traditionally associated, the awakening agents, "spiritel d'amor gentile" (59. 42) or "spiritel novo d'amore" (54. 10), or the awakening by Love described as a birth, "onde ha vita un disio" (67. 20) or "il gran disio . . . fu nato" (68. 40–41).

33. Foster and Boyde, II, 178–81, and *Con.* III. iv. 13.

34. It is no easy job to harmonize the references to the potentially conflicting loves of Beatrice and Lady Philosophy: one must consult the three relevant sonnets of the *Vita Nuova,* "L'amaro lagrimar" (53), "Gentil pensero" (54), and "Lasso, per forza" (55); the canzoni that may allegorize Lady Philosophy (nos. 59, 61, 67, 68, and perhaps others); relevant commentary in the *Convivio;* and references in the *Commedia.* Sometimes, but not always, the speaker calls himself unfaithful to Beatrice.

35. Brandeis, p. 121.

36. See *Purg.* xviii. 55–69, and Foster, "Dante's Idea of Love" (n. 5).

Spitz quotes Freud: "'the original helplessness of human beings is thus the *primal source* of all *moral motives*'" (p. 129; italics mine).

37. Georges Poulet, "The Metamorphoses of the Circle," in *Dante*, ed. John Freccero, p. 161.

38. Foster and Boyde, II, 180, citing Etienne Gilson, *Dante et la philosophie*, p. 119.

39. Brandeis, p. 124.

40. Spitz marvels at the "near-clairvoyant manner" in which a good mother seems to understand what her baby means and needs (p. 127). Dante's "Voi che 'ntendendo" (59) is, of course, addressed to those who have no need of speech.

41. See for example *Par.* i. 100-102; xv. 121-23; xvii. 46-48; xxii. 4-6, 139-44. See also, besides passages already mentioned, *Purg.* ix. 34-63; xi. 63; xxviii. 50-51. In the *Convivio* (I. iii. 20-25) Dante describes himself as "cast forth from the sweetest bosom of Florence (at which I was born and nourished)," and there are similar references in the *Commedia*. For an essentially thematic study of maternal figures in the *Commedia*, see Marianne Shapiro, *Woman Earthly and Divine in the Comedy of Dante* (Lexington: University of Kentucky Press, 1977).

42. Spitz, p. 96.

43. Poulet, p. 159.

44. Perhaps it is to illustrate this paradox that the bowstring metaphor can work backward, in hysteron-proteron; see *Par.* ii. 23-24.

45. Daniel M. Murtaugh, "'Figurando il paradiso': The Signs that Render Dante's Heaven," PMLA, 90 (March 1975), 277-84; cited p. 280.

46. Greene, p. 135.

47. Robert Hollander, "Babytalk in Dante's *Commedia*," MOSAIC 8. 4, 73-87.

48. Many scholars have discussed the emphasis in the *Paradiso* upon metaphor as metaphor. See Brandeis, pp. 143-47, 196; Freccero's introduction to the *Paradiso* (n. 31); Murtaugh.

49. A few lines later, the radiances of this vision reach their flames upward toward Mary, like an infant stretching out its arms to its mother after it has taken the milk (121-25).

50. Brandeis concludes that what remains is the idea of light without specific form; the reader moves toward "some fleeting sense of what it might be to be suffused with truth, yet not to see, feel, taste, touch, or smell" (p. 206). Murtaugh notes that such terms as "poetando" refer grammatically to a process in time and thus exclude themselves and the poet from the supratemporal, supraspatial reality they seek to render (p. 282).

51. See Charles S. Singleton, *An Essay on the Vita Nuova* (Cambridge: Harvard University Press, 1958), pp. 42ff.

Notes to Chapter 5

1. *Letters from Petrarch,* selected and translated by Morris Bishop (Bloomington: Indiana University Press, 1966), p. 19 (*Fam.* I. 1). All passages from Petrarch's letters, the *Epistolae familiares* (*Fam.*) and the *Epistolae seniles* (*Sen.*), are cited in Bishop's translation.
2. See Thomas G. Bergin, *Petrarch* (Boston: Twayne, 1970), pp. 38–39.
3. John Freccero, "The Fig Tree and the Laurel: Petrarch's Poetics," *Diacritics,* 5 (Spring 1975), 35.
4. Bergin, p. 36.
5. *Fam.* xiii. 5, pp. 112–15; Bergin, pp. 33, 79.
6. Oscar Budel, "Illusion Disabused: A Novel Mode in Petrarch's *Canzoniere,*" in *Francis Petrarch, Six Centuries Later: A Symposium,* ed. Aldo Scaglione, NCSRLL, 3 (Chapel Hill: University of North Carolina Press, 1975), p. 150.
7. Bergin, p. 170.
8. Freccero, p. 39.
9. Robert M. Durling, "Petrarch's 'Giovene donna sotto un verde lauro,'" *Modern Language Notes,* 86 (1971), pp. 9–11, 16.
10. Bergin, p. 178.
11. See my article "Petrarch's Courtly and Christian Vocabularies: Language in *Canzoniere* 61–63," *Romance Notes,* 15. 3 (1974).
12. See Robert M. Durling, Introduction to *Petrarch's Lyric Poems,* p. 28.
13. See Leonard Foster, *The Icy Fire: Five Studies in European Petrarchism* (Cambridge: Cambridge University Press, 1969), p. 14.
14. Thomas Greene points out that the characteristic verb tense of the *Canzoniere* is the iterative present: *The Light in Troy: Imitation and Deconstruction in Renaissance Poetry* (New Haven: Yale University Press, to be published in 1982). In my comments about Petrarch's poems, I am indebted to Greene's perceptive readings.
15. Greene has remarked that rhetorical escape from the oxymoronic pattern of these poems can be only momentary.
16. Aldo S. Bernardo, *Petrarch, Laura, and the Triumphs* (Albany: State University of New York Press, 1974), pp. 201, 63.
17. *Trionfo dell'Eternità.* line 95.
18. Foster, p. 74.
19. William J. Kennedy, in *Rhetorical Norms in Renaissance Literature*

(New Haven: Yale University Press, 1978), discusses the rhetorical strategy of the Petrarchan speaker in his first chapter, "The Petrarchan Mode in Lyric Poetry." He says, "By 'vario stile' one may understand the range of tones, moods, and attitudes, that play off one another in balanced patterns of statement and reversal, thesis and antithesis, resolution and dissolution. . . . One could thus characterize the modality of the Petrarchan sonnet by how it involves the reader in the speaker's evolution of thought, feeling, idea, and attitude through multiple statements, shifts, and reversals within a formally limited space of fourteen lines" (pp. 26-28).

20. See for example poems 61-62, 80-82, 141-42, 277-96, as well as those later poems involving Laura's visitations and the Poet-Lover's "conversion."

21. Freccero, p. 37.

22. Bergin, p. 191.

23. Freccero, pp. 37, 38.

24. See René A. Spitz, *The First Year of Life* (New York: International Universities Press, 1965), pp. 98, 135-36.

25. See above, Chap. 1, at n. 59.

26. Durling, "Petrarch's 'Giovene donna,'" p. 5.

27. Bergin, pp. 175-76.

28. Translated by Ernest H. Wilkins, *Life of Petrarch* (Chicago: University of Chicago Press, 1977).

29. If there is an impulse to reparation here, it is very much the *new* presence that is being put together. See above, Chap 1. n. 60.

30. Thomas M. Greene, "Petrarch and the Humanist Hermeneutic," in *Italian Literature: Roots and Branches* (New Haven: Yale University Press, 1976), pp. 211-21. Adelia Noferi, *L'esperienza poetica del Petrarca* (Florence: Le Monnier, 1962), pp. 118-49.

31. Durling, Introduction, p. 32.

32. Budel, p. 144.

33. "We two live together; we will be remembered together." This is *Ep. Met.* I. 7, and is quoted in Bergin, p. 39. Bergin specifies that the number of lines in the poem is equal to the number of years in Petrarch's mother's life.

34. Bergin, pp. 152, 103.

35. Thomas P. Roche, Jr., "The Calendrical Structure of Petrarch's *Canzoniere*," *Studies in Philology*, 62 (1974), 152-72.

36. Freccero, p. 39.

37. Durling, Introduction, p. 26.

38. According to Ernest H. Wilkins in *The Making of the "Canzoniere"* (Rome: Edizioni di Storia e Letteratura, 1951), Chap. 9, poems 292 and

304 were each at one time designed as final poems for the *Canzoniere*. See Table 1, p. 194.

39. See my article "The Evolution of the Poet in Petrarch's *Canzoniere*," *Philological Quarterly*, 57 (Winter 1978).

40. *De Librorum Copia*, in *Petrarch: Four Dialogues for Scholars*, ed. and trans. Conrad H. Rawski (Cleveland: Western Reserve University Press, 1967), p. 35.

41. Bergin, pp. 114, 131.

42. See 359. 64; 268. 40–44, *Trionfo dell'Eternità*, 143–45. The final poem of the *Canzoniere* argues that love for the Virgin Mary should be *proportionately* greater than love for Laura (366. 121–23).

Notes to Chapter 6

1. All quotations from the sonnets are from *Shakespeare's Sonnets* (*SS*), ed. with analytic commentary by Stephen Booth (New Haven: Yale University Press, 1977).

2. J. B. Leishman, *Themes and Variations in Shakespeare's Sonnets* (New York: Hilary House, 1961), p. 217. C. L. Barber, in the introduction to the Laurel edition of *The Sonnets* (New York: Dell, 1960), observes that "the poet's sense of himself hinges on the identification" (p. 24). James Winny, in *The Master-Mistress* (London: Chatto & Windus, 1968), remarks: "Whoever is speaking in the Sonnets is obsessed by a need to integrate himself with an elusive second being" (p. 207). Murray Krieger discusses "love's unreasonable reason" in relation to *The Phoenix and the Turtle* in his book, *A Window to Criticism: Shakespeare's Sonnets and Modern Poetics* (Princeton: Princeton University Press, 1964), pp. 150–54.

3. *SS*, p. 160.

4. See Winifred Nowottny, "Formal Elements in Shakespeare's Sonnets: Sonnets I–VI," in *Discussions of Shakespeare's Sonnets*, ed. Barbara Herrnstein (Boston: Heath, 1964).

5. Giorgio Melchiori, in *Shakespeare's Dramatic Meditations* (Oxford: Clarendon Press, 1976), develops a statistical norm for the sonnets through the high frequency of "you," as "a vital and dramatic I-thou relationship" (p. 18), and then he discusses four "non-You" sonnets which deviate from the norm because they "ignore the ruling theme, Love" and are "dramatic meditations on less conventional subjects" (pp. 31–32). He chooses nos. 94, 121, 129, and 146. See also Carol Thomas Neely, "Detachment and Engagement in Shakespeare's Sonnets: 94, 116, and 129," in *PMLA*, 92 (January 1977), 83–95.

6. Martin Green's provocative reading of sonnet 20 gives the poem a double sexual meaning. See *The Labyrinth of Shakespeare's Sonnets* (London: Charles Skilton, 1974), pp. 59–81.

7. Rosalie L. Colie, *Shakespeare's Living Art* (Princeton: Princeton University Press, 1974), p. 101.

8. See G. Wilson Knight, *The Mutual Flame* (New York: Barnes & Noble, 1955), p. 35, and the entire chapter, "The Integration Pattern," discussing the youth as a symbol of "higher, bisexual integration" (p. 34). See also Leslie A. Fiedler, "Some Contexts of Shakespeare's Sonnets," in *The Riddle of Shakespeare's Sonnets* (New York: Basic Books, 1962), and his discussion of Shakespeare's obsession with escaping the cult of Woman.

9. C. S. Lewis, *English Literature in the Sixteenth Century* (Oxford, 1954), p. 505. Leishman, pp. 117–18.

10. Leishman, p. 163.

11. Stephen Booth in *An Essay on Shakespeare's Sonnets* (New Haven: Yale University Press, 1969) discusses overlapping structural patterns in the sonnets and concludes, "There is a perceptibly distinct octave in 96 of the 152 fourteen-line sonnets" (p. 36).

12. See Winny's comments on the frequency and importance of the term "true" in the sonnets in his chapter "Truth and Falsehood."

13. Edward Hubler, in *The Sense of Shakespeare's Sonnets* (New York: Hill and Wang, 1952), discusses the "homely" language and plain-speaking of the sonnets in the chapter "Form and Matter." Many others have noticed the plain and vivid language of the sonnets.

14. John D. Bernard, "'To Constancie Confin'de': The Poetics of Shakespeare's Sonnets," *PMLA*, 94 (January 1979), pp. 84, 82.

15. Krieger, p. 124.

16. I intend to give no rigorous division, but merely an impression. In the first group I would include sonnets 33–36, 40–42, 49, 57–58, 61, 69–70, 84, 88–96, 99, 109–12, 117–21, and 127–52. In the second group I would include the procreation sonnets, 18–19, 25, 29–30, 37, 49, 52–56, 60, 63–68, 73–74, 81, 97–98, 104, 107, 115–16, and 123–26. Of course, this leaves a number of important sonnets ungrouped, such as some sonnets about poetry, convention, and the "rival poet," and as well several sonnets rich in the language of fusion (22, 24, 39, 62, 76, 105–6, 108–10).

17. *SS*, pp. 191–92.

18. Krieger states of these poems: "As reward for his sacrifice, the poet—through the oneness he has earned by taking another's sin as his own—gains back all he has given up and more. His assumption of guilt has destroyed this otherness, and all the friend's advantages become his too" (*Window*, p. 160).

19. One would suppose that even if the sonnets do encode a homosexual relationship, as Martin Green has worked to demonstrate in his book, such a phrase as the "base infection" of sonnet 94 could hardly refer to the union of Poet-Lover and youth. The dark lady sonnets are another matter.

20. See the excellent article by Janet Adelman, "'Anger's My Meat!': Feeding, Dependency, and Aggression in *Coriolanus*," in *Shakespeare: Pattern of Excelling Nature*, ed. David Bevington and Jay L. Halio (Cranbury, N.J.: Associated University Presses, 1978).

21. G. B. Shaw's preface to *The Dark Lady of the Sonnets* is cited in Philip Martin, *Shakespeare's Sonnets: Self, Love, and Art* (Cambridge: Cambridge University Press, 1972), p. 73.

22. *SS*, pp. 406–8.

23. *SS*, pp. 456, 459.

24. *SS*, p. 466.

25. *SS*, pp. 199–200.

26. *SS*, p. 201.

27. Arthur Mizener, "The Structure of Figurative Language in Shakespeare's Sonnets," in *Discussions of Shakespeare's Sonnets*, p. 139.

28. The texture of sonnet 129 seems relevant here; the poem spits out the various threats of "lust in action," both the adjectives and the verbals, as though to expel them.

29. Mizener, p. 148.

30. *SS*, p. 240.

31. *SS*, p. 419; Mizener, p. 141.

32. *SS*, p. 419.

33. *SS*, pp. 246–47.

34. See for example Knight, pp. 98–99; Booth, *Essay*, chaps. 5 and 6. "Most of the sonnets become decreasingly complex as they proceed" (Booth, p. 130).

Notes to Conclusion

1. Gerald L. Bruns, *Modern Poetry and the Idea of Language* (New Haven: Yale University Press, 1974), pp. 195, 191–92.

2. Bruns, pp. 199, 201.

3. "The Beautiful Is Negative," in *Analects*, trans. Stuart Gilbert, *The Collected Works of Paul Valéry*, XIV (Princeton: Princeton University Press, 1970). pp. 562–63.

Index

QUEEN MARY
COLLEGE
LIBRARY

LOVE WORDS

Designed by Richard E. Rosenbaum.
Composed by The Composing Room of Michigan, Inc.
in 10 point Baskerville V.I.P., 2 points leaded,
with display lines in Baskerville.
Printed offset by Thomson/Shore, Inc. on
Warren's Number 66, 50 pound basis.
Bound by John H. Dekker & Sons, Inc.
in Holliston book cloth.

Library of Congress Cataloging in Publication Data

Regan, Mariann Sanders, 1942–
    Love words.

    Includes bibliographical references and index.
    1. Love poetry—History and criticism.
    2. Literature—Philosophy.   I. Title.
PN1076.R4   1982   809.1'9354   81-15186
    ISBN 0-8014-1415-6   AACR2